Globalization, Culture, and Education in South Asia

Globalization, Culture, and Education in South Asia

Critical Excursions

Edited by Dip Kapoor, Bijoy P. Barua, and Al-Karim Datoo

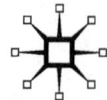

GLOBALIZATION, CULTURE, AND EDUCATION IN SOUTH ASIA
Copyright © Dip Kapoor, Bijoy P. Barua, and Al-Karim Datoo, 2012.

All rights reserved.

First published in 2012 by
PALGRAVE MACMILLAN®
in the United States—a division of St. Martin's Press LLC,
175 Fifth Avenue, New York, NY 10010.

Where this book is distributed in the UK, Europe and the rest of the World, this is by Palgrave Macmillan, a division of Macmillan Publishers Limited, registered in England, company number 785998, of Houndmills, Basingstoke, Hampshire RG21 6XS.

Palgrave Macmillan is the global academic imprint of the above companies and has companies and representatives throughout the world.

Palgrave® and Macmillan® are registered trademarks in the United States, the United Kingdom, Europe and other countries.

ISBN: 978–1–137–00687–5

Library of Congress Cataloging-in-Publication Data

Globalization, culture, and education in South Asia : critical
   excursions / edited by Dip Kapoor, Bijoy Barua & Al-Karim Datoo.
      p. cm.
   ISBN 978–1–137–00687–5
   1. Education—Economic aspects—South Asia.   2. Education and state—South Asia.   3. Education and globalization—South Asia.
   I. Kapoor, Dip.   II. Barua, Bijoy Kumar.   III. Datoo, Al-Karim.
   LC67.S66G56 2012
   338.4′737—dc23   2012013316

A catalogue record of the book is available from the British Library.

Design by Integra Software Services

First edition: October 2012

We dedicate this collection to our beloved mothers: Aruna, Khati, and Chandrima.

Contents

List of Tables   ix

List of Figures   xi

1   Globalization, Culture, and Education in South Asia: Critical Excursions   1
Dip Kapoor, Bijoy P. Barua, and Al-Karim Datoo

Part I   Globalization, Culture, and Education: Urban Priorities and Perspectives and Formal Educational Contexts

2   Indian Higher Education and the Dynamics of Global Collaborations   17
Fazal Rizvi and Radhika Gorur

3   The Global Educational Policy Field and National Education Policymaking in Pakistan   37
Sajid Ali

4   Neoliberal Globalization and Higher Education in Bangladesh   53
Touhida Tasnima and Ehsanul Haque

5   The World Bank, Community Schooling, and School-Based Management: A Political Economy of Educational Decentralization in Nepal   71
Tejendra J. Pherali

6   Global/Colonial Designs, School Knowledge Production, and Students' Cultural Identities: A Critical Ethnographic Perspective from Pakistan   87
Al-Karim Datoo

7   Neoliberal Globalization and Preprimary Teacher Education Policy and Practice in India, Sri Lanka, and the Maldives   103
Amita Gupta

8 Rights and Resistance: The Limits and Promise of Human Rights Education in India 123
   Monisha Bajaj and Bikku Kuruvila

Part II Globalization, Culture, and Education: Rural Priorities and Perspectives and Other Educational Contexts

9 The Barua Community, Globalization, and Colonial Education: The Quest for Sociocultural Identity in Bangladesh 141
   Bijoy P. Barua
10 Performing and Politicizing Education in West Bengal, India 155
   Dia Da Costa
11 Colonization and Decolonization: Resistances and Assaults on Traditional Agriculture in Pakistan 171
   Azra Talat Sayeed
12 Globalizing Capitalism: Accumulation by Dispossession and the Specter of Subaltern Social Movement (SSM) Activism and Anticolonial Pedagogies in Rural India 187
   Dip Kapoor

Author Bios 211

Index 217

Tables

8.1 Excerpts from National Curriculum Frameworks for Teacher Education (1978, 1988, 1998, & 2009; emphasis added) 128
12.1 Lok Adhikar Manch (LAM) 194

Figures

6.1 Saher's Representation of the Local-Global Dynamic and the Self — 93
6.2 Rafique's Representation of the Local-Global Dynamic and the Self — 94

CHAPTER 1

Globalization, Culture, and Education in South Asia: Critical Excursions

Dip Kapoor, Bijoy P. Barua, and Al-Karim Datoo

> Can we have social theory that does not claim universality for a metropolitan point of view, does not read from only one direction, does not exclude the experiences of most of humanity, and is not constructed on terra nullius (land belonging to nobody before the arrival of Europeans—the colonizer's dream)?
> (Connell, 2007, p. 47)

Introduction

Since the critique of anthropology and the exposition of the geopolitics of knowledge (Asad, 1973), the northerness of the sociology of globalization has been described as "a system of categories created by metropolitan intellectuals and read outward to societies in the periphery where the categories are filled in empirically" (Connell, 2007, p. 66). The prognosis includes a *prescriptive* and linear teleology of an inevitable capitalist modernity spreading across the world through a single/global system of connection via capital/commodities markets, information flows, and imagined land/scapes from the heartland in Europe and North America to bring about a "new form of society" (Beck, 1999, p. 2)—a global modern society whose norms of actions, values, and patterns of socialization are centered on individuation (Lefebvre, 1995). What such theorizing has assiduously dodged is the herd of elephants already seeking to explain long distance relations, including colonialism, capitalism, and imperialism; that is, globalization theory fails to theorize colonization; the structuring principle it does not explicitly name is imperialism; and the type of society that never enters its classifications is the colony" (Connell,

2007, p. 37). Modernity is seen as an endogenous change within Europe and is consequently decoupled from the colonial relations of exploitation that are constitutive of modern capitalism and the development of Euro-America (see Giddens, 1984 for this version). Dominant doctrines of globalization continue to downplay the significance of imperialism and the experience of colonized societies while reducing colonial relations and the *coloniality of power* (Quijano, 2000) to a footnote.

At an *analytical* level there is ample cause for skepticism as well, given the ambitious unit of analysis, which is no less than "the global" (addressed by feminist critics skeptical of world-spanning generalizations from the metropole—see Mohanty, Russo, & Torres, 1991, or Moghadam, 2000), and the reliance on obscure, if not largely indecipherable, concepts like integration, intensity, and compression to make the case regarding the same. Attempts to address globalization in these purportedly apolitical systemic/generic terms or in relation to particular/discrete phenomena, such as technologization or migration or culture-knowledge scapes, empty these related categories of their political-economic and historical links and current implication in the ongoing colonial, imperial, and capitalist expansions of this era. As Cooper (2005) has argued,

> The globalization story claims as new what is not new at all, confuses "long distance" with "global," fails to complement discussion of connections across space with analysis of their limitations, and distorts the history of empires and colonization in order to fit it into a story with a predetermined end (p. 10).

Continued flirtation with the term "globalization" in this collection has been prompted by its extensive and continued deployment in the social sciences since the 1990s, after its initial germination in corporate, business, and economic literatures a decade earlier (Fiss & Hirsch, 2005), and in the comparative and international sociology of education[1] over the past decade or so, in an attempt to *examine* and *question* its salience with respect to education on a *South Asian* or *regional scale* (the region is home to well over a fifth of humanity, including countries with population densities of over 1,000/sq. km, for example, Bangladesh and the Maldives) as proposed by Sivaramakrishnan and Agrawal (2003), without subscribing to their preoccupation with and commitment to modernities (*regional* or otherwise). *Regional* could include supple interpretations of multi/national, subnational, and/or supranational multi-scalar linkages and sociopolitical formations variously defined (e.g., see chapters in this collection by *Sayeed* or *Da Costa* or *Kapoor*, which look at rural social action/movement spatio-temporal formations as *regions* in this regard) in relation to globally *intended* interpolations, that is, the in-between possibilities of the otherwise mostly indecipherable global-local polarities *fixed* by the globalization rhetoric. Institutions, events, and actions often operate/occur at different scales, calling for multi-scalar analyses that articulate the relationships between these scales if not the divergent or mixed temporalities at play, each with its own rhythm(s) (e.g., see policy/macro analytical chapters by *Ali* or *Rizvi & Gorur* or *Tasnima & Haque* in this collection). Particular scales (and definitions of *regionality*) become more/less important in examining certain linkages and sociopolitical relations, thereby complicating the matter of *fixing* the spatial referent for *region* as well. However, what is being suggested is an approach that embeds global processes in a regional *formation* (Gupta, 2003) (e.g., see *Bajaj & Kuruvila* in relation to UN-defined human rights education and its limits/possibilities in various *regional*—national/subnational—applications) in order to develop closer mappings (e.g., see *Pherali's* close mapping of the political economy of the un/intended outcomes of educational decentralization around World Bank-initiated privatization and deregulation in education) of the nature and content of relations and social phenomena (e.g., educational) across distances and locales.

> The globalizers are right to tell us to look at long-distance connections. The difficulty is to come up with concepts that are discerning enough to say something significant about them. Like modernization theory, globalization theory draws its power from uniting diverse phenomena into a singular conceptual framework and a singular notion of change. And that is where both approaches occlude rather than clarify historical processes.
>
> (Cooper, 2005, p. 111)

The antinomies of globalization theory (Connell, 2007; Cooper, 2005) in terms of reified polarities and dualities of global/local, homogeneity/heterogeneity, concentrated/dispersed power, and state-transnational loci can hardly be overcome, as various theorists simply chose to emphasize one pole or the other in empirical substantiations for/against (arbitrary conceptual choices) or suggest a mixture such as *glocal*, which simply restates the opposition without necessarily transcending it. Similarly, *hybridization/Third spaces* often end up being exercises in the celebration of diversity for its own sake, accompanied by a deafening silence around histories, forced disruptions, and continuing effects of the same historical/contemporary *structuring forces*, which inevitably *power* the *directionality* of such culture *mixing*, underscoring colonial amnesia and the inadequacy of these analytical tools to analyze anything between, while remaining trapped in the zone of the undecidable (see chapters by *Datoo* or *Gupta* for related attempts that reference power/directionality and/or colonialism/history to reengage these terms/dynamics with respect to teacher training and student identity formations in schooling/classroom spaces).

Insomuch as it considers globalization and education (and education-culture/identity imbrications) that includes the domains of schooling, higher education, and adult education in South Asia, this collection is a likely first (for an exception that specifically considers schooling in South Asia, see Gupta, 2007) in the hopes that it will energize *critical* scholarship in education concerning this *region*. As with any collection of contributions, we cannot claim to have surmounted many of the criticisms and skepticisms pertaining to globalization and globalization education/culture analyses and literature (or the methodological and epistemic politics) foregrounded/shadowed in this introduction, but they have informed this collection to varying degrees in different chapters. Contributors have deployed critique and understanding in relation to their respective contexts/work and *positionality* on these matters, while being vigilant about the problematics of imperial/neoliberal and colonial categories and trajectories at play in globalization and globalization/education scholarship. Lending coherence to the collection, contributors have not written to re/construct "globalization-education perspectives/theories" but have splintered such socio-educational treatment into the stated focus on the *regional,* that is, multi/national (South Asian nation/s) and/or including sub/supra rural/urban formations that are school/system-specific or community (e.g., see *Barua* in relation to the Barua community and colonial politics) or movement-specific spatio-temporal locations and/or engage a multi-scalar analysis of linkages (e.g., policy processes/impacts) that predominantly steers clear of taking the whole globe as the unit of analysis, while taking global/long distance forces into consideration in discussing the *regional.*

We are aware of the absence of chapters addressing (in the *national sense* of *region*) Afghanistan (see Shirazi, 2007) and Bhutan (see Chhoeda, 2007) and acknowledge the brief consideration given to Sri Lanka and the Maldives. However, the contributions together represent a substantial introductory effort by South Asian and South Asian diasporic scholars toward addressing and signaling significant developments in terms of policy, educational/cultural and material processes, and politics pertaining to schooling, higher education, and adult education in India, Pakistan, and Bangladesh, with due consideration of Nepal, while seeking to bring together political-economic and culture/identity analyses germane to globalization/education scholarship.

What does globalization (as global*izing* modernism or capitalism/neoliberalism and/or colonialism) have to do with educational processes and prospects in South Asia *(various regional formations in this geography)* in the current juncture? How are actors and institutions (multilateral, state, community, schools, universities, NGOs, social movements, civil/political society organizations) in these locations making sense of/engaging these interlocutions? How are education and subject formation taking place in these relations in the various spatio-temporal *regionalities?* What can be/is being done educationally and in sociopolitical terms and in whose interests and why in specific *regions* (rural-urban and within/between, for instance)? How should/is this be/ing accomplished?

Organization and Contributions of the Collection

The collection is organized in relation to an apparent positioning around urban-rural regionalities, histories, life/educational priorities, analyses, and politics, while recognizing that these are not firmly bounded/discrete spaces either. Are *urban* slums categorically or distinctly *urban* in all respects (given the spatial referent) or do they constitute a *rural-urbanity* in a political-cultural-social sense of location? In terms of rural-urban *issues* as well, such clear demarcations are hard to decipher or proffer, as in the case of the politics of land acquisition and displacement of village communities in semi-urban spaces (e.g., acquisition of 10,000 acres for a Vedanta University campus and the subsequent displacement of villages or 10,000 families in a Coastal Regulation Zone/pristine ecological environment in the Puri-Konark corridor by the Vedanta Foundation, floated by Vedanta corporation and its CEO, Anil Agrawal. Vedanta is a transnational corporation with considerable mining interests in the state of Orissa, India, and is currently embroiled in litigation over the Vedanta Niyamgiri bauxite mining proposition). That said, urban priorities of consumer/middle and elite classes do tend toward some arrangement or closer alignment with global/long distance forces and their place-specific manifestations, however critical or circumspect (e.g., the proposition of engagement but on national terms if/when plausible), and are arguably more embedded in (often speaking in/for a more inclusive or just modernity/capital if conceivable) and are constitutive of the very socio-educational trajectories being assessed by contributors writing to, from, and for these locations. Part I of the collection brings together these contributions in relation to the formal institutional contexts of higher education and schooling. All contributors grapple with neoliberalism and the global growth in *privatization* agendas in education, while sporadically wrestling with questions of westernization, in/dependence, and post/colonial intrusions with respect to education, religio-culture/student identity, teacher training, and linguistic and curricular formations.

Part II is organized around rural regions, priorities, and social groups/classes (ethnic communities, small/landless peasants, Adivasi/original dwellers, Dalits/untouchable and backward castes, etc.). These contributors rely on analyses that are conspicuously concerned with the coloniality of power/ongoing colonial relations (including current waves of trans/national capitalist-colonial penetrations into rural/agricultural, forest and *seed* spaces, and education/culture) and the role of adult education as politicization (political education) in social action (e.g., in anticolonial assertion and contestation) in the interests of rural spaces, ways/cultures (modes of meaning making), and political economy (modes of production).

In Part I **(Globalization, Culture, and Education: Urban Priorities and Perspectives and Formal Educational Contexts)**, the first contribution, from *Fazal Rizvi & Radhika Gorur* (Chapter 2), examines current shifts in Indian higher education in relation to what the authors reference as "an emerging global architecture of higher education." Explaining recent developments in higher education, partially propelled by the aspirations of the Indian political elite and the middle/consumer classes, the authors focus more specifically on examples of global collaborations (historically contextualized in relation to India's colonial period). They demonstrate key linkages in relation to specific actors and actual and likely developments in national-global terms, while remaining focused on national priorities. New directions are posited for global collaborations, and the authors suggest that "India should engage global possibilities ... without compromising on its national priorities" (such as the distributional benefits of these collaborations or what these collaborations might also have to offer for "those who have been traditionally marginalized"). They underscore the need to develop a framework to guide global collaborations (offer tentative building blocks for the same) in higher education that would pay attention "to a series of fundamental ethical and political questions," which would inform the rationale and purpose for these engagements.

Sajid Ali (Chapter 3) picks up this thematic in relation to Pakistan and its national education policymaking (with respect to all sectors, including higher education) and what he sees as "the arguable development of a global educational policy field." His analysis suggests that "despite weak national capital, which makes it difficult to diverge from the global policy field, national policy making processes and policy in Pakistan does try and assert its own priorities, mainly through aligning and negotiating" with the former. Rather than simply looking "at how to increase the efficiency of the policy," utilizing critical discourse analysis and interview data, the author dissects the politics of policy processes in relation to key global policies/influences and actors (Education For All [EFA], Millennium Development Goals [MDGs], the World Bank, NGOs). This is accomplished in terms of accessing "privatization," "decentralization," and "standardization" in relation to an educational policy development process initiated by the Pakistani Ministry of Education in 2005, which culminated in a White Paper in 2007 and a national educational policy in 2009, in order to address "broader questions of social justice and power" and "the scope of national (in)dependence."

In Chapter 4, *Touhida Tasnima & Ehsanul Haque* continue to weave threads pertaining to policy/macro perspectives on higher education in the region with an ambivalent look at the situation in Bangladesh. Acknowledging that higher education in the country has "undergone a significant shift and this restructuring and redesigning of higher education has been greatly influenced by neoliberal globalization, which encourages privatization and deregulation for more economic efficiency and corporate governance," the authors connect such developments to the wider political-economic shifts taking place in the country, as higher education is central to generating and utilizing human capital to secure the country's share of the global market. They take a look at this transformation through shifts in policies and operations, and new forms of institutionalization (including private and/or public university developments) triggered by globalization imperatives, pressures, and conditions. While recognizing the "public good" of higher education, they "do not propose that neoliberal reforms in the higher education arena are entirely disadvantageous and unrewarding" and argue that changes in this sphere have included "greater openness, transparency, accountability, and communication in relation to educational quality and standards" and that a "balanced approach may help Bangladesh seize opportunities in the new global order," echoing in certain respects the *Rizvi & Gorur* contribution (Chapter 2).

Tejendra Pherali (Chapter 5) continues with the policy discussion in relation to the "global policy discourse of school-based management," in particular, tracking interactions with socioeconomic and political realities in Nepal by relying on funded research and primary data collected in two private and six public schools. His chapter demonstrates the vicissitudes of externally determined and driven managerial schemes in education pertaining to decentralization, highlighting the concomitant development of "excessive politicization, corruption, and related tensions in the school system" produced by such long distance interventions. Considering the political economy of community schooling, he concludes that "the collaboration between the national governments in the past two decades and international development partners has pushed the decentralization policy to the local levels without considering social, political, and economic realities of Nepali society."

Continuing with the focus on schooling, *Al-Karim Datoo* (Chapter 6) examines culture-curriculum links and how "these productions are interpreted, appropriated, and resisted and in turn employed in the self-identity projects by high school youth." With the help of a critical ethnographic study conducted in a higher secondary school in urban Karachi, this chapter analyzes student interpretations of the representations of culture in science and social science texts, "aiming to expose the merger of the global, colonial, and modern in textual constructions and to look at the exclusions/inclusions of the local." Cognizant of contextual and historical shaping of such constructions, one of the conclusions that the author arrives at is that "some of my research participants seem to have been indoctrinated into this knowledge hegemony through their formal education, by studying a curriculum based on western knowledge production" and that "by nullifying the discourse and contributions of Muslim intellectuals, scientists, and thinkers, the curriculum transfers the colonial legacy to the West and in a substantial way excludes the local-self."

Amita Gupta (Chapter 7) looks at preprimary teacher education policies and practices in India, Sri Lanka, and the Maldives on the basis of document analysis, interviews, classroom observations, and a postcolonial theoretical-conceptual framework. Her chapter raises critical concerns for the region in relation to (i) "the impact of western neoliberalism on early education and teacher education from a human capital and for-profit perspective" and (ii) "the resulting cultural incursions that occur due to conflicting pedagogies rooted in different worldviews." After providing a close overview of preprimary teacher education policies and practices in the region, utilizing a postcolonial perspective, she examines particular shifts being driven by key actors/institutions wedded to neoliberalism in relation to privatization and commercialization, westernization, internationalization, and democratization. She proposes that in order to "address the challenges of a globalizing neoliberalism, it seems critical to move forward with an approach to teacher education that would prepare teacher candidates in a theory and practice that is informed by diverse pedagogical ideas; engage teacher candidates with ideas of social justice; create an awareness in teacher candidates of the implications of neoliberalism; emphasize diversity training in teacher preparation; and prepare teacher candidates to recognize the space and moment when a dominant discourse of education begins to encroach upon marginalized voices."

In Chapter 8, *Monisha Bajaj & Bikku Kuruvila* consider the limits and promise of human rights education (HRE) in India. Relying on data from 13 months of fieldwork in India (2008–2010), including observation, document reviews, interviews, and focus groups with over 700 participants (students, teachers, headmasters, activists, and policymakers), this chapter traces HRE and its multi-scalar shaping and possibilities. The authors point to the historical shifts from human capital to human rights approaches in India, tracing key national level HRE initiatives, looking specifically at changes over time in the National Curriculum Frameworks for Teacher Education between 1978 and 2009. They then consider the possibilities/impacts (e.g., students advocating/intervening in situations of abuse) and limits of HRE (e.g., spiritualization of HRE tied to the religious ideologies of specific parties/governments in power or reductionist approaches of NGO-led health campaigns, which failed to consider more pressing political and human rights issues in Adivasi contexts). They conclude that the rise in prominence of human rights discourse in India "has been mediated by a variety of actors on a range of levels, from national- and local-level policy actors, international institutions, and foreign funders, to grassroots activists and NGOs" and that despite the various permutations (e.g., co-optations into other agendas) at play around HRE, "these initiatives have been successful in both stopping actual instances of and changing attitudinal norms around practices such as female infanticide, caste discrimination, child labor, and child marriage."

In Part II (**Globalization, Culture, and Education: Rural Priorities and Perspectives and Other Educational Contexts**), *Bijoy P. Barua* (Chapter 9) explores how "the Barua community has perceived and sustained its social, cultural, political, and ethnic identity in the face of colonial education, westernization, and neoliberal globalization in rural Bangladesh." Recognizing neoliberal globalization as a formation "linked to the power of capital and corporate culture that tends to control others," who are often seen as "backward, inferior, and substandard by the proponents of modernization and globalization," this chapter shows that education driven by such colonial assumptions "has tended to exclude and marginalize indigenous ways of knowing." Based on life experience, field observation, and narratives from research in rural Bangladesh, an "anticolonial approach [that] recognizes the value and merit of cultural heritage, local knowledge, and the realistic/pragmatic experiences of people" is deployed to demonstrate how "neocolonial and neoliberal globalization have been used as political tools to delink space and displace the indigenous, minority communities from their social roots through the practice of mimicry or didactic learning," that is, "learning processes that have tended to dislocate cultural heritage, indigenous knowledge, customary law, and local economics through the infiltration of a market economy and the global commoditization of education and western knowledge" leading to the "detribalization of ancestral lands." The chapter also demonstrates the revival of Theravada Buddhism and Buddhist identity construction and various organized initiatives to reclaim "a cultural identity based on Buddhist ethics and values." Recognizing the challenges associated with this process (e.g., limited access to national and international social movement spaces), the community is rallying toward a "re/discovery of indigeneity [that] does not necessarily contend a return to a primitive or a colonial era" but "invites a search for self-identification and liberation for collective learning and dignity in the contemporary global world."

Dia Da Costa (Chapter 10) maintains the focus on rurality and the *political value* of education (located in *political society*—see *Kapoor* for similar applications in this collection) vis-à-vis rural social action in neighboring (in relation to Bangladesh) West Bengal, India. Posing the question "what kinds of lives do people have reason to value?" and noting the "general urban middle-class disregard for the very possible cultural preferences for living rural futures," the author suggests that "educating villagers can place them at a structural disadvantage because an education biased toward urban futures implies that villagers neither aspire to agrarian livelihoods, nor do they possess the cultural, social, and economic capital to fit into the competitive job environment of the cities." Taking issue with the "unmitigated enthusiasm for education within (human) development thinking, policy and practice," the chapter problematizes EFA commitments to inclusive and diverse education rhetoric and strategy (and the underpinning/informing human rights, development, and capabilities approach) by focusing on Jana Sanskriti's (JS) (a political theater organization of over 1,000 Bengali agricultural laborers) pedagogy based on the author's engaged association and research with this political process. JS pedagogy, as demonstrated in the chapter, has not only enabled rural laborers to believe in their right to access education but has also encouraged people to debate the purposes, meaning, and processes of education, that is, becoming "spect-actors of history." JS's relation to, and epistemological distinction from, the dominant policy enthusiasm for EFA as articulated in global "human development models, world education conferences, and the MDGs" is described as one that "contests the disciplinary regimes and inequalities embedded in a rural education" linked to these urban-civil society-centric developmentalist constructions, while stressing that such "alternative spaces and forms of education place equal importance on the political imagination with which actors respond to structural limitations and inequalities"; a pedagogy of "permanent liberation and permanent critique."

Azra Talat Sayeed (Chapter 11), based on participatory/action research as an NGO actor with Roots for Equity, picks up on the thematic of rural dispossession and colonization in relation to the trans/national liberalization of agriculture and the seed sector in the 1990s in Pakistan, a process whose impacts are being borne by small and landless farmers. Contending that the "increasing poverty, hunger, livelihood insecurity, and migration in the rural economy are a result of the neoliberal globalization (globalization of capitalism) of agriculture," which has simultaneously "advanced the hegemonic control of agro-chemical transnational corporations (TNCs), consolidating their relationship with the feudal, military, and bureaucratic elite in Pakistan," the chapter historicizes/contextualizes and then discusses Roots for Equity small farmer led campaigns and related learning in social action to address "capitalist colonization of agriculture in Pakistan." Tracing the agriculture path taken in pre- and postindependence times as what was touted as the Green Revolution, colonial continuities are excavated in an attempt to demonstrate historical and contemporary links to genetically engineered (GE) cotton/food seeds and the ongoing capitalist colonization of seeds, land, and peasants in the quest for food for profit for feudal trans/national corporate/political elites. The socioeconomic impacts of the model are discussed (e.g., monopolies on research and media and science; culture and class inequalities) and NGO – small farmer campaigns (Pakistan Kissan Mazdoor Tehreek or PKMT) are considered, including radio/community learning, signature campaigns, and awareness raising and organizing work. The chapter also highlights learning for the NGO/Roots for Equity and points to challenges faced by such organizing and education work.

Rounding off the collection and expanding on the focus of *Sayeed's* analysis in the PKMT *region, Dip Kapoor* (Chapter 12) considers similar processes of primitive accumulation or accumulation by dispossession (capitalist colonizations) of Adivasis (original dwellers/Scheduled Tribes), Dalits (Scheduled Castes/the downtrodden), and landless peasants (together referenced as *subaltern* classes/groups in *political society*) in the state of Orissa, India, as a consequence of the post-1991 (neoliberal turn) expansion of mining and industrial development activities by a corporatized state – trans/national corporate – NGO actor complex. The simultaneous growth of subaltern social movement organizing and activism (trans/local) in the state is mapped, as are the contours of popular education processes that have been integral to shaping, sustaining, and scaling up these dis/organized movements, contributing to an anticolonial politics for material and cultural space by subaltern classes and communities *(political society)* in rural and forested regions.

Acknowledgments

The editors of this collection would like to thank Ms. Alison Crump, doctoral student in the Department of Integrated Studies in Education, McGill University, Montreal, Canada, for her invaluable editorial assistance in bringing this collection together. Thank you, once again, Alison.

Note

1. Arnove and Torres (2007), Barua (2010), Burbules and Torres (2000), Choudry and Kapoor (2010), Dale and Robertson (2009), Datoo (2011), Hill and Kumar (2009), Kamat (2012), Kapoor (2009, 2011), Kenway, Singh and Apple (2005), Klees (2002), Lauder, Brown, Dillabough and Halsey (2006), Rizvi (2012), Rizvi and Lingard (2010), Spring (2009), Stromquist (2002), Tikly (2004).

References

Arnove, R., & Torres, C. (Eds.). (2007). *Comparative education: The dialectic of the global and the local* (3rd ed.). New York: Rowman & Littlefield.

Asad, T. (Ed.). (1973). *Anthropology and the colonial encounter.* New York: Humanities Press.

Barua, B. (2010). Ethnic minorities, indigenous knowledge and livelihoods: Struggle for survival in Southeastern Bangladesh. In D. Kapoor & E. Shizha (Eds.). *Indigenous knowledge and learning in Asia/Pacific and Africa: Perspectives on development, education and culture* (pp. 63–80). New York: Palgrave Macmillan.

Beck, U. (1999). *World risk society.* Cambridge: Polity Press.

Burbules, N., & Torres, C. (Eds.). (2000). *Globalization and education: Critical perspectives.* New York: Routledge.

Chhoeda, T. (2007). Schooling in Bhutan. In A. Gupta (Ed.), *Going to school in South Asia* (pp. 53–65). Westport, CT: Greenwood Press.

Choudry, A., & Kapoor, D. (Eds.). (2010). *Learning from the ground-up: Global perspectives on knowledge production in social movements.* New York: Palgrave Macmillan.

Connell, R. (2007). *Southern theory.* Cambridge: Polity Press.

Cooper, F. (2005). *Colonialism in question: Theory, knowledge, history.* Berkeley, CA: University of California Press.

Dale, R. & Robertson, S. (Eds.). (2009). *Globalisation and Europeanisation in education.* Oxford: Symposium Books.

Datoo, A. (2011). Globalization, media and youth identity in Pakistan. In D. Kapoor (Ed.), *Critical perspectives on neoliberal globalization, development and education in Africa and Asia* (pp. 135–152). Rotterdam: Sense Publishers.

Fiss, P., & Hirsch, P. (2005). The discourse of globalization: Framing and sensemaking of an emergent concept. *American Sociological Review, 70*(1), 29–52.

Giddens, A. (1984). *The constitution of society: Outline of the theory of structuration.* Cambridge: Polity Press.

Gupta, A. (2003). The transmission of development: Problems of scale and socialization. In K. Sivaramakrishnan & A. Agrawal (Eds.), *Regional modernities: The cultural politics of development in India* (pp. 65–74). Stanford, CA: Stanford University Press.

Gupta, A. (2007). *Going to school in South Asia.* Westport, CT: Greenwood Press.

Hill, D., & Kumar, R. (Eds.). (2009). *Global neoliberalism and education and its consequences.* New York: Routledge.

Kamat, S. (2012). Neoliberal globalization and higher education policy in India. In R. King, S. Marginson, & R. Naidoo (Eds.), *Handbook on globalization and education.* Cheltanham, UK: Edward Elgar Publications.

Kapoor, D. (Ed.). (2009). *Education, decolonization and development: Perspectives from Asia, Africa and the Americas.* Rotterdam: Sense Publishers.

Kapoor, D. (Ed.). (2011). *Critical perspectives on neoliberal globalization, development and education in Africa and Asia.* Rotterdam: Sense Publishers.

Kenway, J., Singh, M., & Apple, M. (2005). *Globalizing education.* New York: Peter Lang.

Klees, S. (2002). World Bank education policy: New rhetoric, old ideology. *International Journal of Educational Development, 22,* 451–474.

Lauder, H., Brown, P., Dillabough, J., & Halsey, A. (Eds.). (2006). *Education, globalization and social change.* Oxford: Oxford University Press.

Lefebvre, H. (1995). *Introduction to modernity.* London: Verso.

Moghadam, V. (2000). Transnational feminist networks: Collective action in an era of globalization. *International Sociology, 15*(1), 57–85.

Mohanty, C., Russo, A., & Torres, L. (Eds.). (1991). *Third World women and the politics of feminism.* Bloomington, IN: Indiana University Press.

Quijano, A. (2000). Coloniality of power and eurocentrism in Latin America. *International Sociology, 15*(2), 215–232.

Rizvi, F. (2012). *Globalization and education.* New York: Routledge.

Rizvi, F., & Lingard, B. (2010). *Globalizing educational policy.* New York: Routledge.

Shirazi, R. (2007). Schooling in Afghanistan. In A. Gupta (Ed.), *Going to school in South Asia* (pp. 14–36). Westport, CT: Greenwood Press.

Sivaramakrishnan, K., & Agrawal, A. (Eds.). (2003). *Regional modernities: The cultural politics of development in India.* Stanford, CA: Stanford University Press.

Spring, J. (2009). *Globalization of education: An introduction.* New York: Routledge.

Stromquist, N. (2002). *Education in a globalizing world: The connectivity of economic power, technology and knowledge.* Boston, MA: Rowman & Littlefield Publishers.

Tikly, L. (2004). Globalization and education in sub-Saharan Africa: A postcolonial analysis. In A. Hickling-Hudson, J. Mathews, & A. Woods (Eds.), *Disrupting preconceptions: Postcolonialism and education* (pp. 109–126). Mount Gravalt: Post Pressed.

PART I

Globalization, Culture, and Education: Urban Priorities and Perspectives and Formal Educational Contexts

CHAPTER 2

Indian Higher Education and the Dynamics of Global Collaborations

Fazal Rizvi and Radhika Gorur

Introduction

Over the past decade, India has been pursuing a vigorous program of reform to revitalize its system of higher education against the backdrop of its emergence as an economic force on the world stage. India's economic successes have clearly enabled it to reimagine its relevance on the global stage. Yet a palpable nervousness exists in India with regard to the sustainability of its growth rates, and the inequitable and uneven distribution of rewards. These policy anxieties have underscored the need to not only improve but also radically overhaul its system of higher education, especially against the recognition that one of the key drivers of the global knowledge economy is education. There is thus a strong political desire in India to develop a higher education system that matches its recent economic success.

Just as India's economy is now firmly embedded within the global economy, so it is widely believed that its system of higher education needs to become more internationally oriented. And just as liberalization has opened up India's economy to less restrictive trade with the outside world, so it is thought that India's higher education system also needs to engage more purposefully with educational institutions and systems abroad. Reflecting the changing aspirations and ambitions of middle-class India, it is argued that Indian higher education should open itself to global competition. More broadly, it is suggested that policy resources from outside the country have an important role to play in attempts to reform Indian higher education. It is this understanding that has led India to introduce a Foreign Education Providers (Regulation) Bill, potentially permitting foreign institutions to operate in India under certain conditions. While various provisions of the Bill remain contentious, the need to develop links with foreign universities is not contested.

Links between Indian and overseas institutions are, of course, not new. Indian universities have long engaged in collaborative relations with universities abroad, though the scope of these links has been quite limited, and often shaped by asymmetries of influence. This chapter examines the different patterns of engagement and collaboration between Indian higher education and universities abroad, and addresses the current potential of such collaboration. It explores the key challenges faced in developing collaborative arrangements that are mutually beneficial, culturally and politically sensitive, and educationally productive. We argue that if Indian higher education is to derive significant benefits from global collaborations, then it needs to engage the broader conditions under which systems of higher education now operate. These conditions are defined by the shifting discourses of globalization, which are driven by neoliberal ideologies of global markets, but are now also tinged with uncertainty, instability, and a slight loss of confidence in the market system.

In developing its distinctive approach to global collaborations, we suggest, India needs to negotiate this complex terrain so that its perspective on collaborations is not shaped by global market forces alone, but also takes into account national priorities and endogenous policy traditions. India's postcolonial legacy of pluralism and social democracy has become unsettled as national, institutional, and individual interests have become entangled with global forces and influences. In developing its approach to global collaborations, Indian higher education cannot avoid engaging with the dynamics of a globalizing world and the emerging global architecture of higher education, but needs to do this in ways that are consistent with its long cherished political ideals and its priorities for the future. It cannot afford to simply mimic forms of governance established within the western systems of higher education, but needs to develop structures that are negotiated through critical engagement with globalizing discourses and practices and its own emergent ambitions and priorities within this terrain.

Central to Indian higher education's attempts at negotiating global forces, connections, and resources are the issues of social equity. A critical approach to reform cannot afford to perpetuate patterns of inequality in India. Projects of both colonialism and postindependence modernity favored the already privileged in India, enabling them to enjoy global opportunities, both through emigration to richer countries and through entry into high status professions. There is clearly a major risk in India that the current practices of global collaborations will similarly enable its elite institutions and individuals to join an emerging global "club" of universities, while most of India's second tier state universities will be left behind, continuing to offer an education of poor quality and prospects. This pattern is likely to be further institutionalized by policies of privatization in higher education and more specifically through the entry of foreign universities more interested in deriving their own strategic benefits than contributing to India's social needs. The critical question arises then as to how India should structure its programs of reform so that its system of higher education is able not only to develop globally collaborative links and engage global processes but also promote a robust equity agenda, enabling more of its citizens to engage globalization in their own distinctive ways.

The Colonial Legacy

Indian universities have a long history of engagement with universities and scholars overseas. However, it is the colonial influence—and the colonial project of modernizing and reforming India—that has had a significant and lasting overseas impact on its current educational system. From around 1835, the colonial rulers made a conscious and focused attempt to introduce western knowledge and pedagogies and modern practices of governance, gradually replacing indigenous knowledges and practices (Seth, 2007). In 1857, the Universities of Calcutta, Mumbai, and Madras were set up. These universities were modeled on the University of London (Alexander, 1998), with its tradition of affiliated colleges that followed the curriculum and the examinations, and even the texts, prescribed by the university, which conferred the degrees. To a great extent, this system still exists in India and has become a source of major difficulties in attempts to reform Indian higher education.

Education in British India was rife with a variety of tensions. The British project of promoting independent thinking and preparing students for a range of jobs was in tension with the perceived need for producing a compliant and governable workforce, loyal to imperial interests. Another tension was that British education was alien to and disconnected from local customs and traditions (Seth, 2007). At the societal level, the division created through the acquisition of an English education became a new type of caste system. To counter this situation, new institutions like the Muhammadan Anglo-Oriental College (later renamed as Aligarh Muslim University) and the Benares Hindu University were established. But these institutions were shackled greatly by the fact that the certification authority was still in British hands. They could not avoid, to some extent at least, replicating the very institutions they so stridently sought to critique and oppose.

The India that kept its "tryst with destiny" (Nehru, 1947) on the day of its independence from colonial rule was thus already complex and hybrid. Two centuries of British rule had left indelible impressions on India, not least through its institutions and bureaucratic practices. And within this precarious assemblage of a nation, the first Indian government, under the leadership of Nehru, began the ambitious task of "ending poverty and ignorance and disease and inequality of opportunity" (Nehru, 1947) through education and industrialization. Nehru wanted highly trained engineers and scientists to build modern India and sought aid and expertise from UNESCO, West Germany, the Soviets, and the Americans to develop new institutions. The first Indian Institute of Technology (IIT) was set up at Kharagpur, with assistance from the Americans, the Soviets, and the West Germans (Leslie & Kargon, 2006), followed by IITs in Bombay (with Soviet assistance), Madras (with West German assistance), and New Delhi (with British assistance) (Pant & Rajguru, 2003). Massachusetts Institute of Technology provided assistance in the setting up of IIT Kanpur in 1959 (Leslie & Kargon, 2006). The first Indian Institute of Management (IIM) was established in Calcutta in 1961 as a collaborative project between the Sloan School of Management and the government of West Bengal.

These collaborations in the postindependence era followed a neocolonial model in the sense that the developed western universities were assumed to hold the expertise that would be imparted to the fledgling nation. Although brokered at a national level, with not a little arm-twisting and cajoling at the ministerial level in many cases, each of these collaborations was ultimately realized at an institutional level, resulting in the setting up of specific institutional practices that were islands of excellence that stood apart from the rest of the system. Indeed, institutions such as the IITs and the IIMs enjoyed a different status compared with other universities, falling under special policy and regulatory guidelines. These collaborations did little to influence the general policy climate across the system. Moreover, some of these institutions were so alien to local culture, especially in the initial years, that many of their graduates left for overseas universities.

At an individual level, the recruitment of some of the brightest young students in India by overseas universities involved scholarships that were often portrayed as "development assistance." The Colombo and Fulbright Schemes, for example, provided a select group of academically able graduates of institutions such as the IITs an opportunity to go abroad for advanced research training, with an expectation that the graduates would return home and utilize their skills in the projects of nation building. This expectation was underpinned by a "developmentalist" ideology (Peet, 1991), constructed around linear historicist notions of national economic and social development. Educational aid amounted to an ideology designed partly to create a local elite sympathetic to the interests of the donor countries (Pieterese, 2009). The extent to which these arrangements helped India remains an open question. On the one hand, a large number of Indian scholars did not return home and perhaps made a greater contribution to the countries to which they eventually emigrated. On the other hand, these students created a large Indian academic diaspora around the world that now has the potential to assist in the creation of new collaborative arrangements.

The logics of collaboration under both the colonial and the neocolonial "developmentalist" traditions have much in common. Both traditions assumed the purpose of educational collaboration to be the "transfer of knowledge and skills," through which local capacity was to be developed to meet the nationalist aspirations of industrialization and economic development. This assumption was linked to a western modernist ideology that took little account of local knowledge traditions or of the social and economic conditions under which skills learned abroad were to be applied. This form of collaboration largely served the interests of the local elite and of those who became elite through educational opportunities provided abroad. In effect, the ideology of development through educational collaborations reproduced patterns of inequality, both within India and globally (Escobar, 1995).

The Current Scenario

In contemporary India, many of the colonial and neocolonial "developmentalist" framings persist in policy thinking, alongside strident sentiments of postcolonial nationalism that are located within a context of changing economic and political conditions. Under the stresses of an ever-expanding population and a burgeoning student demand, Indian higher education has, over the last few decades, evolved in distinct and divergent streams. Its complexity is reflected—and perhaps perpetuated—by equally complex arrangements of governance. The system coordination is the responsibility of the Ministry of Human Resource Development (MHRD). The Planning Commission draws the funding parameters, while the University Grants Commission (UGC) distributes resources, administers the accreditation mechanism, monitors quality, and promotes reforms. Although these bodies form the framework of the system, state governments establish and oversee most universities. There is, as a result, a messy political tussle for control between the center and the states (Ambani & Birla, 2000).

With 400 public and 40 private universities, nearly 20,000 affiliated colleges, and 250 specialist teaching and research institutions, India now has the third largest higher education system (after the United States and

China). Higher education employs nearly half a million teachers and caters to 11 million students. Since independence, the demand for higher education in India has increased by 4 percent annually and is set to grow at a faster rate in the years ahead. Indeed, the demand for tertiary education has grown so rapidly that it is simply no longer feasible for it to be publicly funded (Agarwal, 2009). This has meant that private education providers, irrespective of their quality, motivations, and operational styles, are tolerated. As a result, a variety of for-profit institutions, including medical and engineering colleges, are in operation. Despite an implied homogeneity in the use of the term "higher education," there is enormous diversity in objectives, commitments, funding sources, structures, and functioning within Indian higher education (Jayaram, 2004).

The insatiable demand and the paucity of places have meant that some institutions have become "rogue" operators, charging exorbitant fees for substandard education. Regulatory mechanisms appear unable to control these institutions (Altbach & Knight, 2007). An accreditation process is in place but is largely ineffective, with no incentive for the institutions to take it seriously. But the challenges of regulation represent simply one level of problems facing Indian higher education. Other problems include a lack of policy coordination, compounded by India's complex federalism; institutionalized corruption; lack of appropriate material and human resources; and dated and poorly constructed curricula, often unaligned to the changing needs of the Indian labor market (Agarwal, 2009). Bureaucratic red tape and loopholes have led to a breakdown in quality. The infrastructure of most universities is dismal. Research as an activity is poorly funded and there is not much of a research culture. Most importantly, there are not enough teachers of high caliber to teach in these colleges and universities.

It is in this context that many viewed India's decision in July 1991 to usher in liberalization and join the world economy, doing away with a raft of restrictions and controls, as a "second independence"—this time from an oppressive and overbearing state bureaucracy (Das, 2002). Having failed to make a mark as an industrial nation, it was believed, India would finally get its chance to become a significant player in the knowledge economy. Indeed, in the decade following the decision to liberalize, another India emerged—one that became increasingly confident and ambitious and one that could glimpse tantalizing possibilities of modernization. However, the effects of liberalization and economic growth on higher education were uneven, as an influential policy report produced in 2000 pointed out:

> While the larger world embraces the information age, the world of education in India encompasses different "worlds" that live side by side. One world includes

only a fortunate few with access to modern institutions, computers, Internet access and expensive overseas education. A second world wants to maintain status quo—teachers, administrators, textbook publishers, students—all have reasons to prefer things to remain as they are or change only gradually. The third world struggles with fundamental issues such as no books, wrong books, teachers desperately in need of training, teachers with poor commitment, rote learning of irrelevant material, classrooms with hundred students, dirty floors and no toilets. India cannot hope to succeed in the information age on the back of such three disparate worlds.

(Ambani & Birla, 2000)

In the decade following the Ambani-Birla report, an entrepreneurial India has clearly emerged, providing new role models and creating and catering for aspirations previously unimaginable. Although a large section of the population is left out of the economic boom story, India's middle class is expanding at a rapid rate. With this, the demand for better institutions of higher education has surged, even as the system lacks the capacity to cope in terms of both number of places and quality.

Over the past decade, this contradiction between demand and supply has created major policy anxieties across most sections of the Indian community. Responding to these anxieties, the National Knowledge Commission (NKC), chaired by Sam Pitroda, a diasporic Indian entrepreneur, outlined a series of priorities and produced an influential template for reform in 2006. Using the language of "global imperatives," the template drew heavily on neoliberal policy ideas circulating globally (Rizvi & Lingard, 2010; Srivastava, 2007), stressing the need to reform Indian higher education so that it could compete globally. The commission proposed a large number of recommendations that urged the adoption of a "knowledge-oriented paradigm of development to give the country a competitive advantage in all fields of knowledge" (NKC, 2006, p. 11). To increase access, it recommended creating over 1,000 new universities, to raise enrolment to 15 percent by 2015, and other measures to better serve disadvantaged communities. It also recommended the establishment of an Independent Regulatory Authority for Higher Education (IRAHE) to promote and monitor quality, and suggested increased public funding and greater diversification in funding sources.

The influence of this report is evident in India's Eleventh Five Year Plan (2007–2012), through which there has been a significant increase in public funds devoted to higher education, with plans to develop 30 new central universities, including 14 world class universities. The notion of "world class" is used to underline the importance of Indian higher education developing its capacity to compete globally. Greater organizational autonomy is accorded to universities, so that they can seek collaborations with overseas universities, industry partners, and other research institutions. Universities will soon have the autonomy to develop their own procedures and systems for admission, course evaluation, and credit award. Recognizing the urgent need to raise the quality of staff, significant salary increases have been effected, with greater opportunities for staff and students to travel abroad to participate in academic conferences and to undertake advanced studies.

Many of these changes are radical for a system that has been moribund for a long time. The pace of change has accelerated under the leadership of the charismatic HRD minister Kapil Sibal, and the unprecedented and significant injection of funds. The Foreign Education Providers (Regulation) Bill, approved by the cabinet and awaiting debate in the parliament, is set to allow overseas education providers far greater freedom in their operations in India. The Innovation Universities Bill is also awaiting a resolution—if passed, it will pave the way for 16 universities that will operate autonomously, outside the purview of the UGC, with the freedom to recruit and pay staff as they see fit, design their own curriculum, and award their own degrees. In effect, these will be "international" universities operating in India, rather than Indian universities, regulated by Indian state and federal bodies. It seems clear, then, that the new policy settings in India are partly designed to encourage universities to explore new ways to respond to the pressures to internationalize, emanating not only from the fast emerging middle class, but also from India's globalizing labor market.

However, social risks associated with these developments are already evident. While the injection of ideas and resources from abroad is widely welcomed, it is also clear that only the elite institutions and individuals are able to access these. When major US, European, and Australian institutions seek to develop collaborative links, they invariably approach the leading Indian universities, such as the IITs and the central universities. The links, once developed, do not benefit the system at large. This further perpetuates the highly damaging hierarchy that exists in India between centrally funded universities and those supported by the states. Indeed, suspicions in India about privatization (and collaborations) are linked to the widely held belief that neoliberal reforms have not produced benefits for all, and have extended the gap between the rich and the poor (Chandrasekhar & Ghosh, 2002). While there is an acceptance in India that its system of higher education must address globalization, hotly debated is the issue of how it might locate itself within the emerging global architecture of higher education.

An Emerging Global Architecture of Higher Education

The fundamental shifts that are occurring in India are located within the broader context of the way higher education is conceptualized, administered, and practiced globally. Propelled by massification and an increased diversity in the student population, they are resulting in changing patterns of knowledge production; new configurations of resource dependencies; greater mobility; a general expansion of possibilities through technology; increasing isomorphism; and changing relationships within society. Internationalization has been both a cause and an outcome of these more widespread and fundamental shifts. For Indian universities to develop their distinctive approach to global collaborations, they need to understand the significance of these shifts in the very nature of what constitutes "higher education" and how it is practiced, how it is linked to the changing practices of the production and dissemination of knowledge, and how it is utilized to develop skills appropriate to what are assumed to be the requirements of the fast globalizing labor markets.

Globally, enrolment in higher education went up by 53 percent between 2000 and 2007, with 150.6 million students enrolled (Altbach, Reisberg, & Rumbley, 2009). At the same time, the movement of people and programs across international borders has reached unprecedented proportions, with 7 million students expected to be studying outside their home countries by 2020 (Altbach et al., 2009). As a result, the patterns of provision, governance, funding, organization, and behavior of higher education institutions are undergoing a transformation. The diversity of students and the pressures of funding, as well as the push from business and industry for certain types of skills, are impacting the courses offered and the pedagogies practiced, giving rise to a range of new patterns such as collaborative program offerings; distance and technology mediated components in teaching; a focus on "communication skills," "team work," and other "21 Century skills"; and a privileging of certain types of subjects. "International experience" is increasingly valued, leading to exchange programs and other arrangements. The increased movement of academic staff also involves working around different rhythms and schedules.

Massification is also giving rise to new patterns of resource dependencies that are redefining the relationship between universities and society. Changes to the public funding of universities, in particular, reflect the pressures to "fundamentally restructure the 'social contract' between higher education and society at large" (Altbach et al., 2009, p. xii). Postsecondary education, previously seen as a public good, which contributes to society "through educating citizens, improving human capital, encouraging civil involvement and boosting economic development" (p. xii), is increasingly being recast as a private good. This has encouraged increasing privatization in terms of both students paying for education and universities becoming more responsible for generating revenue. Institutions engage in "cost recovery" through higher fees and industry partnerships, and now increasingly through attracting overseas high-fee-paying students and through "exporting" education through various means, including collaborative arrangements. This is in keeping with the more widespread move toward privatization in social policy. The distribution of resources between the activities of a university is thus changing, with teaching subsidizing the research activity. Distance and other flexible types of programs that can be offered across national boundaries are also subsidizing universities' other activities.

At the same time as the student body and the funding models are becoming more diverse, the very nature of knowledge production is changing, and universities are caught up in these shifts (Gibbons et al., 1994), and in the changing dynamics of what knowledge is valued and who is authorized to participate in knowledge production. There is a general argument that the types of competencies required in our times are not limited to those that can be encouraged within the traditional boundaries of a university structure (Beerkens, 2002). Old disciplinary boundaries are becoming harder to maintain, and distinctions between university and various other types of organizations—NGOs, commercial research organizations, and industry—are increasingly blurred. As public research funding becomes scarcer, partnerships with industry, business, philanthropic foundations, and with other universities are on the rise. Thus, there is increased cooperation among sometimes competing institutions in order that each might stay competitive.

While specializations continue to be valued, interdisciplinary collaborations are on the rise. There is also a shift in the nature of collaboration between academic researchers (Douglass, 2005). Campus-based communities are increasingly being replaced or supplemented by networked, multisited communities. With new practices of academic and research work, global research communities are developing. This is aided by the increasing use of English as the language of research dissemination. Scholars are now part of an international market (Altbach & Knight, 2007). New collaborative communities are being promoted through international conferences and symposia, specialized journals and special issues of journals, and standardized processes of peer review and publication. The naming of new specializations and the furthering of such specializations through the publication of dedicated journals, special interest groups in various research organizations and departments within universities all channel activities in certain ways to make these distributed communities viable.

To enable this unprecedented movement of students, academics, and programs, a form of social coordination is occurring on a number of fronts, both at the institutional level and at the national and transnational levels. Even as organizations seek to diversify and occupy specialized niches and gain competitive advantage, the very features of such advantage, such as international links, interuniversity partnerships, and a high score on comparative rankings, demand a level of organizational convergence. Making meaningful connections with each other requires a degree of isomorphism and standardization. For long, international collaborations between universities have been hampered by variety in the courses leading to university entrance, and variety in the requirements, course content, methods of assessment, and so on of particular course offerings. "Articulation" between programs has been very difficult to achieve. The conferral of joint awards, for instance, requires that courses be recognized by each of the partner institutions—this is enabled when the style of course writing, the nomenclatures, the credit award system, the duration of courses, the prerequisites, and the quality and level of award are aligned or made comparable. New agreements, such as the Bologna Agreement, are now increasingly facilitating the cross-border movement of students and programs through such articulation (Douglass, 2005). Free from the baggage of a different time, nontraditional and for-profit institutions are able to plan from the outset for an internationally diverse cohort of students, particularly through the use of new communication technologies. In this way, there is an increasing isomorphism occurring globally among institutions, even as competition presses toward unique features to attract students.

Facilitating as well as forcing these changes are various forms of global protocols, processes, norms of practice, standardizations, and other types of formalizations. These shared forms of social coordination are an essential feature of the emerging global architecture of higher education. The framework of global competition is giving rise to international accreditation and quality review processes (Douglass, 2005). This increasing isomorphism at institutional as well as system and policy levels has enabled global ranking systems to spring up, such as the Shanghai Jiao Tong and the Times Higher Education Rankings. The rankings also function as ways of standardizing universities; as universities seek to improve their position on the league tables, they begin to strategically invest in areas that are valued in the rankings, diverting attention from areas they may have previously valued. The increasing convergence of the sector both results from and is enabled by a more general policy synchrony of market-driven policies.

Examples of Global Collaboration

The changes occurring in higher education globally are interconnected and quite fundamental, with universities becoming transformed into international, networked, and multisited organizations. Collaborations have become an inevitable part of these shifts. The question for India is no longer whether or not to engage in global collaborations, but how it might do so to best suit its current and long-term interests, and how it might harness the opportunities not only to address some of the pressing issues, such as expanding access to higher education and tackling inequities, but also to participate meaningfully within the global context of knowledge production and dissemination, beyond merely being a consumer of overseas education exports.

For overseas universities struggling under neoliberal pressures and the rapid shifts in a globalizing knowledge society and looking to expand their "exports," India, with its "youth bulge" (more than 50 percent of India's current population is below the age of 25, and over 65 percent below the age of 35, according to some estimates) and burgeoning and aspirational middle class, represents a lucrative opportunity. A "foreign" education is still highly prized in India, and parents, who support their children's university education as a norm, are willing to invest generously in such education. Although the Foreign Education Providers (Regulation) Bill awaits resolution in parliament, several institutions from overseas are already operating in India through a variety of collaborative mechanisms and structures. A spate of memorandums of understanding (MoUs) have been signed between Indian and overseas institutions. For instance, the University of Illinois at Urbana Champaign lists collaborations with no less than 20 Indian institutions of higher education and research. The Vellore Institute of Technology has collaborations with 60 institutions from around the world. Such arrangements range from joint award of degrees and franchise arrangements to short-term student exchange programs. The number of twinning, franchising, articulation, and exchange arrangements has been growing steadily over the past couple of decades. Indeed, the highly privatized higher education sector in India has jumped at the opportunities for profit offered by such arrangements.

Agarwal (2009) has noted that private higher education in India has grown rapidly in the "low-risk high-profit segment" (p. 112) of higher education. Most private institutions are commercially oriented and claim to prepare graduates for the fast changing labor market. Whether this is a valid claim is an open question, but what is beyond doubt is that they have little difficulty in attracting students, such is the level of student demand and the paucity of places in publicly funded institutions. Privatization of Indian higher education has therefore been a market logic that has been legitimatized by the General Agreement on Trade in Services (GATS). Under GATS, education is now viewed as a tradeable service. And although India has an ambivalent attitude toward GATS, its provisions have steered the dominant understanding of global collaboration within market terms (Tilak, 2011).

This is not to say that all collaborative links in India are now defined in market terms. Rather, many still arise as a hangover from the developmental model, or are driven by the nostalgic aspirations of diasporic Indians. One example is the Cambridge-India Partnership. Citing a long list of eminent Indian Cambridge alumni, including India's first prime minister, Jawaharlal Nehru; the preeminent scientist Sir C. V. Raman; and the Nobel Prize winning economist Amartya Sen, the partnership describes itself as

> a long term, resilient and evolving relationship founded on scholarly and research-based collaborations, two way exchanges at every academic level, and at the interface of academia with NGOs, business, and public policy, commitment to capacity building for a global future in both Cambridge and India and ever strengthening relations with alumni.[1]

The partnerships have not all been two-way, however. Some Indian institutions have seized the opportunity presented by foreign universities looking for outlets in India to internationalize their courses for domestic students. Manipal University's interdisciplinary Study Abroad Program, for example, is designed "for international students from various universities across the globe to showcase Indian culture and traditions, India's place in world affairs and the role of media and communication."[2]

Some arrangements involve the movement of students in the form of study abroad options or mutual exchange of students. While these are seen as important for enhancing student experience and employability, their scope and ambition are fairly modest. Where programs travel—through franchise arrangements or twinning programs—issues of coordination in schedules, course content, and assessment involve a variety of considerations, not least of which are the learning ethos and other cultural considerations. Such arrangements require greater coordination between the faculties of the collaborating institutions. For example, Lancaster University and Goenka Partnership offers Lancaster University Courses on the GD Goenka World Institute campus in Gurgaon, India, leading to Lancaster University awards to, according to its website, about 450 students currently. These are taught jointly by the staff of both institutions.

In many cases, however, collaborations that are advertised on institutions' websites have been no more than symbolic. Many collaborative ambitions have fizzled out after initial promise. Some never managed to get off the ground after the signing of the MoU. Even when successful, such arrangements are limited in both their ability and their ambition to harness the collaboration to significantly enhance their approaches and practices. The motivation remains one of profit, and if the arrangement were to cease, little would have changed in the practices of these institutions.

Collaborations that merely involve the movement of students and programs do not exhaust the range of collaborative links. A wide variety of research links exist, though often on an individual rather than institutional basis. Many overseas academics of Indian background and research students enrolled at overseas universities have developed close links with Indian institutions. Joint academic conferences and workshops have become common, though jointly published papers remain rare. Researchers based at overseas universities also carry out development assistance projects in India for NGOs and aid agencies.

Some more complex arrangements are now beginning to emerge. The Indian Institute of Technology Bombay (IITB) and Monash University, Australia, have, for example, set up a partnership that takes "a collaborative approach to multidisciplinary research that can effectively deliver high impact, integrated solutions to complex research problems for industry, government and the broader research community."[3] Here, the motivation is not merely to take advantage of a market or even to use a more valued or overseas partner to enhance the attractiveness of an Indian institution. Nor is it just a "knowledge transfer" from a better institution to one of lesser quality. Here, two reputed and comparable institutions are engaged in joint research. The joint venture aims to attract over 250 PhD scholars, jointly supervised by the faculty of the two collaborating institutions. The benefits of such arrangements are not measurable only in the immediate term and are open-ended and without a guarantee. Success is not measured merely in terms of money or enrolment rates or successful completions, though these criteria would certainly be necessary.

The launching of India's first exclusive educational satellite, EDUSAT, is offering exciting possibilities. The purpose and ambition of the satellite was to provide a way to overcome the barriers of distance and the problem of numbers in the vast and populous country and deliver quality education remotely to a widely distributed audience. Although the results to date have fallen short of expectations, the presence of the infrastructure could yet result in exciting initiatives. Recognizing the global importance of providing excellent education to talented Indian scientists and engineers, five leading US universities—the University of California at Berkeley and San Diego, Carnegie Mellon University, Cornell University, and State University of New York at Buffalo—are collaborating with Indian institutions led by AMRITA Vishwa Vidyapeetham, the Indian Space Research Organization, and the Department of Science and Technology (government of India) to teach courses in India over EDUSAT. The initiative is funded by Microsoft, Qualcomm, and Cadence. In this arrangement, involving multiple universities, government bodies, and public and private companies, the motivations are varied and complex. Companies like Microsoft expect that highly innovative and productive engineers will be available for recruitment. Universities hope to develop and recruit highly capable graduate students.

Faculty members at the participating institutions have unique opportunities for professional development and capacity building.

Despite the popularity and the promise of collaborations, few are as comprehensive and ambitious as the examples we have cited. Few aim at long-term success that goes beyond the profit motive or the scope of invading a tempting market. Most remain tentative and informal. The more formal arrangements too face several challenges with respect to the delivery of instructional programs. Differences in the articulation of standards (and in some instances, absence of or disregard for standards) have been widely recognized. Cultural differences and differences in infrastructure make straightforward transfer of courses much more problematic than is often assumed. These practical issues need to be more carefully addressed, at the level both of the institutions and of policies governing articulation. More crucially, with critical legislation still pending, most of these arrangements are being forged in a policy vacuum; if anything, policies (or their absence) have become obstacles to overcome rather than guides and facilitating principles that are aligned with national priorities, and ad hoc rather than coordinated. Most of the existing arrangements are purely commercial in nature, and in some cases, the collaborating institutions are of dubious quality.

Toward a New Direction

We have noted that Indian institutions of higher education have pursued collaborations for a variety of different reasons and that their motivations are rooted in an array of traditions. This has led to a haphazard explosion in collaborations, most of which are increasingly motivated by a neoliberal market ideology, often alongside associations where "superior" institutions from overseas render assistance to India in a developmental logic. Accordingly, a globalized discourse of collaboration in a changing world is giving rise to far more complex arrangements and partnerships. In recent years, a number of high-level delegations have visited India with a view to establishing university partnerships and collaborations. These demonstrate an enormous interest in collaborating with India, not only on the part of foreign institutions of higher education but also governments, scientific organizations, philanthropic bodies, and corporations. At the ministerial levels, several resolutions have been passed and intentions reiterated with regard to collaborations.

However, while the activity is extensive, it is less clear what counts as a successful mode of global collaboration and the conditions under which it is potentially achieved. A critical analysis of these questions does not only demand attention to practical issues of governance, but also more fundamentally conceptual, ethical, and political considerations. In what follows we present some tentative ideas. At the practical level of governance, for collaborations to be meaningful, successful, and durable, appropriate mechanisms of coordination at each of the levels of collaboration appear necessary. Both at the national and institutional levels, policymakers need to keep both the immediate and long-term needs in mind as they device ways to not only *regulate* collaborations with a view to preventing exploitative and undesirable collaborations, but also to *facilitate* collaborations that can deliver broader social and educational benefits to Indian universities. The Bill that is being deliberated should not simply be one that arises from a suspicion of collaborators and therefore framed in terms that safeguard Indian institutions against exploitation, though clearly such regulation is important.

At the national policy level, rationales for global collaborations could include human resource development (since internationalization is now much valued globally and can aid mobility); the building of strategic alliances with particular countries; the generation of revenue through "exporting" education or recruiting students from the region and farther afield; nation building; and social and cultural development. At the institutional level, rationales for internationalization could include the enhancement of institutional reputation; student and staff development; the generation of income; and research and knowledge production (Knight, 2004). Although many of these purposes are not mutually exclusive, a clearer understanding of purpose aids decision making about which collaborations would be more useful and should receive priority. Such a framework is also essential since it would serve to develop a coordinated effort toward the fulfillment of long-term national goals. Knight (2004) pointed out that such deliberations are further complicated at the national level by the relationship between internationalization in education and other areas of governance such as foreign relations, trade, immigration regulations, social development, science and technology, and culture and heritage. At a more focused institutional level, frameworks and policies must guide "purpose, licensing, accreditation, funding, curriculum, teaching, research and regulation of post-secondary education ... for all kinds of providers—public and private, for-profit, or non-profit institutions or companies" (Knight, 2004, p. 13).

The expected benefits must be clarified. Often, when MoUs are signed, there is great enthusiasm and a range of possible benefits is identified. However, a prioritized list at the national and institutional level of the benefits visualized is not only important in operationalizing the collaboration, but would also form the basis for evaluating and administering the programs that emerge. These short- and long-term benefits must be taken into consideration. Moreover, unintended benefits (and harms) need to be anticipated and taken into account. When developed, research-mature nations enter into collaborations with India, it is important to be alert to the possibility of a neocolonial approach to the collaboration, where the "advanced" nation assumes knowledge monopoly (Canto & Hannah, 2001). Having been recipients of aid in the past, Indian institutions could default into vertical relationships, where the overseas partner assumes greater knowledge, disregarding the knowledge the other partners might bring, and the contextual particularities of the collaboration.

As Jane Knight (2004) pointed out, while the national deliberations clearly influence internationalization through policy and regulatory frameworks as well as funding arrangements, it is at the level of the institution that most of the action actually occurs. Issues at the implementation level concern administration, regulation, fiscal issues, and cultural and political issues (Edelson, 2003). Many collaborations that are entered into with a great deal of enthusiasm and expectation fall apart after a short duration. A chief reason for this is that the resources and conditions required to sustain such collaborations had not been adequately visualized and provided. At the national level, it is important to build into the regulatory frameworks the requirement to show proof that the institutions involved have taken this consideration into account when planning and have the resources to maintain a successful partnership. At the institutional level, resources and infrastructure should not be taken for granted, but should be clearly specified at the time of entering into collaboration.

Crucially, however, for any of the collaborations to succeed and for India to remain an attractive partner for collaboration, a range of reforms must be urgently instituted that encompass both policy and practices that govern *all* of India's higher education institutions. At the policy level, a new set of ideas is needed that can disband the inherited and unproductive messy hodgepodge of universities, colleges, private providers, and rogue operators that now constitutes the sector. Given India's bid to add 1,000 new universities in the immediate future, this rethinking is urgent if it is to avoid replicating and making the problem bigger. Better mechanisms for quality assurance and accreditations that motivate institutions to perform well are needed. Enhancing teaching and research capacity is critical. Inequity in higher education, which mirrors the rising inequity in the economy, needs to be addressed. In short, "higher education" itself needs to be reimagined.

Beyond these instrumental goals, however, what are undeniably more important are the complicated political conversations about how India should engage global possibilities and local priorities *simultaneously,* and participate in the global discussions about the emerging architecture of global higher education without compromising on its national priorities, especially those related to social equity. Global collaborations clearly provide an opportunity for Indian institutions to speed up and achieve long-overdue reforms. Reform is not however a value neutral concept, but requires delineation of desirable direction and content. If global collaborations are to contribute in reforming higher education in India, then this contribution should not merely apply to elite institutions and individuals but to the system as a whole, and especially include those who have been traditionally marginalized. Developing a framework to guide global collaborations in higher education thus requires close attention to a series of fundamental ethical and political questions related to the rationale for and purpose of collaboration. What would India hope to achieve through such international collaboration? What would be the purpose of such an exercise in the immediate and the long term? Who are the expected beneficiaries? How are the benefits of international collaborations best distributed?

The focus on higher education in the coming five year plan and the setting up of the Education Commission announced by the prime minister in 2011 must be seized as opportunities to create a turning point for Indian higher education, to examine these questions in a most honest, rigorous, and critical manner, addressing not only practical issues but also ethical and political issues concerning the role of higher education in an Indian society that is increasingly connected to discourses, practices, and institutions globally. Successful global collaborations have the potential to support the institution of widespread reforms in Indian higher education by providing examples and bringing in new resources. But these examples and resources need to be carefully selected and applied, mindful of the critical issues facing India—emanating from the uneven and unequal consequences of globalization—which are clearly evident in its system of higher education as they are in all of its other social institutions. Unless reforms are instituted and successfully carried out in ways that are closely aligned to India's commitment to democracy and social equity, many collaborations are likely to fail and the few that remain will, at best, be inconsequential in the benefits that they provide to the nation as a whole.

Notes

1. http://www.cambridge-india.org/about/.
2. http://www.manipal.edu/INTERNATIONALSTUDENTS/STUDYABROAD PROGRAM/Pages/AboutSAPatManipalUniversity.aspx.
3. http://www.iitbmonash.org/.

References

Agarwal, P. (2009). *Indian higher education: Envisioning the future.* New Delhi: Sage.
Alexander, G. P. (1998). *Higher education in India: Critical issues and trends.* Gardena, CA: P&P Publishers.

Altbach, P. G., & Knight, J. (2007). The internationalization of higher education: Motivations and realities. *Journal of Studies in International Education, 11*, 290–305.
Altbach, P. G., Reisberg, L., & Rumbley, L. E. (2009). *Trends in global higher education: Tracking an academic revolution: A report prepared for the UNESCO 2009 World Conference on Higher Education.* Paris: UNESCO.
Ambani, M., & Birla, K. (2000). *A policy framework for reforms in education.* New Delhi: Prime Minister's Council on Trade and Industry.
Beerkens, E. (2002). International inter-organisational arrangements in higher education: Towards a typology. *Tertiary Education and Management, 8*, 297–314.
Canto, I., & Hannah, J. (2001). A partnership between equals? Academic collaboration between the United Kingdom and Brazil. *Journal of Studies in International Education, 5*, 26–41.
Chandrasekhar, C. P. & J. Ghosh (2002). *The market that failed: Neoliberal economic reforms in India.* New Delhi: Left Word.
Das, G. (2002). *India unbound.* New York: Anchor.
Douglass, J. A. (2005). All globalization is local: Countervailing forces and the influence on higher education markets. Retrieved from, Centre for Studies in Higher Education, UC Berkeley: http://escholarship.org/uc/item/3z26h30n
Edelson, P. (2003). *International collaboration in higher education: An overview of critical issues.* Paper presented at the Virtual Education Conference, June 18–20, Miami, Florida.
Escobar, A. (1995) *Encountering development: The making and unmaking of the third world.* Princeton, NJ: Princeton University Press.
Gibbons, M., Limoges, C., Nowotny, H., Schwartzman, S., Scott, P., & Trow, M. (1994). *The new production of knowledge: The dynamics of science and research in contemporary societies.* London: Sage
Jayaram, N. (2004). Higher education in India: Massification and change. In P. G. Altbach & T. Umaakoshi (Eds.), *Asian universities: Historical perspectives and contemporary challenges* (pp. 85–112). Baltimore, MA: John Hopkins University Press.
Knight, J. (2004). Internationalization remodeled: Definition, approaches, and rationales. *Journal of Studies in International Education, 8*(1), 5–31.
Leslie, S. W., & Kargon, R. (2006). Exporting MIT: Science, technology, and nation-building in India and Iran. *Osiris, 21*(1), 110–130.
National Knowledge Commission. (2006). *Report to the Prime Minister.* New Delhi: NKC.
Nehru, J. (1947). *Speech: Tryst with destiny.* New Delhi: Indian Constituent Assembly.
Pant, R., & Rajguru, S. (2003). *IIT India's intellectual treasures: Passage through the Indian institutes of technology.* Silver Spring, MD: Indus Media LLC.
Peet, R. (1991). *Theories of development.* London: Guildford Press.
Pieterese, J. N. (2009). *Development theory.* London: Sage.
Rizvi, F., & Lingard, B. (2010). *Globalizing education policy.* London: Routledge.

Seth, S. (2007). *Subject lessons: The western education of colonial India.* Durham and London: Duke University Press.

Srivastava, R. (2007). National knowledge commission: Meeting social goals or neo-liberal reform. *Economic and Political Weekly, 42*(10), 812–815.

Tilak, J. (2011). *Trade in higher education: The role of the General Agreement on Trade in Services (GATS).* Paris: IIEP UNESCO Publishing.

CHAPTER 3

The Global Educational Policy Field and National Education Policymaking in Pakistan

Sajid Ali

Introduction

The processes of globalization have arguably led to the emergence of a global education policy field, which supposedly pushes for a common world agenda for education (Rizvi & Lingard, 2010). The development of global education targets and international testing regimes, the popularity of the English language, and the import-export of higher education programs across the globe are evidence of this agenda. Nation-states are engaged in an active process of negotiation and trade-offs with this global field through a set of contextual value preferences and what may be referred to as a national education policy field. An important task for policy analysts is to understand these fields and the cross-field effects (Lingard, Rawolle, & Taylor, 2005) in order to better understand the effects of globalization. The policy effects of globalization can only be understood in relation to contextual specificities (Tikly, 2001), although an analysis of a particular case—in this case Pakistan—has important lessons for similar contexts.

In this chapter, I take account of the emerging global education policy field and discuss how it interacts with the specific education policy context of Pakistan. I focus on the current education policy development process, which was initiated by the Pakistani Ministry of Education (MoE) in 2005 and which culminated in a White Paper on education in February 2007 and a subsequent education policy in September 2009. In this chapter, I conduct a critical discourses analysis (Fairclough, 1992, 2006) that focuses on broader questions of social justice and power. This approach allows me to explore the scope of national (in)dependence in the wake of global education policy trends, rather than simply looking at how to increase the efficiency of the policy (Ozga, 2000).

The study from which this chapter draws was carried out between 2005 and 2009. It focused on the policy development process that resulted in a pre-policy document entitled "Education in Pakistan—a White Paper" in 2007 (the central focus of the study and this chapter) and a final policy paper in 2009. Other data sources included 46 policy or policy related documents and 26 interviews with policy review teams, ministry officials, Planning Commission officials, academics, and representatives of donor agencies, NGOs, and INGOs (see Ali, 2009, for more details on the methodology).

Education Policy Context of Pakistan

Pakistan emerged as a postcolonial nation in 1947 after the departure of the British from India. Education was considered one of the most important factors in the development of the new nation, as visible in the first education conference held in November 1947 (3 months after independence). In his inaugural address the nation's founder—Muhammad Ali Jinnah—said,

> There is no doubt that the future of our State will and must greatly depend upon the type of education we give to our children and the way in which we bring them up as future citizens of Pakistan.
> (Ministry of the Interior Education Division, 1947)

However, later events show that this priority to education could not move beyond rhetoric. Several educational plans and policies have been put forward since then but without remarkable results. According to the Federal Bureau of Statistics (2011), the current adult literacy rate is 59 percent and those who go to school either drop out early or suffer a low quality learning experience, with the exception of those who can afford better off private schools.

There are some pertinent education policy issues in Pakistan that need to be understood to appreciate the subsequent discussion. Foremost is the issue of ideology, that is, the role of Islam in curriculum and instruction. Since Pakistan came into being as a homeland of Muslim Indians, the sentiments toward the position of Islam in education have been highly charged (Lingard & Ali, 2009). The current education policy has a whole chapter dedicated to Islamic education (Ministry of Education, 2009). The second significant issue is the language of education, whether it should be Urdu (the national language) or English (the global language) or a local language. Finding the right mix of these has remained a hot issue that often raises high emotions (Mustafa, 2011). Some see a national language as a symbol of national unity; others, however, argue for mother tongue instruction for reasons of identity and familiarity. The role of English for ensuing financial gains is also significant. The third major issue relates to the class-based education system: high quality private schools for elites, low cost private and public schools for the poor, and *madrasas* for the poorest of the poor (Rahman, 2004). Last but not the least is the issue of the government's lack of attention to improving the educational system for the disadvantaged (i.e., rural folk, the poor, and females[1]). The government allocates approximately 2 percent of the GDP for education, which is often not fully disbursed. Policy documents are produced by each subsequent government with high promises but few achievements (Ahsan, 2003).

Recently, there have been some significant constitutional changes that affect education. In 2010, the 18th Constitutional Amendment was passed by the parliament, which has devolved many powers from the center to provincial governments. Pakistan has a federal structure with four provincial and federally administered area governments. Historically, the federal government retained most of the power. The 18th Amendment has given more autonomy to the provinces in several areas, education being one of them. Thus, each province is now supposedly free to devise its own educational priorities and curriculum with minimum federal coordination. This is a significant move for a country where historically curriculum has been tightly scrutinized at the federal level.

Global Education Policy Field

The notion of a global education policy field maintains that a consensual set of education policy themes and processes is emerging above nation-states, which has serious effects on national education systems (Ozga & Lingard, 2007). Rizvi et al. (2005) refer to this as an emerging "educational policy terrain" (p. 5). Lingard, Rawolle, and Taylor (2005) argued that in the era of globalization, the field of education policy is faced with the effects of other fields, such as the economy. A field is not geographically bound, but

> a structured social space, a field of forces, a force field. "It contains people who dominate and people who are dominated.... All the individuals in this universe bring to the competition all the (relative) power at their disposal. It is this power that defines their position in the field and, as a result, their strategies".
> (Bourdieu, 1998, pp. 40–41)

The field of education policy is no longer national in character, but has largely been incorporated within the economic field in many countries; in other words, policymaking theories have to be stretched beyond national levels in order for the effect of the global field of education policy to be recognized (Lingard, Rawolle, & Taylor, 2005).

The constant interactions and tensions between global and national policy fields yield a unique vernacular policy (Appadurai, 2001); therefore, manifestations of local policy need to be understood within the terrain of the emerging global education policy field. However, it is important to recognize that the very nature of globalization and its preferred values are being contested too. Indeed, Santos (2002) pointed out that there are various forms of globalization, representing various ideologies, which are at present dominated by the neoliberal ideology. David Harvey (2005) defined neoliberalism as "a theory of political economic practices that proposes that human well-being can best be advanced by liberating individual entrepreneurial freedoms and skills within an institutional framework characterized by strong private property rights, free markets, and free trade" (p. 2).

These value preferences have led to various education policies and practices that are being globally promoted by organizations such as the World Bank and the Organization for Economic Cooperation and Development (OECD). The result is a prevalence of narrow and economically oriented educational objectives, an emphasis on testing and measuring educational outcomes, the development of globally comparative educational targets, and devolved forms of educational governance. In addition, the global education policy field has created a discursive framework within which education policy is produced at global and national levels (Rizvi et al., 2005); therefore, these global trends and discursive frames set the conditions for national policymaking, but national education policies manifest differently in different countries because of their unique contextual characteristics. In the next section, I discuss the effects of this emerging (neoliberal) global education policy field in Pakistan. This is followed by an analysis of how the global field finds its way into the national policy space and the responses of the Pakistani state.

Effects of the (Neoliberal) Global Education Policy Field in Pakistan

So far I have given an overview of the education policy context of Pakistan and I have argued that the effects of the emerging global education policy field need to be understood within the national education policy space of Pakistan. Briefly, the neoliberal global education policy field privileges the role of knowledge for the service of the economy; it emphasizes competition, measurement, and standardization, and promotes the governance of education through decentralized and privatized structures. In what follows, I provide a deeper analysis of the effects of the global education policy field in Pakistan with respect to three phenomena: privatization, decentralization, and standardization.

Privatization

There is a general and growing preference around the world for private and quasi-private educational services compared with public services. This has given rise to the privatization of entire or partial components of educational services, such as building facilities, teacher provision, or the private adoption of schools with some public support (McCulloch, 2008). Through privatization, schools are run like a marketplace, using a voucher system and similar marketizing strategies (Apple, 2004). This is achieved by showing the ineffectiveness of public schools, and it destroys the social responsibilities that a state holds toward its underprivileged and vulnerable population (Bourdieu, 2003).

In Pakistan, privatization is on the rise, indicating an influence of neoliberal ideals. In 2005, 33 percent of educational institutions were in the private sector (Ministry of Education, 2006), a growth from roughly 18 percent in 2000 (Ministry of Education, 2003). It is estimated that education in urban areas is largely handled by the private sector. There are several government initiatives that encourage private support for public education, most prominently through the work of the Sindh Education Foundation (SEF) and the Punjab Education Foundation (PEF).[2] The initiatives of the SEF and the PEF are financed by the World Bank, an ideologically neoliberal organization. A recent study, sponsored by the World Bank, showed that privatized educational services, even in poor rural communities, are of better quality and more cost-effective than their public counterparts (Andrabi et al., 2008). Several other donor agencies have also promoted public-private partnerships as the right choice for Pakistan.

Although private education has existed in Pakistan since 1947, the emerging privatization trend has several critical issues. The biggest issue with the promotion of private education is that the state becomes complacent about its duty toward its citizens, particularly the disadvantaged. The government's annual expenditure on public education, which has remained around 2 percent of the GDP, indicates a low political interest in this sector. Although it is the state's responsibility to provide equal access to good quality basic education, sadly, the reality is an educational apartheid in Pakistan (Siddiqui, 2007), which guarantees privileges for an elite class, leaving the majority in deprivation.

With government budgets being cut, on the one hand, and increased needs for investments in education on the other, there is little choice but for private involvement in education. In Pakistan, the government has continuously neglected its responsibilities regarding education and has encouraged private and nongovernmental provisions that disadvantage the vulnerable population.

Decentralization

One of the preferred forms of governance promoted through the global education policy is managing through decentralized structures. There has been a steady rise in decentralized forms of government structures since the 1990s (McGinn & Welsh, 1999). Governments are involved in more networked and joined-up forms of governance, which involve several members not only from public but also from private and nongovernmental sectors (Mok, 2005). This move is often referred to as government to governance (Rosenau, 2000) and is influenced by neoliberal views of the free market economy. Decentralization reforms in education are being taken up more readily because of the declining authority of the state, the general agreement on free market principles, and the utilization of ICT and new technologies (McGinn & Welsh, 1999).

Decentralization reforms were introduced in Pakistan in 2001 by the then president Pervez Musharraf. The reforms, particularly in the education sector, aimed to restructure centralized education and devolve decision making to the district level for increased efficiency and autonomy at the local level (Memon, 2003). However, the insufficient capacity of educational managers at the district level raised doubts about the achievement of decentralization objectives at its early stages (Ali et al., 2006). In 2010, the 18th Constitutional Amendment, which devolved powers to the provinces in several domains, including education, was passed.

In a way, decentralization seems logical as it brings decision making to more local levels. However, decentralization does not come as a standalone education reform; rather it is part of a package that not only devolves decision-making authority to a lower level but at the same time distributes the control of educational governance to multiple actors including nongovernmental and private sectors, where the public sector appears quite weak. In Pakistan, the decentralization reforms of the Musharraf government in 2001 were politically motivated too. Through the decentralization of responsibilities at the district level, the federal government achieved more direct control over local affairs, bypassing the middle layer of provincial administration. But the decentralization reforms have also added to the mess of educational management at provincial and district levels. The involvement of various actors—international organizations, funding agencies, and national NGOs—has created a situation where the government is never in full control of the educational policy in its jurisdiction. I recently visited the provincial education and finance ministries to know the actual educational expenditures by various donor agencies. To my surprise the authorities did not know for sure the amount being contributed by donor agencies. This suggests a poor management capacity of the public sector, which allows for the operation of several different streams of educational development without synchronization.

This shifting of responsibility to the local level without providing the necessary financial and human resources has caused serious damage to an already weak governance system in Pakistan. Hence, soon after the departure of the Musharraf government in 2007, the provinces started reverting back to the old commissionerate system in place of local governments. Thus, while decentralized forms of educational governance are pushed by the global education policy field, they do not necessarily result in effective management of the public education system. The case of Pakistan suggests that decentralization has not worked. In fact, in an unjust system, decentralization further deprives the underdeveloped regions in the country.

Standardization

One of the most prominent features of the global education policy field is the importance it attaches to the measurement of outcomes according to well-defined indicators. This has caused a huge surge of educational statistics at the global level. Educational targets are being measured, and tests, such as the Programme for International Student Assessment (PISA) and Trends in Mathematics and Science Study (TIMSS), are conducted to benchmark several countries over a standardized scale. Grek (2009) called this phenomenon "governing by numbers" (p. 23), whereby statistics are used for governing the education sector and for demonstrating performance.

These test scores and indicators show the relative quality of human capital of any particular country and thus are a critical factor in developing the image of a country in the global knowledge economy. These benchmarks also have the potential to create standardization through assessing performance in particular areas and of particular skills, leading to homogenizing curricula and pedagogies. This trend can be seen in Europe's unified "European education policy space" (Grek et al., 2009, p. 5; Lawn & Lingard, 2002, p. 292).

In Pakistan, there have been some developments that indicate a move toward standardization and benchmarking. In 2010, the Higher Education

Commission (HEC) notified the National Accreditation Council for Teacher Education (NACTE) to maintain standards in teacher education. In 2011, the Sindh government likewise notified the STEDA (Sindh Teacher Education Development Authority). Prior to these developments, the MoE established professional standards for teachers in Pakistan in 2009. The length of degrees has also been stretched to fulfill international requirements. Programs for students' assessment at particular grades are also on the rise. In the 2010–2011 academic year, the government of Sindh province assessed all grade four students in language and mathematics through the Provincial Education Assessment Centre (PEACE). There are plans to extend the assessment to other subjects and other grades.

There is also a substantial rise in the development and maintenance of educational statistics in Pakistan, resulting in several publications such as National Education Census 2005; National Education Assessment System's (NEAS) results; provincial assessment results; reports on the achievement of targets of EFA (Education for All) and MDGs (Millennium Development Goals); and annual reports on the state of basic education indicators by the Education Management Information System (EMIS) at the national and provincial levels. The abundance of statistics does suggest a move toward policy by numbers (Grek, 2009). This appetite for numbers will likely continue to increase now that educational decentralization has been passed through the 18th Constitutional Amendment in 2010.

However, critical issues, such as how the standards are set, who determines them, which indicators are chosen, and how are they reported, are not being addressed. This oversight is significant. It is also significant that the standards for teachers in Pakistan have been developed with the support of USAID and UNESCO. The accreditation of teachers is supported by the same agencies. The attention to numbers has led to a system that rewards performativity and does not appreciate excellence because what does not get measured does not matter.

How Did Global Education Policies Seep into National Space?

The global education policy field has affected the national education policy context of Pakistan in several ways (e.g., privatization, decentralization, and standardization). I now discuss how these neoliberal preferences are making their way into Pakistani policy. Dale (1999) highlighted several mechanisms for this shift: harmonization, dissemination, standardization, installing interdependence, and imposition. In Pakistan, the government's support for private education seems to have links with World Bank loans for education (an example of imposition). Other mechanisms largely follow discursive processes, such as persuasion, agenda setting, collective agreements, and membership requirements. These discursive means of policy influence reveal a complex understanding of how the global education policy seeps into the national space (Dale, 1999). For example, the process of reaching collective agreements is not power neutral and the actors engaged in this process are not placed on an equal footing: a donor representative holds much more power than the representative of the recipient country. In fact, discursive processes play a major role in making globalization a reality (Fairclough, 2006). Such means of policy transfer (e.g., persuasion and collective agreements) appear noncoercive on the surface, however, the arena where these policy transfers take place reveals who has the control over resources and who has the power to make decisions.

Relatively more research has been conducted on the effects of aid (a material means) on national policy; the focus of this chapter, however, is on discursive means. In education policymaking in Pakistan, the discursive frame is created through (i) a plethora of reports, research studies, and data; (ii) consulting meetings; and (iii) feedback on drafts of policy.

In 2005, the National Education Policy Review (NEPR) team was created by the MoE, comprising independent consultants and supported by the policy wing of the MoE. The NEPR team developed Green Papers, held several provincial conferences, conducted roundtables, and organized consultations with key education policy actors, including donors, academics, NGOs, and public figures. The White Paper, which synthesizes all these consultations and is considered a pre-policy document, was published in 2007. Later I discuss how the mechanisms alluded to above have created the discursive boundaries for the policy outcome in the White Paper.

An abundance of documents and global policies circulate in the education policy environment of Pakistan. The most prominent global policies are the EFA and the MDGs, both by the United Nations. There are also some country strategy papers produced by international organizations[3] working in Pakistan, which outline the agencies' priorities in relation to education policy developments in Pakistan.

The most common themes that run across these strategy papers are linking educational programs explicitly with poverty reduction strategies; promoting good governance and accountability measures; and achieving the targets set under EFA and MDGs. These concerns have been given a prominent place in the text of the White Paper. The analysis I conducted of the policymaking process of the White Paper suggests that all of these agencies were prominent actors in consultative processes organized by the policy review team. The White Paper acknowledges the power that donor agency representatives have in the national policy context.

Availability of donor support and money also reduces the practical significance of the policy as the priorities identified by these agreements overtake other conditions. Formally, these interventions are not against, or outside, the policy, but these do sometimes distort the priorities.

(White Paper, p. 8, pr. 4)

In an interview, when I asked about donor influence on the policy process, a senior education official said,

I was very particular not to receive any official assistance from any donors at all, but for good reasons. Because in this country it is very fashionable to say that a foreign agenda is being pursued.

The official's response suggests that national policy has been affected by international organizations and therefore the official tried to dispel that idea. However, the priorities set within the White Paper, for example, good governance and achievement of international targets, are some of the prominent demands that are laid out in donors' strategy papers. It is widely believed in Pakistan that donors have a substantial say in education policy in the country either directly or indirectly because of the money that they invest in the sector. In an interview, a member of the policy review team shared the following:

Donors in the sector of education play an extremely important role because they are a major supplier of resources. Therefore, they definitely have a lot of influence.

The participation of various prominent policy actors, particularly from international organizations, also suggests a way through which the policy preferences of global neoliberalism have seeped into the education policy of Pakistan. In an interview, a representative of a donor agency said,

Well, I have to say that this is probably the first time we've seen a highly consultative process for the development of any policy. An elaborate process was engaged by the Ministry of Education and I'm not going to repeat what it was [showing the White Paper document]; I'm sure you must have seen them. The stakeholders, the interviews, I mean that was a district-wide process where the show went on road, so to speak, and provinces and districts were taken into confidence on this particular issue. On the various key areas of education, Green Papers were developed. I think the donors were engaged hugely in reading, commenting, and providing feedback on the Green Papers.

A special Donor Education Group (DEG) was established and the NEPR team and MoE officials interacted with the DEG numerous times. This obviously affects the preferences of the NEPR team in its task of proposing new education policy. Several donor-sponsored roundtables were also organized on the basis of the interests of particular donor agencies. For example, JICA (a Japanese development agency) sponsored a roundtable on technical and vocational education, and UNESCO organized roundtables on literacy and nonformal education, early childhood education, gender and education, and teacher education and accreditation.

Another way global policy preferences influenced national policy was through the feedback and reaction that donors, academics, and NGOs gave on the first draft of the White Paper. The first draft of the White Paper was published in December 2006 and it attracted a lot of feedback from various quarters. A revised version was issued in February 2007 with the following observation:

> The White Paper [first version] has evoked some very valid and well considered comments and observations.... It is recognized that certain clarifications and amplifications are absolutely essential to enlarge its ownership by all concerned. A revised White Paper has, therefore, been attempted to incorporate all valid suggestions to make the pre-policy document more refined.
> (Preface to the revised White Paper, p. ii)

Comparing the two versions shows that the suggestions put forth in the feedback, particularly by international organizations and NGOs, were seriously considered in the revised version. For example, in the revised version there is greater emphasis on the role of the private sector. The revised version proposes introducing a voucher system and public-private partnerships in various areas like textbook publication, higher and vocational education, school inspection, and examination. These examples from the larger study I conducted between 2005 and 2009 show various discursive means of enabling the global education policy field to seep into the national policy space.

The Response of the State

In order to understand the response of the Pakistani state toward the global education policy, it is necessary to first recognize that the global or "travelling policy" comes into the national space that is already loaded with "embedded policy" (Ozga & Jones, 2006, p. 2). There are national specificities, histories, cultures, and politico-economic priorities that interact with the global policy to create a new hybrid form of policy that is unique and vernacular in many ways (Appadurai, 1996; Lingard, 2000). Above all, there is a national pride that national bureaucracies cherish and that can fuel resistance to international pressures. In an interview, the former federal education secretary commented on the control that the Pakistani state feels (or wants to feel):

> Donors have to align with us. I'm very clear about that. We don't align with donors; donors have to align with us. So that's not an issue. The way things happen or should happen, and we try to make sure that it happens, is that which we as a government decide. We may consult the donors, but we as government decide what we want.

Nevertheless, the interaction of global and national education policy fields is filled with tensions. For example, there is a constant pressure for Pakistan to reach the EFA and MDG targets set for 2015, however, it is most likely going to miss these by a big margin. Pakistan's commitment to these targets is a condition for borrowing development money from donor agencies. Pakistan has set the goal of being transformed into a knowledge economy by 2030, which requires a significant investment in the higher education sector. However, donors are in favor of supporting basic education, which will help meet EFA and MDG targets.

There are also tensions around the issue of Islamic ideology, which is quite central to Pakistan's education policy. The events of 9/11 and the subsequent pressures on Pakistan have posed serious challenges for Pakistani education policy with regard to its stance toward Islamic ideology and its place in the curriculum. The government has mostly used Islamic symbolism in the curriculum to promote cohesiveness among the people of Pakistan, who belong to various ethnicities. The official curriculum has always equated being a good Pakistani with being a good Muslim (Durrani, 2008). Thus, the global criticism of Pakistan's overly Islamized curriculum and religious schools has created a tension for national policy.

Overall, the state does not generally receive global policy as a docile agent and the state has encountered numerous tensions within its policy purview. I now return to the White Paper as a specific example of how has the Pakistani state interacted with the global education policy field.

My analysis of the White Paper showed that the Pakistani state has used alignment and negotiation as the two main strategies in dealing with global policy preferences. For example, the policy prescriptions of the White Paper show that government has largely accepted the global priorities of EFA and MDGs, and recommends ways to achieve them. In the case of ideology, the White Paper shows a negotiating strategy, as it does not simply accept the global discourse. In order to achieve an appropriate balance, the White Paper tries to create a discursive rupture between fundamentalist and moderate Islam and gives tremendous attention in its initial pages to suggesting that the current government would be in favor of moderate Islam, which is more aligned with democratic principles, as shown in the excerpt below.

> The Education Policy of every State has an ideological basis at least for a predictable timeframe.... in the context of Pakistan, this ideological base is essentially and historically provided by Islam as an ideology derived from Islam the religion.... However, Islam is not and cannot continue to be treated as a static religious dogma, thriving on ignorance and nostalgia.
>
> (Aly, 2007, p. 3)

The moderate ideological position was taken not simply due to international pressure but also due to the preferred policy of the government and to calm the resistance of national actors (see Silova, 2004; Spring, 2008).

In order to settle tensions between global and national pressures on the issue of the language of education, the White Paper highlights the significance of English over national languages and tries to shed the colonial memories attached with English language, as in the following:

> So English was the official language of authority and the language of the elite and was understandably perceived as a vehicle for social and economic advancement. After 1947, English has continued to enjoy privilege of the British times, though no more considered imperialistic in dispensation. In the meantime in the last half a century or so, the influence of English language has broadened way outside the original English speaking countries. It is no more the language of Anglo-Saxon descent but is now a language of international communication, cosmopolitan life and transnational trade and commerce. English has grown from its colonial aura of luxury and prestige to an international necessity in the globalized world.
>
> (Aly, 2007, pp. 53–54)

Along with this attempt to dispel the colonial legacies of English, the White Paper also suggests the powerful position that the English language has acquired in developing countries as the international language of commerce. English has a push-pull relationship with Pakistan's education policy context. On the one hand, it reminds people of the colonial past and is therefore resisted; on the other hand, it symbolizes economic prosperity to its learners and is welcomed. For example, private schools, which are English medium, have become more and more popular in Pakistan. The prominence of English is not imposed through some explicit foreign policy but has seeped in through discursive means, such as the importance of English in multinational corporations that have lucrative job prospects, the prospects of foreign degrees in English that bring opportunities to Pakistan, and the electronic media which values English conversational skills. These discursive means have helped to firmly establish in the minds of the Pakistani people the idea that a good school is one that enables its students to communicate in English.

Conclusion

In this chapter, I have explored how the global and national education policy fields interact in the education policy formulation in Pakistan. This complex interaction results in a unique vernacular policy; however, the extent to which a state can shape a final policy that disagrees with the global policy depends on its national capital. This is determined by the overall financial, material, human, and political resources a country possesses (Bourdieu, 2003). The Pakistani state, like other developing countries, possesses weak national capital and therefore cannot afford to diverge too much from the global policy field. However, as I found in my critical discourse analysis, the national policy field in Pakistan does try to assert its own priorities, mainly through aligning and negotiating with the global policy field.

Notes

1. The adult literacy rate among females is 46 percent versus 71 percent for males; the adult literacy rate among the rural population is 42 percent versus 75 percent in urban areas (Federal Bureau of Statistics, 2011).
2. SEF and PEF are semigovernmental organizations established by the provincial governments of Sindh and Punjab, respectively, to promote public-private partnerships and innovative models in education.
3. Examples are Asian Development Bank (ADB), World Bank, European Commission (EC), United States Agency for International Development (USAID), Save the Children UK (SC-UK), Japan Official Development Assistance (ODA), Department for International Development (DFID) et cetera.

References

Ahsan, M. (2003). An analytical review of Pakistan's educational policies and plans. *Research Papers in Education, 18*(3), 259–280.

Ali, S. (2009). *Governing education policy in a globalising world: The sphere of authority of the Pakistani state.* Unpublished doctoral dissertation, University of Edinburgh, Edinburgh.

Ali, S., Alvi, U., Babur, M., & Rizvi, M. (2006). *Capacity-building and decentralization at district level: Report on the ESRA research project.* Karachi: Institute for Educational Development, Aga Khan University.

Aly, J. H. (2007). *Education in Pakistan a White Paper revised: Document to debate and finalize the National Education Policy.* Retrieved from http://www.moe.gov.pk/nepr/WhitePaper.pdf

Andrabi, T., Das, J., Khwaja, A. I., Vishwanath, T., Zajonc, T., & LEAPS Team. (2008). *Pakistan – Learning and Educational Achievements in Punjab Schools (LEAPS): Insights to inform the education policy debate.* Washington, DC: The World Bank.

Appadurai, A. (1996). *Modernity at large: Cultural dimensions of globalization.* Minneapolis; London: University of Minnesota Press.

Appadurai, A. (Ed.). (2001). *Globalization.* Durham: Duke University Press.

Apple, M. W. (2004). *Ideology and curriculum* (3rd ed.). New York: RoutledgeFalmer.

Bourdieu, P. (1998). *On television.* New York: The New Press.

Bourdieu, P. (2003). *Firing back: Against the tyranny of the market.* London: Verso.
Dale, R. (1999). Specifying globalisation effects on national policy: A focus on the mechanism. *Journal of Education Policy, 14*(1), 1–17.
Durrani, N. (2008). Schooling the 'other': The representation of gender and national identities in Pakistani curriculum texts. *Compare, 38*(5), 595–610.
Fairclough, N. (1992). *Discourse and social change.* Cambridge: Polity Press.
Fairclough, N. (2006). *Language and globalization.* London; New York: Routledge.
Federal Bureau of Statistics (2011). Pakistan Social and Living Standards Measurement (PSLM) 2010–2011. Government of Pakistan.
Grek, S. (2009). Governing by numbers: The PISA 'effect' in Europe. *Journal of Education Policy, 24*(1), 23–37.
Grek, S., Lawn, M., Lingard, B., Ozga, J., Rinne, R., Segerholm, C., et al. (2009). National policy brokering and the construction of the European education space in England, Sweden, Finland and Scotland. *Comparative Education, 45*(1), 5–21.
Harvey, D. (2005). *A brief history of neoliberalism.* Oxford: Oxford University Press.
Lawn, M., & Lingard, B. (2002). Constructing a European policy space in educational governance: The role of transnational policy actors. *European Educational Research Journal, 1*(2), 290–307.
Lingard, B. (2000). It is and it isn't: Vernacular globalization, educational policy, and restructuring. In N. C. Burbules & C. A. Torres (Eds.), *Globalization and education: Critical perspectives* (pp. 79–108). London: Routledge.
Lingard, B., & Ali, S. (2009). Contextualising Education in Pakistan, a White Paper: Global/national articulations in education policy. *Globalisation, Societies and Education, 7*(3), 237–256.
Lingard, B., Rawolle, S., & Taylor, S. (2005). Globalizing policy sociology in education: Working with Bourdieu. *Journal of Education Policy, 20*(6), 759–777.
McCulloch, G. (2008). Privatisation/marketisation. In G. McCulloch & D. Crook (Eds.), *The Routledge international encyclopedia of education* (pp. 454–456). London: Routledge.
McGinn, N., & Welsh, T. (1999). *Decentralization of education: Why, when, what and how?* Paris: UNESCO, International Institute for Educational Planning.
Memon, M. (2003). *Policy reforms for decentralizing education system in Pakistan: Prospects and challenges.* Paper presented at the International Congress for School Effectiveness and Improvement (ICSEI), August 5–8, Sydney, Australia-.
Ministry of the Interior Education Division (1947). *Proceedings of the Pakistan Educational Conference.* Karachi: Government of Pakistan.
Ministry of Education (2003). *School education statistics.* Islamabad: National Educational Management Information System, Academy of Educational Planning and Management, Ministry of Education.
Ministry of Education (2006). *National education census 2005 – Pakistan.* Islamabad: Academy of Educational Planning and Management, Statistics Division Federal Bureau of Statistics.
Ministry of Education (2009). *National education policy 2009.* Islamabad: Government of Pakistan.

Mok, K.-H. (2005). Globalisation and governance: Educational policy instruments and regulatory arrangements. *International Review of Education, 51*(4), 289–311.

Mustafa, Z. (2011). *Tyranny of language in education: The problem and its solution.* Karachi: Ushba Publishing.

Ozga, J. (2000). *Policy research in educational settings: Contested terrain.* Buckingham: Open University Press.

Ozga, J., & Jones, R. (2006). Travelling and embedded policy: The case of knowledge transfer. *Journal of Education Policy, 21*(1), 1–17.

Ozga, J., & Lingard, B. (2007). Globalisation, education policy and politics. In B. Lingard & J. Ozga (Eds.), *The RoutledgeFalmer reader in education policy and politics* (pp. 65–82). London: Routledge.

Rahman, T. (2004). *Denizens of alien worlds: A study of education, inequality and polarization in Pakistan.* Karachi: Oxford University Press.

Rizvi, F., Engel, L., Nandyala, A., Rutkowski, D., & Sparks, J. (2005). *Globalization and recent shifts in educational policy in the Asia Pacific: An overview of some critical issues.* Bangkok: UNESCO Asia Pacific Regional Bureau for Education.

Rizvi, F., & Lingard, B. (2010). *Globalizing education policy.* Lonon: Routledge.

Rosenau, J. N. (2000). Governance, order, and change in world politics. In J. N. Rosenau & E.-O. Czempiel (Eds.), *Governance without government: Order and change in world politics* (pp. 1–29). Cambridge: Cambridge University Press.

Santos, B. d. S. (2002). *Toward a new legal common sense: Law, globalization and emancipation* (2nd ed.). London: Butterworths LexisNexis.

Siddiqui, S. (2007). *Rethinking education in Pakistan: Perceptions, practices, and possibilities.* Lahore: Paramount Publishing Enterprise.

Silova, I. (2004). Adopting the language of the new allies. In G. Steiner-Khamsi (Ed.), *The global politics of educational borrowing and lending* (pp. 75–87). New York: Teachers College Press.

Spring, J. (2008). *Globalization of education: An introduction.* New York: Routledge.

Tikly, L. (2001). Globalisation and education in the postcolonial world: Towards a conceptual framework. *Comparative Education, 37*(2), 151–171.

CHAPTER 4

Neoliberal Globalization and Higher Education in Bangladesh

Touhida Tasnima and Ehsanul Haque

> Universities are not businesses, however much some administrators and industrial executives would like them to be. For the most part, academics are not motivated by the pursuit of wealth. They are driven by the fulfillment of teaching, the freedom to follow ideas and the collegiality that universities once provided, although no longer.
>
> (Vincent, 2011, p. 339)

Introduction

Higher education plays a vital and growing role in development, the continuum of learning, and the creation of new knowledge. It promotes social mobility, cultural harmony, and community development. However, in this age of globalization, global economic forces are encroaching into the higher education landscape, leading to changes in the philosophies, values, beliefs, goals, and practices in this sector. As a result, higher education has a new dimension vis-à-vis educational governance, financing and delivery, policymaking, curriculum designing, academic work, and student enrollment. While globalization offers unprecedented opportunities for this sector, it poses critical challenges to and raises legitimate questions about higher education and its serving public good.

Higher education in Bangladesh has undergone a significant shift and this restructuring and redesigning of higher education has been greatly influenced by neoliberal globalization, which encourages privatization and deregulation for more economic efficiency and corporate governance. The adoption and implementation of liberalization policy in the higher education sector in Bangladesh have resulted in its unparalleled growth. The new role and value of higher education emphasizes science, technology, communication, business, pharmacy, and other disciplines closely linked with markets. Thus, the role of higher education institutions is central to generating and utilizing human capital to secure a share in the global market (Lynch, 2006). Indeed, the advent of market forces, mechanisms, and competitions has shaped the contours and development of higher education through the dimensions of finance, mission, scope of functions, and the reorganization of national systems as competitive quasi markets (Apple, 2001; C. Torres, 2002). In the past two decades, higher education in Bangladesh has been largely commercialized and commoditized and has turned into a large money-spinning sector under the banner of human capital development, economic growth, and social transformation.

In this chapter, we focus on the transformations in higher education policies, operations, and institutions in general, and particularly in Bangladesh, that have been triggered by imperatives, pressures, and conditions associated with globalization. We put forth a conceptual framework for understanding the various dimensions, levels, and determinants of the globalization – higher education nexus. We explore and examine how these global forces and trends have shaped and defined the development of higher education in Bangladesh. We also analyze some of the institutional responses from both private and public higher education institutions in the fast changing environment.

Conceptual Underpinning and Assumptions

Globalization is a multifaceted phenomenon and its domination of the world marketplace under neoliberal rules represents the most phenomenal global structural change, advanced through structural adjustment programs, since the industrial revolution (Wilson, 2004). Neoliberalism is a popular label for the doctrine of political and economic liberalism that calls for dismantling the typical policies of the welfare state and for the withdrawal of the state from the economy (Hay, 2004; Marginson, 1997). It is a socioeconomic theory that holds that the social good is maximized by unregulated market behavior. As such, it privileges the interests of private property owners and multinational corporations over the interests of society, in a bid to bring all activities under the rules and forces of the market (Harvey, 2005). By propelling market forces, it disregards the social, cultural, and environmental impacts of capital accumulation and supports labor exploitation and causes environmental degradation (Davis, 2008; Giroux, 2002; Lynch, 2006). Minimal governmental regulation, privatization of government-owned enterprises, public spending cuts, and lowering of barriers to international trade and investment play predominant roles in the neoliberal approach (A. T. Torres, 2009). Neoliberal strategies and forms of economic and political organization have featured prominently in the global economic agenda/policy and much of its practices since the early 1990s.

The scope and impact of neoliberalism have expanded to the educational, cultural, and ideological spheres. Higher education is one of the priorities in any public agenda as it is a repository and protector of culture, an agent of change, an engine for national economic growth and development, and an instrument for the realization of collective aspirations and interests (Rena, 2008). However, the forces of neoliberal globalization are pushing the world's education systems toward a universal model. Proponents of neoliberalism find logic in the integration of higher education institutions into the global marketplace; opponents believe that this conflicts with the nature, purpose, and philosophy of such institutions and puts the future of higher education in jeopardy (Currie, 2004; Giroux, 2002). Critics argue that neoliberal ideologies in higher education have altered the conditions for knowledge production, discounted diversity, and undermined professionalism (Grimmett et al., 2009; Robertson, 2007).

Neoliberal ideals are restructuring the fundamentals of higher education, including research, teaching, and the relationship of universities to the public good (Kapoor, 2011). Faculty work is no longer assessed by its academic value, rigor, or intellectual content, but by an economic logic whose primary criterion is the ability for the products of this work to generate revenue (Levin, 2006). Thus, market values are replacing academic values. For example, governments want universities to be managed as if they were businesses, to assess research and curricula in terms of their cost and economic return, and to rely more on larger class sizes and part-time faculty (Axelrod, 2002; Davis, 2008; Jarvis, 2001). Moreover, the slashing of public funding for universities has increased their reliance on corporate funding and commercial endeavors (Yang, 2003).

Slaughter and Rhoades (2004) labeled this phenomenon "academic capitalism," broadly understood as "the involvement of colleges and faculty in market-like behaviors" (p. 37). As resources for higher education deplete, institutions are changing their resource-seeking patterns to vie for new funds, moving away from basic research to applied research while aligning themselves with the market (Slaughter & Leslie, 1997). In particular, institutions are now interested in having contractual relationships with business corporations and some of them collaborate in technology transfers in which knowledge nurtured at the university is sold directly to businesses (Wilson, 2004). Consequently, knowledge is seen as a commodity, professors act like entrepreneurs, university administrators behave like managers, students become customers and consumers, and industry-sponsored research typifies the norm (Giroux, 2007). Undeniably, the unabated commercialization and privatization of the higher education sector has put enormous stress and strain on its social mission.

Trends in many developing countries have included merging of higher education institutions, curbing state monopolies in education, enlarging the diversity of education provisions, redesigning curricula to fulfill market needs, and unleashing forces of competition in the educational sector in order to add to the efficiency and effectiveness of educational services (Lee, 2004; Nguyen, 2007). No doubt, squeezing public funding for higher education undermines higher education institutions and their systems on a global scale (Prichard & Wilmott, 1997).

Higher education has become synonymous with equipping learners for employability (Levidow, 2002), which inevitably causes tensions between the more profitable, applied subjects of science and technology and business disciplines, and the subjects related to arts, humanities, and the social sciences. As Rhoads and Torres (2006) observed,

> Knowledge is now evaluated with the language of finance, and universities are measured by their efficiency in awarding degrees and certificates. Academic leaders are replaced by managers with business backgrounds, and the university shifts from an educational institution to just another business with a bottom line (p. 32).

However, as Barua (2011) observed, the commercialization of higher education, and the sheer profit motive in certain cases, downplays the provision of quality education and wears down traditional values, intellectual exercises, and critical thinking (also Currie, 2004, Singh, 2001). In addition, globalized education gives rise to apprehensions of imperialist attitudes, the erosion of indigenous cultures, and the relentless imposition of western values, which promotes "monocultural economic growth and ignores cultural pluralism" (Barua, 2009, p. 126).

The Pacing and Spread of Neoliberalism in Bangladesh and Higher Education Challenges

In the last two decades, a major shift, influenced by neoliberalism, has occurred in the concept and practices of higher education in Bangladesh, resulting in rapid and fundamental changes in this sector. In fact, Bangladesh is seen as an absorber of market-induced higher education. Researchers and practitioners have attempted to identify the motivation, scope, and impact of this shift and its ramifications on the clientele of higher education (i.e., individuals, institutions, systems, and society). Policymakers have been pushed to incorporate neoliberal principles into the higher education terrain by international financial institutions (i.e., the World Bank, International Monetary Fund [IMF], and World Trade Organization [WTO]), which are neoliberal advocates, and the interests of the political and business elites in the country (Kabir, 2011).

With the liberalization of the country's education sector, global market forces have generated new concerns, dilemmas, and paradoxes for higher education in Bangladesh. In this section, we show how neoliberal assumptions, policies, and programs have warranted reforms in the higher education sector in Bangladesh and how institutions of higher education, their faculty, and their students are being affected by these measures and developments.

State of Public and Private Higher Education

Roughly 6 percent of the population in Bangladesh has access to higher education. This is very limited compared with 12 percent in India, 37 percent in Thailand, and 83 percent in the United States (*The News Today,* 2011). There are 51 registered private and 29 public universities in Bangladesh (University Grants Commission [UGC], 2009). Over the years, student enrollment in the private universities has increased threefold, from 62,856 in 2004 to 182,641 in 2008 (UGC, 2009). In 2008, there were 1,176,969 students registered in public universities (UGC, 2009).

The majority of higher education aspirants prefer and value public universities not only because they provide low-cost education tailored to students' intellectual and professional interests but also because they offer programs in diverse disciplines, such as science, commerce, the liberal arts, humanities, engineering and technology, law, education, and medicine. Additionally, public universities have well-qualified and experienced faculty and the students have access to inexpensive residential facilities (Monem & Baniamin, 2010). In Bangladesh, the tradition—and mission—of public universities has been to ensure generously subsidized quality higher education.

Public universities in Bangladesh are managed and governed by the Acts and Ordinances promulgated by the government. Four universities[1] are controlled by the separate University Acts of 1973. The spirit of these Acts reflects the intention to protect the autonomous character of these institutions. Through the formation of a democratically elected university senate, syndicate, and other statutory bodies, the university administration is accountable to the university community itself, rather than being subservient to the government. The University Grants Commission (UGC) of Bangladesh was set up in 1972 as an intermediary between the government and the universities (Mannan, 2009). The UGC is responsible for funding the public universities. Although private universities do not receive any government funding, they require approval from the UGC to operate and award degrees.

In Bangladesh, private higher education is a recent phenomenon; however, it is a burgeoning sector. The 1992 Private University Act was instrumental in jump-starting private higher education institutions in Bangladesh. For-profit or quasi-for-profit private higher education institutions now represent the fastest-growing sector in the country. The role of these institutions is critical in the revitalization and advancement of higher education in Bangladesh. The main promoters and patrons of private universities in Bangladesh include retired bureaucrats turned academics, private entrepreneurs, senior academics, active/retired politicians, philanthropists, social leaders, and NGOs (Mannan, 2009; Siddiqi, 2011). However, a number of the founders and owners of private universities lack prior experience in managing and running higher educational institutions. Some administer their universities in the model of government offices, others as their business concerns or NGO outfits (Mannan, 2009).

In the past, the government was the main provider and manager of higher education in Bangladesh. However, this changed in the 1990s, when there was a growing demand for and interest in private universities since public universities were unable to accommodate students because of their limited enrollment capacities and the new demands on universities being made by market forces and institutions. Moreover, it was imperative to reverse the trend of a considerable number of students going abroad for higher studies. The government liberalized educational policy by encouraging and supporting the private sector to set up institutions of higher education. As a result, there are nearly twice as many private universities as public universities. After the enactment of the 2010 Private University Act, we expect further growth of private universities. As of December 2011, there were 92 applications (submitted to the government) seeking permission to start new private universities in different parts of the country. The UGC has approved 72 applications and has submitted a report on them to the Ministry of Education.[2] This is a clear manifestation of the ascendancy of business and market ideologies in the higher education terrain of Bangladesh.

The private education sector admits students who cannot qualify for the public institutions, where competition for admission is fierce. Although some selective private universities uphold academic excellence, integrity, and social responsibility, a majority of them serve a mass clientele by fast-tracking students into higher education, which gives a picture of them as mere economic actors, nonselective and non-prestigious (Siddiqi, 2011). In general, the private higher education sector is run on a business model, with power and authority mainly concentrated in the board members and chief executives, while the faculty members hold minimal authority or influence and students are seen as consumers (Altbach et al., 2009). Private universities by and large operate on tuition fees and thus have a strong predilection for those who can afford to pay the outrageous fees, which are often 20 times higher than public university tuition (Masum, 2008). Empirical evidence (Yang, 2003) and our own experiences suggest that private higher education in Bangladesh disproportionately benefits the students from relatively affluent, well-educated, and well-bred families. Student enrollment in these institutions is on the rise because of the obvious benefits accorded to them—rapid and prompt responses to changes in the employment market compared with public institutions, programs tailored to market needs, and clear focus on career preparation.

Modeled after western-style academic organization and management, the curricula in the private universities are confined to market-driven and -oriented programs. Only a limited number of private universities offer courses in the liberal arts, humanities, and the social sciences. The most common courses are computer science and technology, accounting, management, banking, finance, marketing, and secretarial science. These courses fill up quickly as both local and foreign students consider them fitting for the market economy. The number of foreign students (from India, Pakistan, Sri Lanka, Nepal, Bhutan, China, and African countries like Liberia and Nigeria) pursuing higher education in private universities in Bangladesh increased from around 487 in 2004 to around 1,045 in 2008 (UGC, 2009).

Private higher education in Bangladesh is responding to pressures to produce competitive human capital, and provide quality education and opportunities for research and training. As a result, the shift from elite to mass higher education is transforming the private sector higher education in Bangladesh. Since an academic revolution has occurred globally out of neoliberal globalization, developing countries like Bangladesh strive to ensure quality in both public and private higher education at a nationally comparable and internationally acceptable standard.

Neoliberal Processes, Practices, and Discourses

With the growth, expansion, and consolidation of private higher education in Bangladesh, the state has been relegated from its earlier status as the sole provider and manager of higher education to the status of regulator. As such, the state's responsibilities are confined to the supervision and oversight of institutional licensing and program accreditation. The achievement of minimum standard level requirements and of accreditation are based on the course of study, faculty competence, curricula for all disciplines, available facilities, management systems, and rationale for conducting the course of study (UGC, 2008). However, the state cannot allocate funds to these institutions for scholarships and student aid, research, and capital expenditures. Thus, private universities generate their own funds to support such activities.

Market forces drive and fuel the state to initiate policy reforms for achieving excellence, relevance, and marketability of higher education. For instance, as part of improving the quality of higher education in Bangladesh and moving university education to meet international standards, the government devised a 20-year national Strategic Plan for Higher Education (SPHE) for the period spanning 2006–2026. The plan proposes a series of policy reforms and interventions such as depoliticizing public universities, strengthening the UGC, establishing an accreditation council, setting up national search committees for selecting vice chancellors, maximizing support for research, and crafting strategies for retaining and developing quality teaching staff (World Bank, 2009a). A careful review and analysis of this plan indicates an aim of establishing a link between higher education and the neoliberal paradigm within the context of new global norms.

The government clearly supports the role of the World Bank in the higher education sector of Bangladesh. In its efforts to diversify and structurally transform this sector, the government accepted a credit of 81 million US dollars from the World Bank in 2009 under the terms of the Higher Education Quality Enhancement Project (HEQEP), to be implemented by the UGC between 2009 and 2013 (*Financial Express*, 2009). The objective of this project in Bangladesh is to upgrade the quality and relevance of the teaching and research environment in higher education institutions by supporting both innovation and accountability within universities and by enhancing the technical and institutional capacity of the higher education sector (World Bank, 2009b). In essence, this initiative is the reflection of neoliberal beliefs and practices in the country's higher education domain (Kabir, 2011). This shift toward marketplace demands will eventually obliterate the nobility of higher education in general and universities in particular, which are intended to contribute to attaining the goals of national development and identity.[3] As Vincent (2011) remarked,

> A good academic now is one who gains more income than others. A good department is one which maximises external grant income. Students are

implicitly encouraged into a life of self-interest and self-advancement. The idea that a life could be dedicated to public service is now virtually meaningless (p. 335).

Evidently, neoliberal globalization influences teaching and learning in Bangladesh—our educational development is, to a considerable degree, based on a global unified agenda; standardized teaching and learning are encouraged in the name of improving quality and facilitating access. Structural adjustment policies in the education sector have aimed for a transition to global educational standards by benchmarking the entire systems of developing and less-developed countries to those of economically more advanced ones (Sahlberg, 2004). As a distinguished faculty of a Bangladeshi public university noted,

> Market forces have significantly changed our conception of higher education. With the pervasive penetration of neoliberalism, the moral and ethical foundation of higher education in Bangladesh is at stake. As higher education in the country becomes more specialized and academic curricula focus more on the internationally recognized courses and programs, our traditional and cultural values are now vulnerable to the materialism of economic globalization and this standardization eventually conflicts with our institutional traditions and social identity. As a result, the ways teaching and learning are organized in higher education institutions would prove deleterious.
> (Interview, 2011)

Recently, the government introduced the idea of Public-Private Partnership (PPP) arrangements, encouraging the establishment of ties between academia and private industries or firms. Under this arrangement, corporate firms have an unprecedented but coveted opportunity to play a role in the country's higher education sector (Kabir, 2011). Several well-known Bangladeshi companies as well as MNCs operating in the country have sought to increase their presence and influence on university campuses as they have realized the importance of investing in talent, skill, and leadership development to promote their business interests and aspirations. A key figure in a prominent MNC observed that youth employability is a serious issue in Bangladeshi society, as higher education institutions are not training students sufficiently for the business world.[4] In order to cope with this, some private universities have redesigned courses and curricula—supported by, and tailored for, potential employers, thus allowing stakeholders in the business sector to refashion universities in the image of the marketplace. Even some faculty members of a few public universities prefer policy research, consulting, and university – corporate world or industry partnerships. As Noll and Rogerson (1998) and Zumeta (2001) observed, those businesses or industries that provide resources to institutions of higher education possess the capability of exercising power over the direction and outcome of research. Excessive dependence on the part of the institution makes it hostage to the values and goals of the funding source (Slaughter & Leslie, 1997).

The majority of the public universities in the country have introduced four-year undergraduate programs and one-year graduate programs in accordance with western academic norms, standards, and priorities, which are compatible and integrated with the neoliberal agenda and global standard. Similarly, private universities have embraced a western (primarily North American) education model. Several of the courses are designed by foreign universities, think tanks, or professional bodies that have an interest in promoting neoliberal ideologies and enforcing neoliberal, market-led strategies.[5] English dominates as the language of instruction, scholarship, research, and communication in the fields of business, science and technology; thus, when private universities use English, it gives the impression that they deliver quality education and strong, promising career outcomes that are being propped up by the west. However, this makes it possible to overlook the critical issue of students' actual competencies in English.

Private sector universities take pride in their efforts to blend western values with eastern traditions. In fact, students of both public and private universities look at the western education model as being the exemplar of great learning and teaching, leading to high employability. They are motivated by and enthusiastic about western thought and western scholars; on the contrary, native institutions and their education systems are seen as traditional, backward, colonial, and ill suited for developing students' potential for the job market. The neoliberal model of higher education, in reality, leads to the students' denigration of their own historical and cultural heritage.

The country's receptivity to globalized higher education is reflected in the branch campuses of some foreign universities, institutions, and colleges (American, British, Canadian, Australian, Thai, and Malaysian) that have been set up mainly in Dhaka. Supporters of neoliberal globalization see these branches as an opportunity to meet massive demands for quality education, defray huge expenses of overseas education, benefit from the professional services and outstanding academic programs of international educational institutions, and improve the overall quality and standard of higher education in Bangladesh. The foreign universities/institutions lend their names and curricula, providing some extremely limited supervision and nominal quality control to local academic institutions and business firms. Thus, the operation of the foreign higher education institutions in the country has given rise to much controversy and debate. Critics consider foreign university branches as low-grade institutions and argue that the fee-paying students are receiving the degrees but not the same level of education offered in the countries of origin of those universities (*The Independent,* 2011; *The News Today,* 2011).

Amidst these allegations, in 2007, the UGC blacklisted 56 foreign university branches in Dhaka and four other cities, declaring them unauthorized/illegal as they were operating in violation of the 1992 Private University Act and the 1998 Amendment Act; however, a majority of them are still running with backing from influential quarters. They are commonly seen as degree/diploma mills with questionable commitment to quality education, and have roughly 20,000–25,000 students (*The Independent,* 2011; Debnath, 2007). Nevertheless, the 2010 Private University Act promotes the idea of Cross Border Higher Education (CBHE), which facilitates offshore campuses of foreign universities/institutions in Bangladesh. However, there is a deep division over this issue among policymakers, academics, politicians, and businessmen.[6] The Association of Private Universities of Bangladesh (APUB) is vehemently opposed to allowing the activities of foreign universities at least on two grounds: first, the 2010 Private University Act forbids the Bangladeshi private universities to operate branches in the country; and second, foreign universities promote commoditization of education (*The News Today,* 2011). Because education provided at these branches does not conform to national norms, beliefs, and practices, students trained by them are not socialized to want to contribute to the social and cultural richness of the nation.[7]

Neoliberal ideology puts pressure on the country's higher education sector to produce decontextualized and human capital – oriented knowledge. Lamenting the current state of higher education in the country, a veteran Bangladeshi educationist remarked,

> The neoliberal economic policies and practices of the government adversely affect higher education in Bangladesh. In the name of unified global education, western values, norms, beliefs, and institutions are injected into our curricula, which run counter to our expectations, customs, sensibilities, and social development priorities. It is an affront to our national pride. And in the sphere of teaching, there is a radical departure from the liberal intellectual tradition where education was about learning. This sort of education not only harms our achievements but also mars the prospect of our potentialities.
>
> (Interview, 2011)

For that matter, higher education, as it is organized and managed in Bangladesh today, loses its appeal as a social good with intrinsic value and is looked at as a commodity that can be bought for material gains, augmenting human capital and thus securing a well-paid job. Woefully and abysmally, the nonprofit character of educational enterprise is hamstrung by the pervasive nature of market-induced globalization.

Whither Higher Education?

Even after four decades of independence, the issue of reforming and overhauling the tertiary education system in Bangladesh is a high priority concern that merits attention and evaluation. As our analysis demonstrates, higher education in the country confronts a multitude of challenges, including inadequate and under-resourced teaching, flight of skills and concomitant human capital deficiency, and academic curricula that are poorly fitted and unresponsive to local needs, expectations, interests, and conditions. As compared with the western countries, in terms of their research prowess and reputation for academic excellence, there is a decline in the quality of teaching and research in Bangladesh. Many do not consider teaching an intellectually demanding and socially challenging enterprise and there is a belief that research is devoid of sociocultural values and norms, and ethical issues. This has social and economic consequences and adversely impacts the development sector. Moreover, it is a daunting challenge for higher education institutions in Bangladesh to maintain their footing on the global higher education stage. Higher education institutions are under pressure with respect to accountability, access, and quality. In fact, embracing the overwhelmingly neoliberal educational agenda conflicts with the core objectives of higher education in terms of its obligations to transmit knowledge and promote the intellectual and moral development of people. Surely, the values and goals of higher education are markedly different from those of businesses; rather, they play an important role in generating social cohesion. Higher education institutions cling to idealism, not profit, and expenses for education are heavily subsidized (Birnbaum, 2000). Granted, the neoliberal educational agenda and its outcomes jeopardize the universities' traditional values of social justice and development. Consequently, tensions grow between national realities and international trends.

In spite of the perilous nature of the neoliberal paradigm, many defend the privatization of higher education at the national and global levels. They argue that deregulation and market orientation will put more power in the hands of education consumers by easing research restrictions, enrolling a greater number of students, and supporting foreign collaboration in the university sector. In essence, decentralized educational governance and control are crucial for enhancing efficiency by giving more responsibility to the private sector, which is expected to increase motivation and accountability. However, Currie (2004) cautioned that for creating healthier and wiser societies, outright deregulation should be averted and public funding for the universities should be supported. Moreover, universities should be allowed to enjoy the right to "freedom of inquiry and persist in their role as critic and conscience of the nation" (pp. 59–60).

Concluding Remarks

It appears that the role of higher education as a public good is essentially important. We do not propose that neoliberal reforms in the higher education arena are entirely disadvantageous and unrewarding; rather, we argue that changes in this sphere were motivated by the desire for greater openness, transparency, accountability, and communication in relation to educational quality and standards. Ironically, this has not been the case since the neoliberal restructuring, diversification, planning, and governance of universities has turned them into economic engines. The increasing tendency to treat higher education as a commercial enterprise is altering the meaning, purpose, and role of the university to a considerable extent. As Vincent (2011) deplored, "higher education is a private, not a public, good" (p. 337).

Reforming higher education through a gradual yet balanced approach may help Bangladesh seize opportunities in the new global order. However, an apprehension haunts us—neoliberal globalization precipitates the degradation of humanistic values, of cultural, moral, and spiritual dimensions in teaching and learning processes. Given this, there is a need to develop professional management and sensitive leadership. Moreover, the higher education enterprise is expected to provide strong, vibrant institutions to keep up with the knowledge economy as well as transmit knowledge indispensable for both social mobility and economic progress. As the neoliberal narcissistic culture tends to standardize almost everything to the point where unique cultural identities and their values and practices erode, higher education programs need to be more attuned to pressures and opportunities in the national context.

Notes

1. University of Dhaka, University of Rajshahi, University of Chittagong, and Jahangirnagar University.
2. Personal communication with a UGC official, 2012. Moreover, a popular vernacular daily in Bangladesh, *Prothom Alo,* ran a report on this on January 3, 2012.
3. Personal communication, 2011.

4. Personal communication, 2010.
5. Observation based on our experiences.
6. See, Daily *New Age,* December 11, 2011, Daily *Shamokal* (a vernacular), December 26, 2011, January 1, and January 9, 2012, for debates and controversies over the question of granting permission to foreign universities to open branches in Bangladesh.
7. Opinion given by a senior academic and administrator of a public university. Personal communication, 2011.

References

Altbach, P. G., Reisberg, L., & Rumbley, L. E. (2009). *Trends in global higher education: Tracking an academic revolution.* A report prepared for the UNESCO 2009 World Conference on Higher Education. Paris: UNESCO.

Apple, M. W. (2001). *Educating the "right way": Markets, standards, God, and inequality.* London & New York: Routledge.

Axelrod, P. (2002). *Values in conflict: The University, the marketplace, and the trials of liberal education.* Montreal and Kingston: McGill-Queen's University Press.

Barua, B. (2009). Non-formal education, economic growth and development: Challenges for rural Buddhist communities in Bangladesh. In A. Abdi & D. Kapoor (Eds.), *Global perspectives on adult education* (pp. 125–140). New York: Palgrave Macmillan.

Barua, B. (2011). Critical perspectives on development and learning in community action in Bangladesh and Thailand. In D. Kapoor (Ed.), *Critical perspectives on neoliberal globalization: Development and education in Africa and Asia* (pp. 171–186). Rotterdam: Sense Publishers.

Birnbaum, R. (2000). *Management fads in higher education: Where they come from, what they do, why they fail.* San Francisco: Jossey-Bass.

Currie, J. (2004). The neo-liberal paradigm and higher education: A critique. In J. K. Odin & P. T. Manicas (Eds.), *Globalization and higher education* (pp. 42–62). Honolulu: University of Hawaii Press.

Davis, E. (2008). Citizenship, higher education, and neo-liberal globalization. *Research Review, 2*(1), 39–53.

Debnath, S. (2007, June 13). Low quality foreign university branches "selling" degrees. *The Daily Star, 5*(1078). Retrieved from, http://www.thedailystar.net/2007/06/13/d7061301128.htm

Financial Express, The (2009, April 6). WB provides $ 81m credit for an edn improvement project. *The Financial Express,* Dhaka. Retrieved from, http://www.thefinancialexpress-bd.com/2009/04/06/63215.html

Giroux, H. (2002). Neoliberalism, corporate culture and the promise of higher education: The University as a democratic public sphere. *Harvard Educational Review, 72*(4), 1–31.

Giroux, H. (2007). Neoliberalism and the vocationalization of higher education. Online article. Retrieved from, http://www.henryagiroux.com/online_articles/vocalization.htm

Grimmett, P. P., Fleming, R. & Trotter, L. (2009). Legitimacy and identity in teacher education: A micro-political struggle constrained by macro-political pressures. *Asia-Pacific Journal of Teacher Education, 37*(1), 5–26.

Harvey, D. (2005). *A brief history of neoliberalism*. New York: Oxford University Press.

Hay, C. (2004). The normalizing role of rationalist assumptions in the institutional embedding of neoliberalism. *Economy and Society, 33*(4), 500–527.

Independent, The (2011, November 10). Body formed to probe foreign university branches in city. *The Independent,* Dhaka. Retrieved from, http://theindependentbd.com/paper-edition/frontpage/129-frontpage/78976-body-formed-to-probe-foreign-university-branches-in-city.html

Jarvis, P. (2001). *Universities and corporate universities: The higher learning industry in global society.* London: Kogan Page.

Kabir, A. H. (2011). *The politics of neoliberalism in the higher education sector in Bangladesh.* Unpublished Master's Thesis, College of Education, University of Canterbury, New Zealand.

Kapoor, D. (2011). Neoliberal globalization, saffron fundamentalism and Dalit poverty and educational prospects in India. In D. Kapoor (Ed.), *Critical perspectives on neoliberal globalization, development and education in Africa and Asia* (pp. 69–86). Rotterdam: Sense Publishers.

Lee, M. N. N. (2004). Global trends, national policies and institutional responses: Restructuring higher education in Malaysia. *Educational Research for Policy and Practice, 3*(1), 31–46.

Levidow, L. (2002). Marketizing higher education: Neoliberal strategies and counter strategies. In K. Robins & F. Webster (Eds.), *The virtual university? Knowledge, markets and management* (pp. 227–248). Oxford: Oxford University Press.

Levin, J. S. (2006). Faculty work: Tensions between educational and economic values. *The Journal of Higher Education, 77*(1), 62–88.

Lynch, K. (2006). Neo-liberalism and marketisation: The implications for higher education. *European Educational Research Journal, 5*(1), 1–16.

Mannan, A. (2009). *Higher education in the 21st century Bangladesh.* Retrieved from, http://www.articlesbase.com/education-articles/higher-education-in-the-21st-century-bangladesh-1017170.html

Marginson, S. (1997). *Markets in education.* Sydney: Allen & Unwin.

Masum, M. (2008). Higher education in Bangladesh: Problems and policies. *Journal of the World Universities Forum, 1*(5), 17–30.

Monem, M. & Baniamin, H. M. (2010). Higher education in Bangladesh: Status, issues and prospects. *Pakistan Journal of Social Sciences, 30*(2), 293–305.

News Today, The (2011, December 12). Government urged to prohibit entry of foreign universities. *The News Today,* Dhaka. Retrieved from, http://www.newstoday.com.bd/index.php?option=details&news_id=46881&date=2011-12-12

Nguyen, H. T. (2007). *The impact of globalisation on higher education in China and Vietnam: Policies and practices.* Paper presented at the 4th Education in a Changing Environment Conference, September 12–14, University of Salford, UK.

Noll, R., & Rogerson W. (1998). The economics of university indirect cost reimbursement in federal research grants. In R. G. Noll (Ed.), *Challenges to research universities* (pp. 105–146). Washington, D.C.: Brookings Institution Press.

Prichard, C. & Wilmott, H. (1997). Just how managed is the McUniversity? *Organisation Studies, 18*(2), 287–316.

Rena, R. (2008). Financing education and development in Eritrea: Some implications. *Manpower Journal, 43*(1), 73–97.

Rhoads, R. A. & Torres, C. A. (2006). Introduction: Globalization and higher education in the Americas. In R. A. Rhoads & C. A. Torres (Eds.), *The university, state, and market: The political economy of globalization in the Americas* (pp. 3–38). Stanford: Stanford University Press.

Robertson, S. L. (2007). "Remaking the world": Neo-liberalism and the transformation of education and teachers' labour. In L. Weis & M. Compton (Eds.), *The global assault on teachers, teaching and their unions* (pp. 11–36). New York: Palgrave Macmillan.

Sahlberg, P. (2004). Teaching and globalization. *International Research Journal of Managing Global Transitions, 2*(1), 65–83.

Siddiqi, Hafiz G. A. (2011, April 11). Private universities: A half-full glass. *The Daily Star.* Retrieved from, http://www.thedailystar.net/suppliments/2011/anniversary/part9/pg9.htm

Singh, M. (2001). Re-inserting the "public good" into higher education transformation. Paper presented at the Conference on Globalization and Higher Education: Views from the South, March 27–29, Cape Town, South Africa.

Slaughter, S., & Leslie, L. (1997). *Academic capitalism: Politics, policies, and the entrepreneurial university.* Baltimore: Johns Hopkins University Press.

Slaughter, S. & Rhoades, G. (2004). *Academic capitalism and the new economy: Markets, state and higher education.* Baltimore: Johns Hopkins University Press.

Torres, C. (2002). Globalization, education and citizenship: Solidarity versus markets? *American Educational Research Journal, 39*(2), 363–378.

Torres, A. T. (2009). *Education and neoliberal globalization.* New York: Routledge.

University Grants Commission (UGC) (2009).*University Grants Commission Annual Report-2008* (in vernacular). Dhaka: UGC.

Vincent, A. (2011). Ideology and the university. *The Political Quarterly, 82*(3), 332–340.

Wilson, M. G. (2004). *The global hegemony of neoliberal values: The challenge to social work.* Paper prepared for presentation at the Annual Conference of the Alberta College of Social Workers, Calgary, Alberta, Canada. March 18–20. Retrieved from, http://www.acsw.ab.ca/pdfs/global_showdown_maureen_wilson.pdf

World Bank (2009a). *Bangladesh: Country summary of higher education.* Washington, DC. Retrieved from http://siteresources.worldbank.org/EDUCATION/

Resources/278200-1121703274255/1439264-1193249163062/Bangladesh_countrySummary.pdf

World Bank (2009b). *Bangladesh: Higher education quality enhancement project.* Washington, DC. Retrieved from http://web.worldbank.org/external/projects/main?pagePK=64312881&piPK=64302848&theSitePK=40941&Projectid=P106216

Yang, R. (2003). Globalization and higher education development: A critical analysis. *International Review of Education, 49*(3–4), 269–291.

Zumeta, W. (2001). Public policy and accountability in higher education: Lessons from the past and present for the new millennium. In D. E. Heller (Ed.), *The states and public higher education policy: Affordability, access, and accountability* (pp. 155–197). Baltimore, MD: Johns Hopkins University Press.

CHAPTER 5

The World Bank, Community Schooling, and School-Based Management: A Political Economy of Educational Decentralization in Nepal

Tejendra J. Pherali

Introduction

Community involvement in educational development in Nepal is nothing new. Even during the Rana oligarchy (1846–1950), when public education was considered a threat to the regime and educational initiatives were a punishable act, local communities made efforts to establish schools and learning centers, often risking their lives to do so. In 1951, there were 321 primary schools and 11 secondary schools in Nepal; this number had increased to 4,000 by 1971, when the Panchayat (local government) polity (1960–1990) introduced the National Education System Plan (NESP) to nationalize all public schools. The NESP has been referred to as the "most politically significant education policy" (Caddell, 2007, p. 15) in Nepal. Centralized education was to replace dominant educational traditions with a supposedly egalitarian model of education that would involve technical support and funding from the government to improve the quality of education.

However, the political motive of the NESP was "to strengthen devotion to crown, country, national unity and the *Panchayat* system" (MoE, 1971, p. 1) and legitimize the regime and its ideologies (Apple, 2004) by homogenizing the country's diverse cultural and linguistic traditions. A national curriculum was introduced to "synthesise diverse socio-economic interests, negotiate ethno-lingual heterogeneity and convert the geopolitical entity of Nepal into an emotionally integrated nationhood" (Mohsin, 1972, pp. 35–36). Textbooks were centrally produced and distributed to all schools throughout the country and reflected the Panchayat ideology—monarchy, Hinduism, and Nepali language (Onta, 1996).

Nevertheless, despite significant policy reform and national investment, the quality of public education and the efficiency of school management remained relatively poor compared with the private schools established in the late 1990s. These private schools continuously outperformed government schools in the School Leaving Certificate (SLC) examinations (World Bank, 2003). Hence, over the years, the national education system has strengthened elitism and led to the systematic marginalization of indigenous nationalities, minority ethnic groups, and Dalits (the untouchable castes).

In response to the weak performance of public schools, the Seventh Amendment of the Education Act was introduced in 2001, which allowed for a transfer to school-based management. This did not emerge only in the context of Nepal's struggle for educational reforms; it was also greatly influenced by the global discourse of neoliberalism, which rationalizes decentralization as a means of enhancing accountability, quality, ownership, and efficiency in the public sector (World Bank, 2003).

In this chapter, I discuss how the global policy discourse of school-based management interacts with local socioeconomic realities and political scenarios in Nepal. I draw on interviews I conducted with SMC (school management committee) members, parents, teachers, and political leaders as part of a multi-agency funded study into the political economy of education in Nepal. These interviews were carried out in two private and six government funded schools in Dhanusha, Kapilvastu, Kathmandu, and Rupandehi districts of Nepal and primarily focused on identifying political economy drivers of educational management within the context of decentralization in education. I argue that unintended outcomes of decentralization in education have manifested in the form of excessive politicization, corruption, and tensions in the school system.

School-Based Management: A Global Policy Discourse

The publication of the World Bank document *Priorities and Strategies for Education* (World Bank, 1995) marked the formal beginning of the global drive for educational decentralization. These bank priorities have primarily impacted educational reforms in the developing world. The document is inspired by neoliberal concepts of deregulation, privatization, and marketization in education. In this document, the funding mechanism of public education was proposed as involving

> local rather than central government taxation; cost-sharing with local communities; the use of block grants; the charging of fees at higher levels of education; the encouragement of revenue diversification; the use of "portable" capitation grants, vouchers and student loans; and funding based on output and quality.
> (World Bank, 1995, p. 131)

Most developing countries are already struggling to manage their public services and have had no choice but to subscribe to this policy shift. The gradual process of state withdrawal from education has hence become a major symptom of a neoliberal attack on already malfunctioning education systems in the developing world.

School-based management is considered a radical form of educational decentralization that enhances participation of local stakeholders. It involves "the transfer of decision-making authority, responsibility and tasks from higher to lower organizational levels or between organisations" (Hanson, 1998, p. 112; McGinn & Welsh, 1999). Educational decentralization is often argued "to increase both the productivity and efficiency of educational delivery systems, based on a presumption that local actors are better equipped to make appropriate decisions for their local context and better able to hold local actors accountable" (Edwards, 2011, p. 69).

Decentralization is often driven by the motives of governments or international agencies and is based on the assumption that policy aims and objectives are shared by all stakeholders at community levels (McGinn & Welsh, 1999); however, this can lead to problems in terms of access to and quality of education, teacher professionalism, and participation of civil society in the provision of education (Carnoy, 1999; Poppema, 2009). As Carney, Bista, and Agergaard (2007) argued, "most decentralisation initiatives have struggled to realise their goals" (p. 614) due to a disconnection between policy aims and local capacities. As a result, policy aimed at mobilizing parents and communities fails to reach its intended stakeholders or the authority devolved to the local level is captured by unintended agents, who manipulate policy reforms to work in their favor (Edwards, 2011).

When education is decentralized, local communities in low-income countries are burdened with the responsibility of school management (Poppema, 2009). Since structural inequalities threaten stability, devolution of authority is seen as a strategic intervention of the neoliberal state to neutralize political opposition and reduce the chances of outbreak of violent conflicts (Cornwall & Brock, 2005). Clearly, this approach to conflict prevention ignores the fundamental problems of social injustice in these societies. Hence, delegation of educational responsibility to local communities perpetuates the status quo in the society and exploits the poorest by making them contribute to the state's fundamental duty of providing basic education to its citizens (Poppema, 2009). Local educational reforms, however, are influenced by the complex processes of globalization, which are dominated by the ideologies of international organizations such as the World Bank (Watson, 2000).

On the global scale, political and economic processes of globalization have contributed to a massive growth in knowledge industries, leading to "differential effects" on nation-states and their educational institutions (Zajda & Geo-Jaja, 2009, p. xix). As a result, the major goal of educational reforms has been to maximize efficiency and economic productivity by internationalizing educational processes (e.g., access to education, standardization of curriculum and assessment techniques, meritocracy, etc.). This largely undermines the agenda of educational equality. In addition, the advancement of information technology and innovation in the global market calls for a multitasking, flexible workforce (Carnoy, 1999); and education systems are expected to fulfill the needs of the world market. In particular, education systems in the developing world are under pressure to produce an educated labor force that can attract global financial capital, which is seen as the only rescuer of world poverty. This comes with a "private sector bias" that promotes market competition, smaller public sectors, and often dismantling of the welfare state (Carnoy, 1999, p. 16). As a consequence, there is indirect pressure on the governments of developing countries to promote mechanisms that reduce public spending while expanding the provision of education. This can only be done by devolving authority and ownership of educational institutions to communities, who are then held accountable to their governments for public education. Hence, education decentralization involves not just the devolution of power to indigenous people or communities, but also an ideological action that facilitates systematic delegation of financial responsibilities, which promotes economic and self-functioning mechanisms that are expected to produce public returns at the public's cost. Thus, the ultimate beneficiary of neoliberalism is the private sector and the mega structures of global capitalism where the educated workforce is likely to be absorbed.

Educational Decentralization in Nepal

Proponents of educational decentralization often argue that educational development in Nepal, which has included establishing and managing public schools, has mostly been community driven. However, since the Education Act of 1971, which nationalized all the schools that were initially established by local people and managed using mainly local resources, the relationship between communities and schools gradually became ceremonial. Also, the notion of community is problematic, since communities in Nepal represent ethnic and caste-based hierarchies and are not homogeneous (Carney et al., 2007).

In the post-1950 period, privileged social groups (mainly Brahmins, Chhetris, and Newars) were able to seize the opportunity of educational freedom and establish schools and learning centers in their own neighborhoods, thus providing education for their children, and consequently exacerbating horizontal inequalities (Stewart, 2008) along caste and ethnic lines. Despite increased provision of education and the consistent improvement in school enrolment, educational outcomes in Nepal are usually inequitable across different castes and ethnicities. Upper caste groups, males, and hill-based ethnic groups have been the principal beneficiaries of the education system as compared with the subordinate castes (e.g., Dalits), indigenous nationalities, and Madheshi (the ethnic people in the Southern flatlands). These disparities are not solely explained by economic factors, however, but also by the varied social and cultural capital of these groups, which do not have the *habitus*—a set of socially acquired dispositions, skills, and ways of cultural interaction (Bourdieu, 1984)—needed to achieve their full potential in education.

Educational decentralization in Nepal was taken up aggressively in 2001 with the Seventh Amendment of the Education Act of 1971. The amendment renamed all government schools as community schools and established a policy to delegate authority of school management to the district and village development committees. As a result, the role of SMCs became significant in each school's operation, as well as in supervising teaching and learning, recruiting teachers, managing the school budget, and mobilizing local resources. There were also a number of other policy regulations that laid the foundation for the systematic transfer of school management authority to local communities. For example, the *Education Rules 2002,* the *Operational Manual for Community Managed Schools 2002,* and more importantly, the World Bank funded *Community Schools Support Project (CSSP)* collectively created a policy framework for community schooling.

However, there are two fundamental challenges within this policy reform. First, the assumption of the community as a homogeneous entity and characterized by fellowship, harmony, and social cohesion is highly problematic (Carney et al., 2007) in Nepal. Nepali communities represent tremendous diversity along sociocultural, economic, religious, ethnic, caste, and linguistic lines. Unequal power relations and social hierarchies among groups mean that the degree of influence in community participation can vary significantly.

In Nepal, there is a strong patronage system, meaning that the involvement of local communities in school management processes is highly selective and is often motivated by the political and economic interests of stakeholders at different levels.

A second challenge to the policy reform is the limited extent to which local communities can be involved in the functioning of the school. For example, schools must follow the national curriculum and use the prescribed textbooks published by the government. In addition, the district education officer, who is accountable to the Department of Education, has full authority to dissolve the SMCs that cannot deliver their responsibilities at prescribed standards. This means that the decisions of the SMCs are always under the influence of the district education officer, who oversees the implementation of the policy.

In contrast, the private education sector, which educates roughly 14 percent of students (DoE, 2010), is unaffected by most education policies (e.g., decentralization, education in mother tongue). The majority of politicians, bureaucrats, policymakers, social elites, and the urban rich educate their children in fee-paying English-medium private schools. This means that most policy interventions affect the children from the bottom of society while children from wealthier and more privileged backgrounds benefit from what tends to be seen as better quality education. The consistent underperformance of government schools has significantly damaged the reputation of public education. As a result, there has been a significant increase in the number of private schools in the last decade (DoE, 2010).

However, in the interviews I conducted, teachers from both private and public schools revealed that private schools promote western values and lifestyles, which are generally "away from dominant social and cultural realities of Nepal" (interview with a private school teacher in Kathmandu). There is also increasing evidence that suggests that private education reproduces elitism and perpetuates social divisions and injustice in society (Dorling, 2011). For example, private education is viewed as a marker of social status and those with English-medium private school education can seize economic opportunities in the English-language market (i.e., private businesses such as banks and the massive INGO sector).

The perceived superiority of private education and its western orientation indicates an increasing influence of external factors on the national education system. That is, education is becoming synonymous with serving the purpose of the global economic market, rather than the local economies, through relevant education and skill training. As a result, modern educational processes are less appreciative of indigenous knowledges and the needs of local economies such as cottage industries and sustainable agriculture. Thus, youth measure their educational successes against parameters set by the global economic market rather than against the social and economic needs of their local settings.

When neoliberal policy prescriptions travel to local levels, they tend to interact with various political economy drivers, leading to disconnections between national and global as well as local and national levels, often producing unintended outcomes such as corruption, politicization, and "capture" (Edwards, 2011) of the benefits of decentralization. In the following section, I discuss some of these tensions in education from the political economy perspective.

The Political Economy of Community Schooling

Political economy analysis is concerned with "the interaction of political and economic processes in society: the distribution of power and wealth between different groups and individuals, and the processes that create, sustain and transform these relationships over time" (Collinson, 2003, p. 3). While education decentralization has given local communities access to school funds, it is the traditionally privileged groups (mainly the upper castes) that usually hold political prominence in the community and are most likely to influence the selection of the SMCs. Because schools are "the site(s) of political and social influence" (Edwards, 2011, p. 78), decentralization contributes to sustaining and reproducing traditional power relationships rather than transforming them in favor of marginalized groups such as women, Dalits, Tharu, Madheshi, and other indigenous nationalities. The decade-long civil war (1996–2006) has often been rationalized as a means to transform the rigid horizontal inequalities across these social and cultural groups (Tiwari, 2010) and to achieve a more just and equitable social order (Bhattarai, 2003). However, the absence of elected government bodies at local levels for over a decade created political spaces in schools where the struggle for political dominance, for example, through the SMCs, became a common phenomenon. The return of peace as a result of the peace accord simply reduced the amount of direct violence but the fundamental causes of social inequalities, uneven development, and economic grievances (Bhattarai, 2003; Deraniyagala, 2005) have not yet been dealt with. Thus, any policy initiative in the education sector that does not fully appreciate the social context is likely to serve the interests of the privileged groups in society rather than promote equality and social inclusion.

Most SMC members who were interviewed by me had close affiliations with political parties, and many of them held responsible positions in the local or regional party committees. The analysis of interviews with parents, teachers, and members of the SMCs revealed that there are social and political benefits to being involved in local educational committees such as SMCs, parent-teacher associations, or Social Audit Committees. An SMC chair in Kapilvastu mentioned that his responsibility in the SMC provided him with an opportunity to serve the community in other avenues of social services, such as politics. In most schools that participated in my study, the SMC chairs belonged to upper castes and were influential personalities in the local communities. Edwards (2011) likewise noted that the SMC chair usually has a high social status in the community and it is considered "a place to gain political prominence" (p. 79). As SMC chairs usually hold reputable positions in their political parties, they have a significant influence over teachers and parents in the community. In theory, the SMC should reflect a wide range of stakeholder interests, including representatives of women, Dalits, and other marginalized groups in society, but, in reality, the SMC chair dominates the committee and the regulations about its functions are often undermined.

For example, in a secondary school in Kapilvastu, where 95 percent of the children come from Tharu communities, the SMC chair belongs to a non-Tharu ethnic group. He is able to secure this role because of his social prominence and political affiliation to one of the national political parties. In a community school in Kathmandu, the SMC chair is an influential businessman and is highly regarded in his local community for his significant financial contribution to the development of the school playground. Neither of these SMC chairs is the guardian or parent of any child in the school. A study conducted by the Research Centre for Educational Innovations and Development (CERID, 2006) found that only 34 percent of the SMC chairs were parents or guardians of children in the school and although the government has clarified the regulation specifying that only a parent could be eligible for the SMC membership, this rule is mostly ignored or manipulated.

Interestingly, the analysis of interviews with SMC members and head teachers shows that educational success is measured in terms of infrastructural development such as construction of school buildings, playgrounds, and fences around the school. Teachers and SMC members in Dhanusha strongly argued for a fence around the school to prevent children from escaping during school hours. Most SMC members felt that the physical barrier around the school would oblige children to stay inside the school and learn. However, none of the members had ever observed the poor quality of teaching and learning that took place inside the classroom. In the interviews, SMC members and head teachers rarely mentioned children's learning, teacher development, or the quality of educational experience.

Another perceived measure of school development for both head teachers and SMC chairs was a school upgrade, which would not only provide higher-level schooling for children locally, but also help SMC chairs and head teachers gain social prestige for their achievement. However, an educational officer in Kathmandu mentioned that school upgrading and the subsequent construction of extra classrooms often involved corruption. He revealed that

> we often receive complaints from opposing groups of the SMCs about the misuse of school funds. This is more likely to happen where the head teacher and the SMC chair have a good working relationship and share the same political views. Even the district education officer [DEO] is sometimes involved in this kind of corruption.
>
> (Education officer in Kathmandu)

In the southern districts of the Terai (southern plains bordering India), corruption and malpractice are reported by SMC members to be pervasive in the process of teacher recruitment and redeployment. One SMC member in Kapilvastu stated that "there are different rates for recruitment in different teaching grades: 100,000, 200,000, and 300,000 Nepalese rupees for a primary-, lower secondary-, and secondary-level post, respectively" (focus group interview with SMC members and local politicians in Kapilvastu). It appears that this type of corruption is pervasive in these schools and occurs at different levels, involving SMC chairs, DEOs, head teachers, and school auditors. Community schooling seems to have been perceived as a means to gain increased access to school funds rather than achieve improved educational quality by enhancing local capacities and better engaging teachers and parents in children's learning. This suggests that there is a disconnection between policy aims and sociopolitical realities at the local level.

Local Capacities, Teachers, and School Management

The nationalization of schools and pedagogies in 1971 gradually disconnected communities as a whole from educational processes and systematically centralized the educational authority. The increasing horizontal inequalities across different ethnic and caste groups, fueled by a biased education system (e.g., medium of instruction, teaching workforce, cultural references in pedagogies, etc.), structurally resisted inclusive representation and community empowerment. This simply perpetuated social and political disparities within communities, where only the privileged social groups were able to influence community decision making. In this context, educational decentralization, designed at the national level and influenced by external agencies, largely ignores the realities of local-level capacities and interests to manage schools. As noted elsewhere, the roles and responsibilities of SMCs lack clarity within the policy guidelines (Carney et al., 2007; World Bank, 2010), which may potentially lead to management uncertainties among local stakeholders. SMC members who participated in the interviews in Kapilvastu, Dhanusha, and Kathmandu were unaware of any training available to them in order to support their school management role. Even though the policy states that SMC members can also observe lessons, only the SMC chairs who were educated and genuinely interested in the educational processes were likely to do so. Most SMC members I interviewed reported that they did not observe lessons. While head teachers and SMC members liked the idea of observation, they were not clear about what to observe (e.g., teaching methods, classroom setting, behavior management, student engagement in learning activities, etc.). Most importantly, the majority of SMC members in rural schools were not necessarily educated or trained to an extent that they could provide constructive feedback to qualified teachers on teaching and learning. Hence, most SMCs monitored teacher absenteeism and focused their work on infrastructural development of the school, depending on availability of funding.

There tend to be underlying tensions between teachers and SMCs since the teacher unions have always resisted the transfer of school management to local communities, citing this as a state policy of gradual disengagement in the delivery of public services and, most importantly, as a threat to their job security. Almost all teachers are affiliated to a teachers' association that operates under the umbrella of different political parties. With their political connections, teachers can neutralize the risk of their unintended transfer by the DEO and create a favorable working environment where they can enjoy the privileges of a flexible timetable and reduced workload. For example, in Kathmandu's public schools, most secondary-level teachers have second jobs in private colleges. A deputy head teacher in Kathmandu revealed in an interview that some teachers had abused their profession with the patronage from their political parties.

> We have a fulltime teacher who arrives at 12PM and leaves at 4PM. Sometimes he disappears from school during his teaching hours without even informing the head teacher. I think he works in a private college during his fulltime teaching hours here. The school management cannot do anything to him because he is associated with a Maoist teachers' union.
> (A deputy head teacher in a community school in Kathmandu)

Even the DEOs are unable to stand up to the teacher unions, which undermines the DEOs' work of monitoring and supervising schools and delivering continuing professional development opportunities for teachers. In a few districts in the southeastern part of the Terai, most of the officials have given up trying to do their jobs and remain in the district office. The state failed to provide personal and professional security to teachers in most rural parts of the country during the decade-long civil war. Since the peace agreement, the state has not yet regained full trust from teachers, who have responded to their traumatic experiences by negotiating their loyalty with political associations that extend teachers' professional security.

Politicization of School Management Committees

Because the role of an SMC chair generally provides political and economic benefits, the SMC chair has become a competitive position. As a result, many schools hold elections for their SMC. Especially in the Terai, securing the position of SMC chair has become the subject of intense political competition, especially where there are school lands and properties that generate extra income. In the absence of elections for local governments, the election of SMC chairs presents practically the only opportunity for political parties to measure their strength. The ferocity of these elections may arise from this factor rather than from any concern for education. A recently elected SMC chair, who is also a senior political leader of a Terai-based political party, lamented that

> I had to spend NRS.40, 000 [US$500] to win the election for the SMC chair. Other parties also supported me in this election as I had helped them gain a good number of votes during the elections for the Constituent Assembly. It [the election] became an issue of my social and political prestige.
> (An SMC chair in Kapilvastu)

It is interesting to observe that the SMC elections take place in the same manner as parliamentary elections and likewise involve expensive political campaigns. The SMC chair cited above is also a district president of the regional party and running for chair also became a test of his political influence in the district. However, getting a consensus to hold elections is also not without hassles. A head teacher from a community school in the north of Kapilvastu revealed the difficulty of forming a new SMC.

> A former UML [local] leader who has been the SMC chair of my school still intends to continue but now there are two other candidates—one from the Maoists and the other from Nepali Congress—interested in the post. It is likely that elections will be held this time. But the present SMC members, who are mainly linked with UML, would not allow me to invite parents for a boarder consultation to form a new SMC and the school inspector, who represents the

SMC selection committee, was warned by local political leaders not to interfere in the selection process.

(Head teacher from a secondary school in Kapilvastu)

The District Education Office (DEO) has been converted into a "Complaint Office": officials are mostly occupied in dealing with complaints from schools. Mainly, these are about political favoritism of the SMC in temporary teacher recruitment, corruption in teacher recruitment, misuse of school funds by the head teacher or SMC or both (e.g., not distributing scholarships), failure to form the SMC due to tensions between contesting groups, unfairness in the election of the SMC, and grievances against a previous DEO's decisions. For example, it was reported that 25 relief quota teachers recruited by one of the previous DEOs in Kapilvastu district did not teach in any school but were paid a full salary and attended district-level training to gain additional daily allowance.

Issues with Community School Management: A Political Economy Analysis

The vignette below, drawn from my diary during the fieldwork, represents a typical political tension that occurs in rural districts.

> It is 11AM; a group of teachers from a secondary school were picketing at the entrance of the District Education Office [DEO]. No DEO staff members, apart from an office assistant, have arrived yet, even though work was supposed to start at 10AM. The DEO was reported to be on leave for four days and had given his charge to a lady officer, who arrived only around 1PM. The story of the teachers' protest in front of the DEO unfolded interestingly. They had not been paid for the past four months due to school-based tensions related to the appointment of a new head teacher. The previous head teacher had recently retired, giving his deputy the authority of headship. The new head teacher, although able to acquire an appointment letter from the DEO, was rejected by most teachers but the SMC chair. However, the school accounts had not been transferred to the new head teacher, so he could not sign the cheques for teachers' salaries. The school generated some additional income by renting out its properties, including to some shops. Clearly, there was a potential for economic gains from school funds, which encouraged a struggle for the post of SMC chair and head teacher.
>
> To achieve a new political combination of the head and the SMC, an individual who had support from a prominent regional political party forcefully replaced the SMC chair and illegally captured the SMC. Now, the new SMC, with support from the newly appointed DEO in the district, transferred a

secondary-level teacher from a different school into this school to replace the new head. But the head teacher was not prepared to renounce his post as he claimed that he had been formally appointed to the post. The new DEO could not approve the transfer of school accounts to anyone in this situation, and hence the teachers' salaries were withheld. The school had been closed for the past week, as the teachers demanded the appointment of a new head teacher and the payment of their salaries without further delay. The current head teacher had the patronage from a teachers' union as well as from the Nepali Congress Party. The DEO was suspected of being bribed and was therefore hesitating to make a decision.

The position of SMC chair provides a significant opportunity to control resources and extend patronage networks. While the SMC chair may have strong political links and simultaneously hold positions in the party, this is not so evident in the case of head teachers, even though they might hold positions in teacher associations that are linked to different political parties. This arrangement makes it possible for the two key figures to work together in the SMC. In practice, one or the other is dominant. The analysis of interviews in my study also showed that in the schools where head teachers were enthusiastic and provided strong leadership, the quality of education was better than in other schools in the region. SMC chairs usually took the lead in the (highly politicized) Terai, while head teachers appeared more likely to take the lead in the hilly areas. A range of political causes were identified behind the politicization of SMCs, some of which are stated below:

- There is a political vacuum at the local level due to the absence of local government. As government institutions, schools provide a platform for exercising local political power. Political parties endeavor to maintain their local profile through representation in the SMCs.
- Holding SMC positions, particularly the chair, provides social and political status, which contributes to a political career in the party.
- Schools have become places for expanding political ideologies. SMCs can influence teachers, students, and parents to pursue their political agendas.
- SMCs can have indirect economic benefits (e.g., bribes) in teacher recruitment.
- Schools receive direct funds from government and the SMCs have influence on how to manage those funds. Supporting investment in school development (e.g., building classrooms) helps them gain social credibility.
- SMCs are not clear about their roles and do not receive any training

Therefore, there are a number of political and economic motivations for competing for the SMC positions, especially the chair. The aggressive decentralization processes inspired and assisted by development partners and project-based educational programming have influenced the trajectories of Nepal's education policies. Politicization in the education system is one of the unintended outcomes of the interaction between the global drive for educational decentralization and incompatible local contexts.

Conclusions: Disjuncture between "Centralized Decentralization" and Political Localities

The post-1990 governments in Nepal have adopted liberal economic policies creating a space for neoliberal policy reforms in public sectors, including education. Several state owned companies were privatized to reduce public spending and enhance efficiency and accountability. The long-term effect of Nepal's educational decentralization policy seems to be the transfer of responsibility of public education to the poor people, while preserving private education, which maintains an elite system of education. This policy choice has been influenced by the neoliberal market economy through international organizations, particularly the World Bank, the largest education aid provider to Nepal. Nepal's bureaucracy and political leadership are dominated by high castes and traditionally privileged social groups, who educate their children in private schools, have bought into the idea of decentralization without adequate analysis of local realities, nor through the "piloting of the policy initiative" (World Bank, 2010). Hence, the collaboration between the national governments in the past two decades and international development partners has pushed the decentralization policy to the local levels without considering the social, political, and economic realities of Nepali society.

In this chapter, I have argued that educational decentralization has a hidden motive of privatizing education in a bid to reduce public spending while encouraging competition, accountability, and participation at local levels. These global policy prescriptions accompany development funding, which can easily attract weak economies that have structural inequalities and elitism. Subsequently, these developing countries fall into the trap of dependency on international aid. Decentralization in this situation provides socially privileged groups with access to local resources and power. It serves primarily their interests, and thus reproduces political and economic structures and reinforces social hierarchies. Education decentralization does not necessarily empower marginalized groups in communities; rather it reinforces the traditional power of social control exercised by privileged groups in a different form. Finally, with no appreciation of local political economies, the consistent policy thrust from the center could create tensions among local and mid-level educational institutions and foster the development of a damaging culture in the education sector.

The interactions between relative poverty, postwar transitional politics, and unjust sociopolitical structures characterize the political economy of Nepal. The devolution of authority to local and regional levels cannot unconditionally benefit a community that harbors horizontal inequalities along caste and ethnic lines.

References

Apple, M. (2004). *Ideology and curriculum* (3rd ed.). London: Routlege Falmer.
Bhattarai, B. R. (2003). The political economy of the "People's War". In A. Karki & D. Seddon (Eds.), *The people's war in Nepal: Left perspectives* (pp. 117–164). New Delhi: Adroit Publishers.
Bourdieu, P. (1984). *Distinction: A social critique of the judgment of taste*. London, UK: Routledge and Kegan Paul.
Caddell, M. (2007). Private schools and political conflict in Nepal. In P. Srivastava & G. Walford (Eds.), *Private schooling in less economically developed countries: Asian and African perspectives* (pp. 187–207). Oxford Studies in Comparative Education. Didcot, UK: Symposium. Retrieved from http://oro.open.ac.uk/2892/1/CaddellSympChpt.pdf.
Carney, S., Bista, M. & Agergaard, J. (2007). "Empowering" the "local" through education? Exploring community-managed schooling in Nepal. *Oxford Review of Education*, 33(5), 611–628.
Carnoy, M. (1999). *Globalization and educational reform: What planners need to know*. Paris: United Nations Educational, Scientific, and Cultural Organization (UNESCO).
Collinson, S. (Ed.) (2003). *Power, livelihoods and conflict: Case studies in political economy analysis for humanitarian action*. London: Overseas Development Institute.
Cornwall, A. & Brock, K. (2005). What do buzzwords do for development policy? A critical look at "participation", "empowerment" and "poverty reduction". *Third World Quarterly*, 26(7), 1043–1060.
CERID (2006). *Education for all formative research report. Synthesis report of the case studies conducted in 2006*. Tribhuvan University: Research Centre for Educational Innovation and Development.
Deraniyagala, S. (2005). The political economy of civil conflict in Nepal. *Oxford Development Economics*, 33(1), 47–62.
DoE (2010). *Flash I Report 2067 (2010–011)*. Sanothimi, Bhaktapur: Department of Education, Nepal.
Dorling, D. (2011). *Injustice: Why social inequality persists*. Bristol: The Policy Press.
Edwards, R. M. (2011). Disconnect and capture of education decentralisation reforms in Nepal: Implications for community involvement in schooling. *Globalisation, Societies and Education*, 9(1), 67–84.

Hanson, M. (1998). Strategies of educational decentralization: Key questions and core issues. *Journal of Educational Administration, 36*(2), 111–128.

McGinn, N., & Welsh, T. (1999). *Decentralisation of education: Why, when, what and how?* Paris: United Nations Educational, Scientific, and Cultural Organization (UNESCO).

MoE (1971). *The national education system plan for 1971–76.* Kathmandu: Ministry of Education.

Mohsin, M. (1972). Interview with Mohammad Mohsin. In I. Baral (Ed.), *National education plan: As they see it* (pp. 34–50). Kathmandu: National Education Committee Office.

Onta, P. (1996). Ambivalence denied: The making of Rastiya Itihas in Panchayat era text-books. *Contributions to Nepalese Studies, 23*(1), 213–254.

Poppema, M. (2009). Guatemala, the Peace Accords and education: A post-conflict struggle for equal opportunities, cultural recognition and participation in education. *Globalisation, Societies and Education, 7*(4), 383–408.

Stewart, F. (Ed.) (2008). *Horizontal inequalities and conflict: Understanding group violence in multiethnic societies.* New York: Palgrave McMillan.

Tiwari, B. N. (2010). Horizontal inequalities and violent conflict in Nepal. In M. Lawoti & A. Guneratne (Eds.), *Ethnicity, inequality and politics in Nepal* (pp. 55–92). Kathmandu: Himal Books.

Watson, W. (2000). *Multiculturalism.* Buckingham: Open University Press.

World Bank (1995). *Priorities and strategies for education: A World Bank review.* Washington, DC: World Bank.

World Bank (2003). *NEPAL: Community school support project* (Updated Project Information Document (PID)). Kathmandu: World Bank.

World Bank (2010). *Project Performance Assessment Report Nepal, Community School Support Project* (CR. 3808). Retrieved from http://lnweb90.worldbank.org/oed/oeddoclib.nsf/DocUNIDViewForJavaSearch/FFBF09CBD4E802D185257788005B9EFA/$file/PPAR_Nepal%20-%20Community%20School%20Support%20Project.pdf

Zajda, J., & Geo-Jaja, M. (2009). *The politics of education reforms.* London: Springer.

CHAPTER 6

Global/Colonial Designs, School Knowledge Production, and Students' Cultural Identities: A Critical Ethnographic Perspective from Pakistan

Al-Karim Datoo

Introduction

In the wake of globalization, culture is in motion losing its local moorings (Appadurai, 1996). Curriculum is drawn from culture (Stenhouse, 1967) and this raises the critical question of whose culture is produced through the curriculum, and what its implications could be on students' self/cultural identities. In this chapter, I explore the culture-curriculum link in a high school context in urban Pakistan and analyze how globalization and processes of cultural globalization influence curricular meanings and texts related to global and local cultures. I also look at how these productions are interpreted, appropriated, and resisted and in turn employed in the self-identity projects by high school youth. I pay special attention to the roles of global and colonial projects in shaping school knowledge in the high school curriculum. In this respect, I analyze students' interpretations of the representations of global/local culture in science and social science texts. The aim is to expose the merger of the global, colonial, and modern in textual constructions and to look at the exclusion or inclusion of the local. I discuss local cultural bases and references of knowledge and their implications for the students' sense of self and other identities in the context of a globalizing world.

The analysis is based on a selected data set generated through a critical ethnography conducted in a higher secondary school setting in urban Karachi, a metropolis of Pakistan. The data is drawn from focus group discussions and semi-structured interviews with the students (used to generate their initial views, and to begin a dialogic engagement); visual texts produced by the students; and a critical analysis of the curricular texts (informed by critical globalization and postcolonial stances).

Education-Culture Interplay in a Globalizing World: Explicating Power

Education is primarily a cultural and social practice (Masemann, 2003). Formal education represents a link with a social institution like a school or university that deals with knowledge production in a society and that socializes students into the culture(s). At another level, the content and processes of education are drawn from the culture in terms of knowledge, ways of knowing, symbolic resources, culturally situated meanings, and visions of beings. Put simply, culture becomes a source-bed of education, and once formalized and institutionalized, education adopts the role of cultural transmission and transformation. In this sense, education can be regarded as both the product as well as the producer of culture (Retallick & Datoo, 2005). This also shows how deeply education is embedded in the politics of culture (Apple, 1996).

The selection of culture in curriculum, as with any selection, involves judgments, such as the judgment to include or exclude knowledge. It involves the decision of what counts as knowledge and what does not; thus curriculum is an embodiment of power (Apple, 1995). Knowledge and power are central to understanding the production of the political economy of culture through education. Knowledge defines what constitutes "truth" in a given society; it therefore also defines what is false. In this respect, the knowledge/truth claims of a culture constitute an ideological discourse that propagates the hegemony of the dominant over the subordinate culture/self (Apple, 1998).

In the context of schooling, Apple (1998) discussed how dominant ideologies shape the content, form, and processes of school knowledge through overt and hidden curricula. He pointed out how the discourse of the New Right excludes certain forms of knowledge. This selected knowledge becomes legitimate curricular knowledge, in which western civilization is seen as superior and is therefore in a position to civilize the "Other" (Apple, 2004). As such, certain groups of people, connected by their common ideological lenses, have great power over the nature of what takes place in schools. Apple (2004) identified the neoliberals, neoconservatives, authoritarian populists, and professional middle class as being powerful, sometimes unknowing, participants in promoting the dominant culture. With the power of numbers and financial resources, they are able to shape students' day-to-day experiences in schools. Through this ideological discourse, the dominant culture exerts (western) cultural hegemony through epistemic hegemony (Mignolo, 2000). Values are judgments of right and wrong, while norms are behavioral definitions of the values. Ideology—a set of beliefs, values, and norms—(Apple, 2004) gets embedded in the curriculum and is conveyed through socialization in education (Masemann, 2003).

In the context of globalization, the politics of cultural production acquires a spatial dimension. Globalization, especially through media and migration, has generated a process of de/territorialization, which has set cultures in motion (Clifford, 1997). In this respect, experiences, and thereby cultural meanings, are no longer limited to one place, but have been reinscribed in spatiality (Giddens, 1990), creating an intermingling of cultural traffic (Inda & Rosaldo, 2002). This hybridized nature of culture forms the character of a culture. It influences the nature and content of the curriculum and the types of cultural capitals it produces. This nexus between globalization, culture, and curriculum influences and controls the meaning-making processes of students, and thus their lives and identities. Hence, the curriculum can be seen as a pressure site—a site of production, reproduction, contestation, and resistance structured at the liminal zones of micro-macro or structure-agency contexts.

The knowledge dynamic referred to earlier gets played out in and through school curricula. These curricula are shaped by the politics of knowledge implicated by the local-global interplay. According to Eisner (1994), all schools teach three types of curricula: (a) intended, which is explicitly advertised and written; (b) unintended or hidden; and (c) null. I regard the first type (intended) as the official curriculum in Apple's (1993) sense because it highlights the political dimension of knowledge production, legitimization, and representation processes that shape school curricula. Put simply, the official curriculum determines the knowledge that a school selects and legitimizes. Through legitimization, this curriculum makes available the knowledge of a certain select tradition or certain cultural groups, that is, a curriculum that is rooted in their ideology/hegemony and is represented as official. The term "official" is crucial for conceptualizing my research and the global-local dialectic implications for the construction of official school knowledge. It raises the question as to whose knowledge becomes included in the official curricula. And conversely, whose knowledge is nullified in the wake of the local-global dynamic?

The "null" curriculum refers to "that knowledge which schools do not teach" (Eisner, 1994, p. 97). In identifying a null curriculum, two dimensions need to be considered: one is "the intellectual processes that schools emphasize and neglect"; the other is "the content or subject areas that are present and absent in school curricula" (p. 98). Cultural hegemony in curricula is exerted through the exclusion of certain forms of knowledge, especially those of a subordinate culture. In such exclusion, the history (and memory) of a particular community gets lost. The critical task of curriculum discourse construction then is to recover the memory and history of the "subordinates" in ways that make it possible for individuals to politically act for their rights (Kincheloe & Pinar, 1991).

Postcolonial View on Eurocentric/Occidental Knowledge

The postcolonial perspective sees the global/modern project as culturally hegemonic. It assigns a valid and superior status to western forms of knowledge as compared with the diverse knowledge forms of non-western societies, which are assigned a subaltern status. This hegemony of western forms of knowledge, science, and rationality was spread through colonization, and heavily influenced the educational systems of the colonies. This shadow continues to haunt postcolonial societies.

Edward Said's *Orientalism* (1978) unearthed how colonial knowledge discourse construed the categories of Orient and Occident: the Orient was rationalized as needing to be civilized by the Occident, through the knowledge systems of the latter. Much of the educational policies and curricula in developing countries (including Pakistan) are still shaped by this colonial educational legacy, which has a tendency to suppress the value of local knowledge (Geertz, 1993). This creates a disjuncture in students' minds about their locatedness vis-à-vis their own histories, cultures, and epistemic and interpretative traditions and experiences, thus influencing their identities.

From a postcolonial perspective, globalization is seen as a perpetuator of Enlightenment epistemologies, which are steeped in the history and cultures of the West and promote the role of reason and rationality as the only valid form of knowledge. This assigns a subaltern status to all other forms of knowledge, which are treated as folk-wisdom (Mignolo, 2000). Consequently, the education of the South is controlled by the North (the western world) (Stromquist, 2002), which defines what is valid knowledge and true academic scholarship (Nandy, 2004).

Moreover, a postcolonial critique points to the notion of colonial difference manufactured by colonial masters (Mignolo, 2000), who count knowledge as defined by Enlightenment rationality and exclude local cultural knowledge as non-knowledge. For example, empiricist epistemology would disqualify forms of local knowledge that do not subscribe to the authority of reason and are not verifiable by human senses, since their sources may not be found through other a-rational epistemologies (e.g., the role of intuition in the mystic tradition). Mignolo (2000) criticized this universalizing tendency of Occidental reason, as it subjugates other forms of knowledge as subaltern. He viewed this as the modern/colonial project of knowledge and called for the development of a discourse about gnosis, or border thinking, which highlights colonial difference in knowledge production. The discourse of globalization should be sensitive to this exclusion and should be open to plural epistemic discourses. Mignolo (2000) argued for the importance of bringing local (non-western, non-Enlightenment) epistemologies to the fore.

Overall, the postcolonial perspective champions the role of the historical, the political, and the local, and the role of agency within these. It rejects the universality of globalization and exposes its colonial and imperial intent. This view critiques and problematizes the globalist agenda and the power behind it. This colonial difference (Mignolo, 2000), or the juxtaposition of western knowledge forms and "the rest," needs to be theorized (Kapoor, 2007).

Education and Cultural Identity: Local-Global Dynamics

The notion of identity is central to one's becoming and being. Holland, Lachicotte, Skinner, and Cain (2001) define it as follows:

> People tell others who they are, but even more important, they tell themselves and then try to act as though they are who they say they are. These self-understandings, especially those with strong emotional resonance for the teller, are what we refer to as identities (p. 3).

Developing self-understanding, and therefore identity, involves a relationship between self and other. The development of these self-understandings involves the interplay of history, culture, and power. Hence, identity is a matter of being that is always becoming and remains in constant transformation rather than being a fixed entity frozen in time.

Education, as a mode of cultural production, significantly contributes to the development of these self-understandings. In the wake of globalization, with the rapid growth of information and communication technologies, students' lived worlds are substantially being shaped by formal education and media. Youth, in particular, are heavily engaged with these educational sites and associated activities (Datoo, 2011). These contexts constantly put self and other in contact, and in turn, shape and reshape the students' self-understandings (identities). The student self is encountering the cultural other at an increasingly accelerated pace, and therefore self-identity is created on a more active basis than before (Giddens, 1991).

Globalization, with its dis-embedding mechanisms and complex connectivity (Tomlinson, 1999), has opened up new social spaces for interaction. But, at the same time, this has brought anxieties, as there is a sense of the "invasion of local space with distant social forces and processes" (Niezen, 2004, p. 38), and hence of delocalization. The invasion in the form of, for instance, urbanization, industrialization, and/or dis-embedding mechanisms creates a forced coexistence of modernity and tradition (Niezen, 2004). Thus, locality has lost its ontological traditional base (Appadurai, 1996). These changes are significantly influencing the local rootedness of the self. This underscores the interrelationship between education and culture, and how this relationship is shaped by cultural globalization, especially in a postcolonial educational context.

Having set the theoretical backdrop, in the following section, I present some key findings about and discussions around the merger of the global and the colonial in curricular texts as well as in the students' perceptions and interpretations. I also discuss how students responded to these interpretations as they attempted to make sense of their own identities, and situate themselves in the contemporary globalizing world.

Global-Modern Complex: Students' Perceptions of the Global, the Local, and the Self

Modernity has desired universality and is for the most part expressed in the terminology of the West. Therefore, in individual imaginations, the global, the modern, and the West are often seen as synonymous; these references are at play in an individual's interpretation of their cultural identity. This Eurocentric perspective is clearly seen in the visual productions that the student research participants made when they were instructed to represent how they view the global and the local, and the relationship of the self with these. In what follows, I present two of the students' visuals and provide the transcription of the students' views on those representations. This is followed by my own interpretations of those constructs, especially highlighting the knowledge structures that may have influenced the students' perceptions and interpretations.

Saher and the Local-Global World

Saher comes from a working-class family. Her mother is the principal of a school called Mama Baby Care. Saher has traveled to Kampala, Uganda.

Al-Karim Datoo • 93

Figure 6.1 Saher's Representation of the Local-Global Dynamic and the Self

She imagines Paris to be the most beautiful city in the world and wishes to travel to Paris in the future. Saher's immediate family lives in Karachi, but her extended family is in the United States, Canada, and the United Kingdom. Saher does not like communicating via MSN or the Internet but prefers face-to-face connections. Saher wants to become a doctor.

Once the visual was produced (Figure 6.1), Saher started explaining her representation:

> This is a bridge [pointing to the visual]. Modern has crossed the bridge and has come here [to the local], so the local welcomed it [the global]. This [global] is very rude, but the local has changed it. The local has changed the global through its love and friendly behavior, so the global became intermingled with the local, and her nature and behaviour got changed. And when the local went to the global, the global did not welcome the local. I actually agree with this point. There was one program on TV, "George ka Pakistan" [George's Pakistan]. In that they showed that there was a foreigner, who came to Pakistan and the local welcomed him, but the westerners are not ready to welcome the local. There are many TV programs which show that Whites are running after Blacks/Asians [chasing them as suspects].
>
> (Student's presentation, April 19, 2007)

Rafique and the Local-Global World

Rafique was born in Karachi, Pakistan. In his very early years, he migrated to the United States with his parents. He completed his elementary and junior

94 • Global/Colonial Designs, School Knowledge Production

Figure 6.2 Rafique's Representation of the Local-Global Dynamic and the Self

high schooling there. After 9/11, he returned to Karachi with his family. In 2008, he and his family migrated to Canada. Rafique enjoys watching television, playing the guitar, and listening to popular music (Pakistani, Indian—Bollywood—and western), and communicating with friends and family via the Internet (Figure 6.2).

FZ[1] Local people are so weird people and wear those long, long, long *Shalwar Kurtas* and *Burqaas* and everything and like this is a local gun and drum.
　　　[Here the conversation between Rafique and myself began in question-response form.]
AKD It's written here in this bubble that [local people] "Always do farming." So, who says that?
FZ　 The old people say that, they are the local people.
AKD But who says that?
FZ　 I say that.
AKD Okay.
FZ　 "Children should sleep early."
AKD Tell me about that? [Sound of laughter while asking that.]
FZ　 Like [local] people are so weird.
AKD Okay, what does weird mean to you?
FZ　 Strange and bizarre.
AKD Strange in which manner?

FZ   They always tell their children to sleep, like they don't want their children to wake up and have fun, they want them to sleep.
AKD Okay, and what is happening in global?
FZ   And global people like, they are all fashionable and everything, they listen to iPods, they like to play the guitars and like the girls wears the skirts and everything, like they are so developed, they are very advance, like they have started using the Bio [biological sciences] and all the things and we have discovered all these things.
AKD Okay, now, who are "we"? Where do you see Rafique in this whole scenario?
FZ   I am here [pointing at the heading: Global]. (Student's presentation, April 19, 2007)

Knowledge and Global/Colonial Difference: Sense of Exclusion, Student Knowledge, and Nostalgia

The West has come to be regarded as synonymous with scientific technology and advancement. The knowledge power of the West creates a sense of cultural superiority. This superiority has been manufactured by colonialism, which has been a tool for globalization. The West took up a civilizing mission of the rest of the world, which was the self-justifying logic of the colonial project. The students in my research felt this sense of cultural difference (Mignolo, 2000). One remarked, "There is something hidden in West culture that makes them scientifically advanced and progressive. We need to know, what is there that most of the people are attracted by the West" (Focus group discussion, February 28, 2007).

Sense of Exclusion and Culture Loss

One theme that emerged in my research was a feeling of exclusion from the West, especially with respect to knowledge. One student remarked,

> When I read modern books about sciences, I find all reference of western scientists, and hardly any of Muslim scientists, although Muslim scientists did make great contributions in science. I think that this is conspiracy from the West, that it has suppressed contributions of our Muslim scientists.
> (Focus group discussion, February 28, 2007)

The power of knowledge production and reproduction has created a cultural anxiety that has penetrated student agency which has caused disjunctures among students at various levels, in part through a sense of exclusion.

The Student and Knowledge in a Globalizing World

Globalization has accelerated the pace of knowledge flows across contexts. As a result, students are able to access knowledge with relatively greater ease. In this respect, the students also acknowledge that their options to travel abroad have opened up:

> Due to globalization we can go to study abroad easily, which was not possible a few decades back. We can go to other countries, gain knowledge, and educate ourselves.
> (Focus group discussion, February 28, 2007)

Another student added,

> The US is leader in science. We wish to go there and see what is hidden in their culture. How come they are producing so many scientists? So if you wish to go abroad for studies, meaning the science that is so much progressing, that is progressing in the western culture—so if you wish to gain good scientific education, then you have to go abroad.
> (Focus group discussion, February 28, 2009)

A majority of the student participants expressed similar views.

Nostalgia

Paradoxically, the force of modernity/global generated a sense of nostalgia in students as they tried to fill the cultural/technological gap by resorting to their own history—the golden past. As one student remarked,

> We [Muslims] were very advanced. In the past we had lots of scientists. People like Ibn-e-Haytam, Ibn-e-Sina, whose work was copied and taught in western universities. Today we are left behind. Today West is where we were few centuries back. So then West learnt from us, now we have to learn from West.
> (Focus group discussion, February 28, 2007)

In such a state, torn between past and present, nostalgia and future, local and global, students are responding to the local-global cultural dynamic and the resulting disjuncture by aligning their identities with either a complementary or a counter discourse to global cultural power and supremacy.

Political Economy of Knowledge and Culture: Theoretical Interpretations

In the first visual, by Saher, the spatial metaphor of the global is represented as a geopolitical metaphor: West is seen as modern. Hence, the global is equated with modern and the West, and by the same token, the local is implied to refer to the East. Similar views were cited by the majority of the participating students, for whom "East is local, West is global" (Focus group discussion, September 20, 2006). The students located themselves in the local context (i.e., the East), and the "Other" as the West. In grounding themselves in the East and the global as the West, the students were articulating not only their location in the international world, but also their relationship with the global other.

The second visual, by Rafique, constructs the binary opposites of the global (as modern/progressive) and the local (as conventional/traditional/backward in terms of development, as defined by the so-called development discourse). In doing so, Rafique is self-Orientalizing, meaning that he comes to see his own local context in the terminology of Orientalism. One contrast in the visuals is that Rafique, unlike Saher, wishes to regard himself as belonging to the global, and not the local (Focus group discussion, September 20, 2012).

How could these perceptions have developed? What role might knowledge and education have played? The dichotomy between the global and the local on the one hand, and the conjoining of the global/West/modern is a historical and epistemological/political product that Edward Said (1978) referred to as Orientalism. He explained that the Orientalist discourse creates an opposing dynamic between the East and the West. It is a discourse used by the West to create a sense of self-recognition and promote its own superiority and power over the other. In her visual of the local-global dynamic, Saher presented these binary positions and located herself in the local, defined as the East, and positioned the Other in the global (i.e., the West).

Arkoun (2000) explained that equating the global with being modern and coming from the West is an eighteenth-century Eurocentric Enlightenment tradition. This view excludes other "modernities" that took place in other civilizations. The students appear to have accepted this Eurocentric definition of enlightenment. They have either failed to see modernity within their own civilization or do not assign it with the same value and importance. Their frame of reference for modernity comes from the criteria espoused by the West, which is in line with Said's argument (1978).

How is it that such a discourse is prevalent today? In analyzing the school curricular texts, I noticed that the historical discourse focuses on the superiority of the western Enlightenment and the subjugation of the colonized world. The contributions of the colonized world are not given the same value or power and are intentionally or unintentionally perceived as being either insignificant or inferior by the students. Such education instills ignorance by design, where the intellectual contributions and cultural achievements of other civilizations are not taught within the curriculum. Hence, there are only two binary options of reference: the West, which is seen as modern and superior, and the East, which is perceived as traditional and inferior.

Knowledge and Colonial Difference: Theoretical Reflections

Colonial difference for students is a space where the knowledge hegemony of the West in the shape of science and technology is, on the one hand, accepted, indoctrinated, and reproduced, and on the other, resisted, argued against, and criticized for its exclusionary approach toward knowledge production throughout history (Mignolo, 2000). As a result, local knowledge becomes suppressed and western epistemic supremacy becomes hegemonic. The West becomes a desired and idealized place and is seen as advanced in science and technology. This disjuncture in science and technology discourse, which the students felt, colonizes the East. It generates a dichotomy between West and East through various markers of knowledge production, sometimes in the name of scientific inventions and sometimes through the creation of dichotomized and binary categories such as developed and underdeveloped; modern and traditional; and progressive and backward (Escobar, 1995).

Some of my research participants seem to have been indoctrinated into this knowledge hegemony through their formal education, by studying a curriculum based on western knowledge production. By nullifying the discourse and contributions of Muslim intellectuals, scientists, and thinkers, the curriculum transfers the colonial legacy to the West and in a substantial way excludes the local-self. Through this, the knowledge hegemony brings in nostalgia, whereby students can only glorify their cultural and intellectual heritage to negotiate and reinvent their future.

Concluding Remarks

In the context of globalization, culture is an adulterated site where there are exo-local forces at play. These forces appear to reproduce global and colonial designs, encroaching the role and place of the local culture.

The students' perceptions and articulations reflected the hegemonic nature of the global/modern/colonial mind-set, which is an active signifier of cultural power vis-à-vis the local culture. Modernity seems to be acquiring universal reach through neocolonial, education, media, and development discourse. These often converge in the school curriculum, yet as my research shows, they are also resisted and reappropriated by the students.

Within this power nexus, curriculum is becoming a site for cultural contestation, reproduction, and resistance. It is a site where the structuration

(Giddens, 1990) between knowledge (as embodied in the curriculum) and agency (as expressed in the students' perceptions and interpretations of the curricular knowledge) is active and filled with power dynamics. In high school, curricular knowledge, especially of science, seems to produce colonial difference, that is, a knowledge and innovation gap between the West and the rest. This has been achieved through historiography of the knowledge called science, which in the current parlance has been associated with and articulated in the terminology of the West. The historiography excludes other human intellectual contributions/heritages and by doing so produces and reproduces a hegemony and cultural supremacy. This creates a sociopsychological condition where the less dominant begin to self-judge and self-verify vis-à-vis that complex. Thus, colonial difference perpetuates a sense of backwardness, a qualitative feeling that is manipulated by the international developmentalist discourse: the curriculum reinforces and reproduces the difference.

The urban high school youth of Pakistan felt a sense of cultural loss and experienced ambivalence in the context of globalization. This loss has been reacted to in a variety of ways. One of the responses is engagement with nostalgia. The students remembered and lamented the golden days of the past when Muslim civilizations were leaders in science and technology. Using nostalgia as praxis (Dirlik, 1996), the students seemed to negotiate and reinvent their identities.

Overall, this chapter has highlighted the importance of a new sociology of curriculum, especially in postcolonial/globalization contexts. This approach needs to pay critical attention to the politics of Orientalism and neo/colonial epistemology to expose and critique the production of colonial difference, with a view to creating space for indigenous/pluralistic epistemologies. These can provide an anchor for local/cultural identities, which is essential in reconciling the global and the local in education.

Note

1. Rafique's responses are depicted as FZ, and I am AKD.

References

Appadurai, A. (1996). *Modernity at large: Cultural dimensions of globalization.* Minneapolis: University of Minnesota Press.

Apple, M. W. (1993). *Official knowledge: Democratic education in a conservative age.* New York: Routledge.

Apple, M. W. (1995). *Education and power* (2nd ed.). New York: Teachers College Press.

Apple, M. W. (1996). *Cultural politics and education*. New York: Teachers College Press.
Apple, M. W. (1998). Under the new hegemonic alliance: Conservatism and educational policy in the United States. In K. Sullivan (Ed.), *Education and change in the Pacific Rim: Meeting the challenges* (pp. 79–99). Wallingford: Triangle Books.
Apple, M. W. (2004). *Ideology and curriculum* (3rd ed.). New York: Routledge Falmer.
Arkoun, M. (2000). Present-day Islam between its tradition and globalization. In F. Daftary (Ed.), *Intellectual traditions in Islam* (pp. 179–221). New York: I. B. Tauris & Co Ltd.
Clifford, J. (1997). *Routes: Travel and translation in the late twentieth century*. Cambridge, USA: Harvard University Press.
Datoo, A. (2011). Globalization, media and youth identity in Pakistan. In D. Kapoor (Ed.), *Critical perspectives on neoliberal globalization, development and education in Africa and Asia* (pp. 135–149). Rotterdam: Sense Publications.
Dirlik, A. (1996). The global in the local. In R. Wilson, & W. Dissanayake (Eds.), *Global local: Cultural production and the transnational imaginary* (pp. 21–45). Durham: Duke University Press.
Eisner, E. W. (1994). *The educational imagination: On the design and evaluation of school programs* (3rd ed.). New York: McMillan.
Escobar, A. (1995). *Encountering development: The making and unmaking of the third world*. Princeton, NJ: Princeton University Press.
Geertz, C. (1993). *Local knowledge*. London: Fontana Press.
Giddens, A. (1990). *The consequences of modernity*. Stanford: Stanford University Press.
Giddens, A. (1991). *Modernity and self-identity: Self and society in the late modern age*. Cambridge: Polity Press.
Holland, D., Lachicotte, W., Skinner, D., & Cain, C. (2001). *Identity and agency in cultural worlds*. Cambridge, MA: Harvard University Press.
Inda, J. X., & Rosaldo, R. (2002). A world in motion. In X. J. Inda, & R. Rosaldo (Eds.), *The anthropology of globalization: A reader* (pp. 1–34). Oxford: Blackwell Publishing.
Kapoor, D. (2007). Editorial introduction: International perspectives on education and decolonization. *International Education, 37*(1), 3–8.
Kincheloe, J. L., & Pinar, W. F. (1991). Introduction. In J. L. Kincheloe, & W. F. Pinar (Eds.), *Curriculum as social psycho analysis: The significance of place* (pp. 1–23). Albany: State University of New York Press.
Masemann, V. L. (2003). Culture and education. In R. F. Arnove, & C. A. Torres (Eds.), *Comparative education: Dialectic of the global and the local* (pp. 115–132). Maryland: Rowman & Littlefield Publishers.
Mignolo, W. (2000). *Local histories/global designs: Coloniality, subaltern knowledges and border thinking*. Princeton, NJ: Princeton University Press.
Nandy, A. (2004). *Bonfire of creeds: The essentials Ashis Nandy*. New Delhi: Oxford University Press.
Niezen, R. (2004). *A world beyond difference: Cultural identity in the age of globalization*. Oxford: Blackwell.

Rettalick, J., & Datoo, A. (2005). Transforming schools into learning communities: Focus on Pakistan. In J. Rettalick & I. Farah (Eds.), *Transforming schools in Pakistan: Towards the learning community* (pp. 1–25). Karachi: Oxford University Press.

Said, E. W. (1978). *Orientalism.* New York: Vintage Books.

Stenhouse, L. (1967). *Culture and education.* London: Nelson.

Stromquist, N. P. (2002). *Education in a globalized world: The connectivity of economic power, technology, and knowledge.* New York: Rowman & Littlefield Publishers.

Tomlinson, J. (1999). *Globalization and culture.* Chicago: University of Chicago Press.

CHAPTER 7

Neoliberal Globalization and Preprimary Teacher Education Policy and Practice in India, Sri Lanka, and the Maldives

Amita Gupta

Introduction

In this chapter, I present current trends in preprimary teacher education in India, Sri Lanka, and the Maldives and discuss the implications of neoliberal globalization for these policies and practices. The terms early childhood/preprimary education are used interchangeably, as are teacher education/preparation/training. The critical proposition advanced here is that the commercialization and westernization of educational institutions as a result of neoliberal globalization promote a human capital perspective on child development and educational aims, which often conflicts with the local understanding of these issues. Postcolonial theory frames the argument that neoliberal advances in education and teacher education lead to neocolonialism through the imposition of the dominant western discourse that is influencing educational decisions in South Asia. An overview of preprimary teacher education in India, Sri Lanka, and the Maldives is followed by a discussion on ways in which post-neoliberal shifts are evident in these changing landscapes. Critical concerns in two broad areas are raised for discussion: the impact of western neoliberalism on early education and teacher education from a human capital and for-profit perspective; and the resulting cultural incursions that occur due to conflicting pedagogies rooted in different worldviews. Recognizing the pervasive nature of neoliberal globalization,

I recommend a hybrid third space in teacher education theory for South Asia that may be used to empower rather than colonize.

Conceptual Frameworks

Globalization is the idea that there are flows between international, national, regional, and local boundaries with an interconnectivity between cultural and economic lives (Giddens, 1990). Globalization of education refers to the "worldwide discussions, processes, and institutions affecting local educational practices and policies" (Spring, 2009, p. 1). These flows, or global forces, cause rapid shifts empowering some groups while marginalizing others through new forms of exploitation and political and economic domination (Carney, 2009; Kamat, 2002). Neoliberal trends in education evident in the market economies of capitalism in the developed world and now being globalized to regions in the global South, are not very different from classic colonial education, which promulgated a western version of education in the colonies (Kapoor, 2011).

Postcolonial theory not only allows for a discussion of the "colonial" encounter within the context of contemporary globalization, but also draws attention to previously under-researched areas, thus challenging existing theoretical perspectives (Crossley & Tikly, 2004). It focuses on the continuing negotiations and lingering transactions between the ideas and philosophies of the colonized and the colonizing, the modern and the traditional, the center and the margins (Bhabha, 1994; de Alva, 1995; Gandhi, 1998; Pratt, 1992; Trivedi, 1993) resulting in a transcultural mixing and exchange (Tikly, 1999). Bhabha (1994, 2009) suggested that it is helpful to view cultural categories not as binaries opposing each other but as having fluid boundaries that interact with each other: the exchange is essentially a form of cultural translation as ideas from one culture are modified and embedded into another culture, and the process of transformation leads to the creation of a hybrid third space or grey area that holds possibilities for alternative theoretical frameworks. Like postcolonialism, globalization elicits the notion of hybridity as the transactions between global and local foster two-way negotiations in newly created hybrid spaces; and within these spaces a new, more empowering discourse becomes possible.

Current educational dialogue on good teacher quality, which is perceived as being key to high student outcomes, has resulted in a flurry of activity worldwide to reexamine and reevaluate teacher preparation processes. Globalization has led to concerted efforts in several "Third world" countries to improve local education and teacher preparation approaches. Much of the discourse of international educational development is shaped by western research and debates and this often compels local efforts to be more aligned with global (meaning western) trends in teacher education. Therefore, systems of schooling and teacher training are practices shaped by both western and local discourses.

Since the early 1990s, the work of several governments, private sectors, and NGOs in the field of early education has been impacted by the widespread ratification of the Convention on the Rights of the Child and Education for All. The need for a professional, nationally organized field of early childhood education is currently a high priority on the policy agendas of governments and international organizations. Equally important is the need for early childhood teachers to be professionally prepared; governments in India, Sri Lanka, and the Maldives are working on creating university-related degree programs to this end. This is a shift from earlier thinking that teachers of young children do not require a university degree in education.

International organizations that fund education in the developing world such as the World Bank, the IMF, and the UN approach the education and development of the young child as part of a larger policy discourse on building human capital. Investing in children is integral to their broader social and economic investment projects. The approach of world organizations that sponsor early childhood care and education in South Asia has been closely defined by a child development discourse rooted in American research on neuroscience, behavioral science, and developmentally appropriate practice (Mahon, 2010). The dominant discourse stresses a future-oriented rationality that views the child as human capital in the making (Dahlberg & Moss, 2008). For example, the World Bank (2011) referenced Nobel Laureate economist James Heckman, whose work has demonstrated the economic returns of investing in early childhood education (ECE). Reports such as those published by Legal Momentum's Family Initiative and the MIT Workplace Center (Calman & Tarr-Whelan, 2005) and by the Institute for a Competitive Workforce (2010) emphasized that the first five years are the most critical in the child's brain development; achievement gaps develop well before children begin kindergarten and high quality preschool programs significantly impact all children, but especially those from low-income families. The reports recommended that good early learning programs for younger children reduce costs later in life while enhancing economic growth; thus high-quality early childhood education can help break the cycle of poverty. These ideas have been shaping ECE policy decisions in the developed world as well; investing in quality ECE is currently a priority in the Obama Administration.

In financially supporting NGOs, community-based schools, vouchers, and public-private partnerships to benefit the very poor, the World Bank maintains a neoliberal discourse on social policy (Mahon, 2010). Under this influence, education and teacher education in general are becoming positioned as regulated markets governed by neoliberal policies where test scores are a measure of student performance and good teaching. Educators are measured by their students' performance on academic tests rather than by their professional knowledge of how children learn and develop (Brown, 2009). This follows trends in the United States where teacher education programs are being increasingly shaped by standards-based accountability reforms in which teacher candidates are taught how to deliver curricula specific to a local district and how to comply with specific assessment systems (Mayer et al., 2008). In increasingly globalizing world systems of schooling, economic considerations have led to a push to impose neoliberalism and conservative reforms in the form of both global and local standards (Apple, 2001; Green, 2005; Ross & Gibson, 2007). In this chapter, I address some of the resulting tensions and challenges in practice that emerge from neoliberal and culturally diverse sources that are both global and local.

Overview of PrePrimary Teacher Education Policies and Practices in the Region

This chapter draws on the findings of a qualitative inquiry of issues in preprimary teacher education in India, Sri Lanka, and the Maldives. Methodology included a bibliographic investigation, a document investigation and review of institutional and policy, and an empirical investigation (interviews and classroom observations). Data were collected from policymaking organizations, research institutions, colleges/departments of education, teacher-training centers, NGOs, and preprimary schools.

Although the size, demographics, political orientations, and dominant spiritual influences in India, Sri Lanka and the Maldives are vastly different, the existing structural and organizational nature of teacher education systems is similar. In all three countries there were clear goals and efforts in place for the preparation and development of preprimary teachers, which has not so far existed in any organized form. Policy trends are commonly characterized by increase in privatization, competition and choice; and viewing citizens as consumers of fee-paying services in privatized sectors, reflecting neoliberal ideology. These trends were evident in the field of teacher education as well, such as increased privatization of schools, stricter entry requirements for teachers, more stringent measures for teacher assessment, and decreased teacher autonomy. In the sections below, I discuss each country separately.

India

This predominantly Hindu country with a population of almost 1.2 billion has been undergoing huge shifts in its economic-political agenda, directly impacting its educational reforms from preprimary to higher education. After the restructuring of the National Curriculum Framework in 2005, which aimed to move the educational system in India from being traditionally teacher directed to being a progressive learner-oriented one, the NCERT (National Council of Educational Research and Training, 2007) and the NCTE (National Council for Teacher Education, 2009) proposed massive parallel changes in the domain of teacher education as well.

Public (government) education starts with Class 1 (age five years), although recently some government schools have started preprimary classrooms for 4-year-olds. A range of preprimary education settings in India include private nursery schools; private day cares; mobile crèches; and the government-sponsored Integrated Child Development Services (ICDS) *Anganwadis,* although the last is focused more on health and nutrition (Gupta, 2007). Since preprimary education has not been a government mandate no government universities offer a degree in preprimary teaching. Centers for the State Council of Educational Research and Training (SCERTs) have so far provided only primary and secondary teacher training, and early childhood/preprimary teacher education in India has been limited to certificate and diploma awarding bodies. Preprimary teacher training programs fall within government, NGO, or private sectors (Datta, 2001). Some ECE Diploma/Certificate courses are offered by distance learning institutions like Indira Gandhi National Open University (IGNOU) and National Institute of Open Schooling (NIOS). India's eleventh Five Year Plan (2007–2012) urged the development of early childhood care and education, and ministries are still scrambling to put into place formal degree programs at the undergraduate and graduate levels to prepare teachers to work effectively with young children. Private training centers have mushroomed all over the country in response to this need, but many of these centers lack quality pedagogical standards and are being run like substandard shops and businesses.

The NCTE was established in 1995 as a licensing body to "achieve planned and coordinated development of teacher education throughout the country and for the regulation and proper maintenance of Norms and Standards" (NCTE, 2011). Four regional committees of the Council approved the recognition of teacher-training institutes throughout the country, permitting them to run teacher-training courses. In 2010, NCTE accepted sweeping changes in teacher-training curriculum for all grade levels. Although not necessarily within the area of preprimary education, some of these reforms included raising the minimum eligibility criteria; raising the minimum qualifications for faculty and lecturers; a national level entrance examination for candidates who wish to qualify for university teaching jobs; strict checks to curb the growth of private substandard teacher training centers around the country; and more stringent criteria for recognizing and licensing a private school by mandating that it hire teachers with a degree from an NCTE-recognized teacher education institution.

Sri Lanka
This predominantly Buddhist country of almost 20 million people is poised to bring back stability and security to a society marked by years of violence and tension between the Hindu Tamils and the Buddhist Sinhalese. Undoubtedly, with the end of the civil war, educational reform and teacher education are important goals in Sri Lanka. A brief overview of the history of education and schooling in Sri Lanka can be found in Jayaweera (2007).

For the period of 2005–2009 primary school enrollment was at about 99 percent and the national average of early childhood/preschool enrollment at about 90 percent (UNESCO, 2011; UNICEF, 2010). While the Ministry of Education oversees primary education, preschool education is overseen by the Children's Secretariat (CS) under the umbrella of the Ministry for Child Development and Women's Empowerment. Even though certified teachers now staff many preschools, this does not always imply high quality teaching practices, as the standards of many institutions awarding ECE certificates are questionable.

Sri Lanka's thirteenth Amendment of the Constitution positioned preschool education as a devolved subject placing it within the jurisdiction of the provinces (Ministry of Social Welfare, 2003). Though the provinces have authority over the registration and functions of preschools, careful coordination between committees at the national, provincial, district, divisional, and village authorities is provided by the National Co-ordination Committee on ECCD within CS. The latter, however, provides the funding. Some provinces offer preschool teacher-training programs managed by the provincial education ministry or department, or sometimes by an independent authority. Curriculum development falls within the jurisdiction of the National Committee. Currently, there are only guidelines, as there is not yet a comprehensive national curriculum.

The central government does not run preschools, but local government authorities may offer preschool programs, run by urban or village councils. Generally, preschools are in the private sector with a large number being Montessori schools, and many of the private preschools tend to be merely moneymaking enterprises. As in India, there is a grave need for quality preprimary teacher education programs and the gap is being filled by the mushrooming of private enterprises. The conundrum in both cases is that there is a dearth of experienced and qualified early childhood teacher educators to teach in these teacher education programs.

A recent policy change now requires teacher-training institutions in Sri Lanka to be registered with the CS in order to be approved by the provinces. At the time of this inquiry, about 22 teacher-training programs had been registered with the CS. Provinces to not recognize preschools that employ teachers who have been trained at nonregistered institutions. During this transition period, teachers will be given time to complete their credentials, but new teachers will not be recruited unless they are appropriately qualified. The definition of appropriately qualified raises another issue in the formal training of teachers. Currently, students can be admitted if they have completed their A-level. However, research participants noted that teaching requires certain dispositions in addition to a formal college degree, thus entry criteria to identify preferred dispositions in teacher candidates need to be used. This is a current concern in global teacher preparation debates as well.

The Maldives

This Islamic archipelago of 1,192 islands and about 400,000 people is also experiencing the growing pains of a new democracy. With the threats of global warming inducing rising sea levels, Maldivians are concerned about educating a generation of children who will be faced with these environmental issues. Other important developments in the Maldives are the new constitution written in 2008 and a president who came to power in 2008 after democratic elections were held for the first time in 30 years. This, and subsequent political changes, considerably influenced current educational policies. Another issue is distance education as some islands are very remote.

In Malè, the capital island-city of the Maldives, most preschools are nongovernmental institutions (Latheef & Gupta, 2007). As in India and Sri Lanka there has been no preprimary teacher training at the college level so far. The Faculty of Education at the Maldives College of Higher Education has offered teacher training programs for primary and secondary levels only. Preschool teachers in Malè are largely untrained at the moment, or if they are they have been trained in another country. However, schools do offer procedures to support the ongoing professional development and assessment of their teachers.

The country's first 4-year undergraduate degree program in early childhood education started in 2009–2010 by the Faculty of Education. This was catalyzed by two events. First, the government elected in 2008, closely aligned with UNICEF's strong thrust on ECE, proclaimed an educational mandate to support early childhood education to ensure that all children were enrolled in preschool by the end of 2010 and that all preschool teachers would be certified professionals. These policies have created a high need for preprimary teacher training. The second impetus came from the Faculty of Education's decision in 2009 that courses on early childhood development and education should be a part of all teacher education based on the belief that optimal early development of children fosters more successful primary school experiences. Consequently, there have been sustained government efforts toward offering early childhood/preprimary teacher training. However, there is not yet a formal educational guiding policy or curriculum for the early years. Like all reforms, this will be a slow process and curriculum guidelines will need to be designed thoughtfully and in detail before an effective program can be offered at the college.

Clearly, preprimary teacher education is in flux in the three countries discussed above. New policies and practices are being implemented in all of them, many of which are directly linked to effects of neoliberal globalization.

Neoliberal Globalization: Current Shifts in Teacher Education Policy and Practice in the Region

The influence of neoliberal globalization in India, Sri Lanka, and the Maldives is apparent in three processes: visions of and implementation of preprimary teacher education reforms in South Asia; pedagogical shifts from traditional teacher directed toward progressive learner oriented; and the borrowing of concepts from the western discourse of early education. I highlight these neoliberal shifts in the following sections.

Privatization and Commercialization

Privatization and commercialization of education are strong offshoots of neoliberal globalization, which has promoted open markets, changing economic reforms, corporatization, and advances in information and communication technology (Anjali & Archana, 2003). In light of an acute teacher shortage, educational agencies in South Asia are actively inviting foreign collaborations with the United Kingdom and the United States, especially with regard to curriculum development and teacher training. To fill the gap, private and nongovernmental institutions for early education and teacher preparation are mushrooming in South Asia. These are usually shaped by the agendas of their funding agencies, such as the World Bank, whose human capital conceptualization of child development and the economic reframing of childcare (Prentice, 2009) feed into the increasingly neoliberal ethos of the emerging economies.

With the Right to Education Act of 2009, which promises free and compulsory elementary education in India, there has been a surge of student enrollment and the shortage of teachers in schools has become even more acute. The establishment of more private schools only adds to this crisis by increasing the number of schools but worsening the backlog of teachers. A corresponding increase in private teacher education institutes helps to meet the demand for trained teachers, but unfortunately, many of these institutes are substandard. Thus the privatization and commercialization of teacher training raises serious questions of access and quality.

One of the research participants, the head of the department of education at an established university in India, observed that education has shifted from being a philanthropic enterprise to a service that charges and people pay for, "and by way of market intervention anyone who is able to invest can provide education." This intervention is facilitated by the emphasis on Information and Communication Technology (ICT) and other vocational areas like fashion design and event management, which keep candidates away from the teaching profession.

Recent policy initiatives in India, such as the Foreign Educational Institutions Bill 2010 and the Universities for Innovation Bill 2010, have serious implications for teacher education, specifically with regard to stronger private-public partnerships, industry-academia collaboration, and the possible wide-ranging freedoms available to these universities, like differential salaries to faculty. This will only help private promoters and corporations seeking to take advantage of the provisions of this draft bill. More educational institutions will be established by commercial companies whose ulterior motives often conflict with the philosophical aims of education and who view education as a venture to ensure attractive profits.

An example from the Maldives serves as another illustration of the neoliberal shift in education. A formerly public primary school in Malè that received financial help from the Japanese government was recently bought by a private citizen from India. Newly admitted children now must pay a monthly fee of about US$250 whereas the 1,500 children already enrolled before it became private will have the difference in their monthly fee bridged by the Maldivian government, paid for by taxpayers' money.

Westernization

The impact of western education is clear in India, Sri Lanka, and the Maldives. Educational reforms in all three countries are couched in the core ideas of the discourse of early childhood education in the west: child-centered, developmentally appropriate practices, cooperative learning, constructivism, Multiple Intelligences, Vygotsky's sociocultural theory of learning, play-based pedagogy, performance assessment, choice-time, and circle-time.

In Sri Lanka, early education is influenced by educational trends and policies in the United Kingdom. Some schools have been established and named after the Gateway preschools in the United Kingdom, and many schools are using texts and curricula directly from the United Kingdom. In the Maldives, the Center for Open Learning (COL) received input and guidance from UNICEF, which has been concerned with the global development of early education and care since 1997. UNICEF has been involved in the development of an early childhood curriculum for the Maldives and plans to fund training for implementing it in schools. The Faculty of Education and COL are partnering in this initiative and working together to develop the four-year program. The courses in the first two years will be offered by COL in their distance education program as an online diploma.

The discourse of child-centered, activity-based, joyful pedagogy has been positioned as a national policy discourse to address issues of student retention and achievement in South Asia. However, western concepts cannot be readily and easily implemented in practice and are often given mere lip service. A study of child-centered teaching in rural India demonstrated that using the democratic language of child-centered discourse did not necessarily equate with handing over control to children; in addition, teachers were influenced by institutional systems, and the hierarchy and social inequalities remained prevalent in rural India (Sriprakash, 2010). My current study in all three countries showed that several preprimary classrooms exhibited a noticeable shift toward a progressive learner-centered pedagogy, but the shift was manifest mostly in the physical environment of classrooms displaying colorful children's work. The teaching strategies, adult-child interactions, roles and responsibility of teacher, large class sizes, and curriculum content still reflected a distinct teacher-centeredness.

The limited success of creating learner-centered classrooms in South Asia stems from the cultural contexts of preprimary classrooms. The core tenets of a progressive learner-centered pedagogy, which is built on the assumptions that children are free to engage with activities related to their interests; are able to make choices with regard to their engagement with classroom life; and will start school equipped with the decision-making skills essential to successfully navigating a choice-based classroom (Gupta, 2011), challenge the nature of the child-adult relationship in Asian society. South Asian childrearing is based on a group-oriented worldview. The imposition of individualism on a collectivist mind-set is certainly a cultural incursion.

Another example of a cultural divide emerges as a result of surging primary school enrolment in India due to the Right to Education Act. On the one hand, the surge in school enrolment has enabled India in moving toward its Constitutional goal of providing free and compulsory education for all children till 14 years of age. On the other hand, a large number of the children in classrooms represent formerly marginalized sections of Indian society. Teachers are not only inadequately prepared to teach these children but many teachers exhibit strong prejudices against the children's cultural backgrounds. This reflects cultural conflicts between socioeconomic classes at the local level in addition to conflicts between the local and western worldviews.

Internationalization

Internationalization can result in a form of neocolonialism. Viewing English as a global language can lead to linguistic imperialism; the compulsion to learn and teach English, and to adopt a western discourse of ECE can be seen as forms of colonization leading to handing over control of local forms of knowledge production and research. The perception of English as a global/international language and its spread was very apparent in India, Sri Lanka, and the Maldives. Private classes and tutoring agencies claiming to teach spoken English were advertised widely in large urban centers, small hill towns, rural villages, and along narrow roads. The most striking occurrence across all three countries was the visible mushrooming of schools being described as international, world-class, or global. English classes and the rapidly growing international schools are marketed as being necessary for leveling the playing field by preparing South Asian children in the language and skills prioritized in the global job market.

In India the language of instruction in private schools is English and in government schools it is the language of the region where the school is located; in the Maldives the language of instruction is English. In Sri Lanka, the educational reforms of the 1940s replaced English with either Tamil or Sinhala as the instructional language. This Sri Lankan reform facilitated educational access at many levels: it allowed rural children to attend schools, increased the student enrollment in schools, increased the number of students who appeared for public examinations, and increased the number of total universities in the country. However, the reform also led to a decrease in English-language speakers in the country. In the current socio-political-economic climate, this is perceived as a disadvantage in the global job market and there is a demand to reintroduce English as the language of instruction in schools and for teacher training.

One of the consequences of globalization is widespread parental desire among rich and poor to send their children abroad to study. To this end, many South Asian families want their children to begin their English education at the preprimary level, even if it means the preschool teaches only English nursery rhymes. A popular demand is thus placed on preschools to teach English; poor families view this as a way out of poverty for their children. But the implications of teaching all children in a foreign language need to be carefully considered.

Preprimary institutional quality is measured against international standards and currently the quality of many preschools does not meet the expected standards. In efforts to improve this, Children's Secretariat in Sri Lanka is identifying substandard centers and helping upgrade them by providing classroom materials, outdoor play equipment, books, and other resources. The national goal in Sri Lanka is to ultimately transform all preschools into child-friendly institutions prescribing minimum standards for basic administrative and physical facilities, furniture/equipment, learning and psychosocial environment, and teachers' qualifications and professional development (Ministry of Child Development and Women's Empowerment, 2006). The National Committee determined these standards after several discussions and a careful study of curricula of other countries. The policy was finalized and consolidated with UNICEF support. These parameters have been shaped largely by the ECE standards in the west and are now being articulated in the most recent ECE policy handbook in Sri Lanka.

Efforts toward creating "world-class" institutions are occurring in the Maldives as well. The first grade supervisor of a primary government school in Malè explained that the school had recently changed its mission statement and was now positioning itself as a "world class school," defined by an extended school day, a single shift system (most of the schools in the Maldives have at least two to three shifts to accommodate all children due to an acute paucity of land), provision of meals to children during school hours, and more activity-based teaching. This last parameter would seem a challenging goal as all the classrooms observed had 28–30 children.

Democratization

Recent political shifts in Sri Lanka and the Maldives have moved these societies toward democracy, as defined by the west. In Sri Lanka, after the end of a civil war that lasted 26 years, the first post – civil war presidential elections were held in January 2010, and in the Maldives the new President was democratically elected after thirty years in 2008.

Several research participants in the Maldives felt that changes in society came too quickly after democracy was announced. The democratic elections resulted in the formation of a coalition government under which conservatism has been gaining strength. For example, in 2010, it was ruled that women must wear thigh-length tunics over their trousers, which troubled the more moderate Maldivian women. The shift toward democracy has not been easy and people are struggling with many aspects of a new political system based on a culturally different worldview. Maldivians have been recently introduced to the democratic principle of the rights of the individual and seem to enjoy exercising this principle in their day-to-day lives. But they are also encountering the tension between individualism and collectivism and are beginning the process of resolving this tension and finding a balance between the two. One early childhood educator explained that school parents now had the right to contact their child's teachers anytime and school administrators were requiring teachers to provide their mobile numbers to families. This, she felt would make children less responsible for their own tasks as they would increasingly rely on their parents to contact teachers directly to inquire about school assignments.

Child-centered pedagogy is based on the principles of progressive education, which emerged within the context of a middle-class, democratic, capitalist west. It is based on the notion of individual rights, choice, assertiveness, confident self-expression, and advocacy. These raise questions when juxtaposed with, say, the Buddhist worldview of Sri Lankans, which promotes qualities such as loving kindness, compassion, sympathetic joy, and equanimity. Implementing a true democratic child-centered pedagogy in these countries can only happen if existing cultural worldviews are transformed, which in itself is a colonial consideration.

Neoliberal Globalization in Preprimary Education Policy and Practice: Critical Concerns in the Region

There are critical concerns relating to neoliberal shifts/ influences in preprimary teacher education with regard to the implications of approaching early childhood education from a human capital perspective; and what is lost when economic profit determines how we teach young children and what we teach them. The skill set required to succeed in capitalist knowledge economies is different from that required to flourish in a well-being-based community. These are grave questions that have to be grappled with.

Neoliberalism frames education within the discourse of consumerism; consequently, the learning experiences of young children are increasingly quantified and evaluated in terms of economic profit. Quality of early education centers is measured in terms of the academic performance of its students. This is used as a selling point for its consumers. An emphasis on academic achievement often results in teaching to the test, which dominates children's learning experiences in the classroom, sometimes to the detriment of their social-emotional well-being.

The measure of good teaching is another issue. The head of the early childhood and primary education program at a Sri Lankan university perceived teaching to be

> a born talent...all cannot be teachers. They must love their profession. They must love the children...So maybe teacher training programs are not so effective...They are getting the certificate but I think we have failed somewhere.

This line of thought questions the increasing emphasis on professionalization requirements such as certifications in the making of a teacher, recognizing that preprimary teaching requires a stronger emphasis on children's socio-emotional skills rather than academic skills. A neoliberal approach views schools as businesses and favors an assessment system, which evaluates teachers based on the academic success of their students. This form of evaluation cannot be used for teachers whose success should be marked by the happiness and well being of the very youngest.

Teacher training should also address the fact that globalization leads to local events being closely shaped by global happenings. The local cultural context and worldviews in South Asia will not necessarily support the core ideas of child-centered teaching. Here is another example of the inevitable tension between conflicting worldviews that is embedded within this global-local transaction. In the collectivist communities of much of Asia, parents and children live together for an extended period resulting in a longer adult-child continuity and this interdependent worldview shapes local ideas on child development (Gupta, 2006; Viruru, 2001). What parents in collectivist well-being based cultures want their children to develop in terms of skills and attitudes may be different from the western skills of independence and self-reliance. One of the research participants, a Sri Lankan early childhood specialist, described a study she had conducted across urban, rural, and plantation communities in the country to survey how parents perceived their child. Parents commonly expected their child

> to be obedient and to be educated...and when the child grows up, to look after them...It has something to do with our own tradition...even the present generation depends so much on parents.... With all the ladies

employed they leave their children with parents...even with all the day care centers and everything, we prefer to keep our children with our parents [grandparents].

Interdependence between generations and the vital role that grandparents play in raising grandchildren and helping their own children is commonplace in Asia (Gupta, 2006).

Although developmental expectations are quite different in diverse cultural contexts with respect to developmental milestones, education and teacher education in Asia continue to be held to western standards as evident in an assessment of early education in Sri Lanka: "Pre-school education in Sri Lanka has developed a style of its own that is uniquely out of step with the more widely accepted Early Childhood Education theories and practice valued in most developed countries" (King, 2010). Clearly, published research is an important source of knowledge and creates a particular discourse. The knowledge that shapes early childhood teacher education policy decisions in South Asia mostly draws on research conducted on children, issues, and concepts that are situated in the west. Educational reforms that infuse an educational system with dominant ideologies and neoliberal knowledge and values work toward colonizing that educational system (Loomba, 2005). A globalized teacher education system as a function of power and privilege is also a form of colonialism dictated by neoliberal forces (Adams et al., 2008; Canella, 2004; Gupta, 2006; Loomba, 2005; Viruru, 2001).

The roles that world organizations have played in influencing the imposition of neoliberal policies on developing countries cannot be denied and the continuing dominance of neoliberal policies indicates that those who benefit from these policies have gained control over public debates and policymaking (Hursh & Henderson, 2011). The soft loans offered by organizations, such as the World Bank and its networks, come "wrapped in policy advice that admonishes dependent countries of the South to follow "best practices" of the advanced capitalist countries" (Mahon, 2010, p. 188). The resulting increase in privatization of educational institutions increases economic inequality, thus widening the gap between those on the socioeconomic continuum. The central mission of neoliberal states to create a good business climate (Harvey, 2006) turns the focus of educational reforms toward efficiency and accountability and this has come at a cost to improving learning (Ravitch, 2010). The individualism of capitalist countries is evident in curricular reforms and this is what gets imposed onto the collectivism of many developing countries, despite the research that documents the varied bodies of knowledge, skills, and attitudes that children are expected to learn in different sociocultural contexts.

Concluding Reflections

Two things are apparent: first, the current state of teacher education in South Asia is outdated and needs to be reconceptualized and reenergized by drawing on local as well as global research on children's learning and development, and second, the powerful forces of neoliberal globalization seem all-pervasive. Thus, there is a need to build a body of scholarship that will allow for efforts to be made that will "go beyond what common discourse describes as "appropriate" early childhood education and look for other possibilities and ways of knowing" (Viruru & Cannella, 2001, p. 145).

Findings from my earlier research (Gupta, 2006) indicated gaps in teacher education in India that were largely due to the fact that it has been is a colonial construct based on Euro-American design and discourse with primarily imported theories of education; and it has been much too didactic and technical, failing to offer teachers experiences in sociocultural learning. Teacher education in South Asia has not evolved through the same stages as it has in the west, where it moved from the technical training model to models based on stage theory, constructivism, reflective teaching, multicultural and social reconstructionism, and teacher socialization (Gupta, 2006). Recognizing the inevitable western and Indian cultural transactions continuing in Indian society and schools, my recommendation is to work toward a postcolonial model of teacher education that draws from both local and global educational philosophies and psychologies.

> Not only is it important for teachers in India to know about current educational research and discourse in the west, but it is also essential to equip them with an educational discourse that will validate the underlying strengths of their own culture... An enlarged frame of relevance in teacher education that takes into account existing connections between historical, social, and cultural perspectives will lead to a deeper understanding between knowledge and power. This model of teacher education in India will not only enable teachers to better understand and name their own and their students' world views and help them recognize their own cultural values and biases but also ease the tensions that the teachers face in their struggles to balance Indian and western worldviews in their classrooms.
>
> (Gupta, 2006, pp. 221–22)

To address the challenges of globalization and neoliberalism, it seems critical to move forward with an approach to teacher education that would prepare teacher candidates in a theory and practice that is informed by diverse pedagogical ideas; engage teacher candidates with the ideas of social justice; create an awareness in teacher candidates of the implications of neoliberalism;

emphasize diversity training in teacher preparation; and prepare teacher candidates to recognize the space and moment when a dominant discourse of education begins to encroach upon a marginalized voice. A third form of formal educational discourse supported by a postcolonial perspective will emerge from this hybrid space in teacher education. It is an alternative to current teacher education theories and actively acknowledges the many imbrications of South Asian and western knowledge flows. This, then, has the potential to provide the basis for teaching that is empowering rather than colonized.

References

Adams, J., Luitel, B. C., Afonso, E., & Taylor, P. C. (2008). A cogenerative inquiry using postcolonial theory to envisage culturally inclusive science education. *Cultural Studies of Science Education, 3*(4), 999–1019.

Anjali, K., & Archana, T. (2003). The metamorphoses of education in the era of globalization. International Conference on Globalization and Challenges for Education: Focus and Equity. National Institute of Educational Planning and Administration (NIEPA). February 19–23, 2003. New Delhi, India.

Calman, L. J. & Tarr-Whelan, L. (2005, April). An early childhood investment for all: A wise investment. Recommendations arising from a conference "The Economic Impacts of Child Care and Early Education: Financing Solutions For The Future". Sponsored by Legal Momentum's Family Initiative and the MIT Workplace Center. Executive summary retrieved from, http://web.mit.edu/workplacecenter/docs/Executive%20Summary.pdf

Apple, M. (2001). *Educating the "right" way: Markets, standards, God, and inequality.* New York, NY: Routledge Falmer Press.

Bhabha, H. (1994). *The location of culture.* London, UK: Routledge.

Bhabha, H. (2009, Winter). An interview with Homi Bhabha: Cultural translation and interpretation: A dialogue on migration, identity, and ethical responsibility: An argument against fixed identities. *Sangsaeng, 26,* 32–35. Asia-Pacific Center of Education for International Understanding: UNESCO.

Brown, C. P. (2009). Confronting the contradictions: A case study of early childhood teacher development in neoliberal times. *Contemporary Issues in Early Childhood, 10*(3), 240–258.

Canella, G. S. (2004). *Childhood and postcolonization: Power, education, and contemporary practice.* New York, NY: Routledge.

Carney, S. (2009). Negotiating policy in an age of globalization: Exploring educational "policyscapes" in Denmark, Nepal and China. *Comparative Education Review, 53*(1), 63–88.

Crossley, M., & Tikly, L. (2004). Postcolonial perspectives and comparative and international research in education: A critical introduction. *Comparative Education, 40*(2), 147–156.

Dahlberg, G. & Moss, P. (2008). Beyond quality in early childhood education and care: Languages of evaluation. *New Zealand Journal of Teacher's Work, 5*(1), 3–12.

Datta, V. (2001). *A study of urban early childhood programs*. Report sponsored and published by UNICEF.
de Alva, J. J. K. (1995). The postcolonization of the Latin American experience: A reconsideration of "colonialism", "postcolonialism" and "mestijaze". In G. Prakash (Ed.), *After colonialism, imperial histories, and postcolonial displacements* (pp. 241–275). Princeton, NJ: Princeton University Press.
Gandhi, L. (1998). *Postcolonial theory: A critical introduction*. New York, NY: Columbia University Press.
Giddens, A. (1990). *The consequences of modernity*. Stanford, CA: Stanford University Press.
Green, C. (2005). *The privatization of state education: Public partners, private dealings*. Abingdon, Oxon: Routledge Falmer Press.
Gupta, A. (2006). *Early childhood education, postcolonial theory, and teaching practices in India: Balancing Vygotsky and the Veda*. New York, NY: Palgrave.
Gupta, A. (2007). *Going to school in South Asia*. Westport, CT: Greenwood Press.
Gupta, A. (2011). Play and pedagogy framed within India's historical, socio-cultural and pedagogical context. In S. Rogers (Ed.), *Rethinking play and pedagogy in early childhood education: Concepts, contexts and cultures* (pp. 86–99). Oxford, UK: Routledge.
Harvey, D. (2006). *Spaces of global capitalism: Toward a theory of uneven geographical development*. New York, NY: Verso.
Hursh, D. W., & Henderson, J. A. (2011). Contesting global neoliberalism and creating alternative futures. *Discourse: Studies in the Cultural Politics of Education, 32*(2), 171–185.
Institute for a Competitive Workforce (2010). *Why business should support early childhood education*. Institute for a Competitive Workforce: U.S. Chamber of Commerce.
Jayaweera, S. (2007). Schooling in Sri Lanka. In A. Gupta (Ed.), *Going to school in South Asia* (pp. 167–194). Westport, CT: Greenwood Press.
Kamat, S. (2002). Deconstructing the rhetoric of decentralization: The state in education reform. *Current Issues in Comparative Education, 2*(2), 110–119.
Kapoor, D. (Ed.) (2011). *Critical perspectives on neoliberal globalization in Asia and Africa*. Rotterdam, The Netherlands: Sense Publishers.
King, D. (2010). Failure of preschool education in Sri Lanka. Retrieved from, http://www.srilankaguardian.org/2010/01/failure-of-pre-school-education-in-sri.html
Latheef, M., & Gupta, A. (2007). Schooling in Maldives. In A. Gupta (Ed.), *Going to school in South Asia* (pp. 112–125). Westport, CT: Greenwood Press.
Loomba, A. (2005). *Colonialism/postcolonialism*. New York, NY: Routledge.
Mahon, R. (2010). After neo-liberalism? The OECD, the World Bank and the child. *Global Social Policy, 10*(2), 172–192.
Mayer, D., Luke, C., & Luke, A. (2008). Teachers, national regulations and cosmopolitanism. In A. Phelan & J. Sumsion (Eds.), *Critical readings in teacher education: Provoking absences* (pp. 79–98). Rotterdam, The Netherlands: Sense Publishers.
Ministry of Child Development and Women's Empowerment (2006). *Starting right: Guidelines for child development centers*. Colombo, Sri Lanka: Ministry of

Child Development and Women's Empowerment. Retrieved from, http://www.childwomenmin.gov.lk/web/index.php?option= com_publication&Itemid= 50

Ministry of Social Welfare (2003). *National Policy on Early Childhood Care and Development Colombo, Sri Lanka.* Retrieved from http://www.childwomenmin.gov.lk/web/index.php?option= com_publication&Itemid= 5

National Council for Teacher Education (2009). *National curriculum framework for teacher education: Toward preparing a professional and humane teacher.* New Delhi, India: NCTE. Retrieved from, http://www.ncte-india.org/publicnotice/NCFTE_2010.pdf

National Council for Teacher Education (2011). *NCTE at a glance.* New Delhi, India, NCTE. Retrieved from, http://www.ncte-india.org/theintro.asp

National Council of Educational Research and Training (2007). *National Focus Group on Teacher Education for Curriculum Renewal. National Curriculum Framework 2005 Position paper.* New Delhi, India: NCERT.

Pratt, M. L. (1992). *Imperial eyes: Travel writing and transculturation.* New York and London: Routledge.

Prentice, S. (2009). High stakes: The "investable" child and the economic reframing of childcare. *Signs: Journal of Women in Culture and Society, 34*(3), 687–710.

Ravitch, D. (2010). *The death and life of the great American school system: How testing and choice are undermining education.* New York, NY: Basic Books.

Ross, E. W., & Gibson, R. (Eds.) (2007). *Neoliberalism and education reform.* New York, NY: Hampton Press.

Spring, J. (2009). *Globalization and education.* New York, NY: Routledge.

Sriprakash, A. (2010). Child-centered education and the promise of democratic learning: Pedagogic messages in rural Indian primary schools. *International Journal of Educational Development, 30*(3), 297–304.

Tikly, L. (1999). Postcolonialism and comparative education. *International Review of Education, 45*(5/6), 603–621.

Trivedi, H. (1993). *Colonial transactions: English literature and India.* Calcutta, India: Papyrus.

The World Bank (2011). Why invest in early childhood development. Retrieved from, http://web.worldbank.org/WBSITE/EXTERNAL/TOPICS/EXTCY/EXTECD/0,,contentMDK:20207747~menuPK:527098~pagePK:148956~piPK:216618~theSitePK:344939,00.html

UNICEF Statistics (2010). Sri Lanka statistics. Retrieved from, http://www.unicef.org/infobycountry/sri_lanka_statistics.html

UNESCO (2011). World data on education. Retrieved from, http://unesdoc.unesco.org/images/0021/002113/211312e.pdf

Viruru, R. (2001). *Early childhood education: Postcolonial perspectives from India.* New Delhi, India: Sage Publications.

Viruru, R., & G. S. Cannella (2001). Early childhood education and postcolonial possibilities. In R. Viruru (Ed.), *Early childhood education: postcolonial perspectives from India* (pp. 137–156). New Delhi, India: Sage Publications.

CHAPTER 8

Rights and Resistance: The Limits and Promise of Human Rights Education in India

Monisha Bajaj and Bikku Kuruvila

> The strength of the insurrection in India is its diversity, not uniformity.
> (Arundhati Roy, 2011)

Introduction

The decline of the institutional left domestically (Bag, 2011; Vanaik, 2011), not to mention the political and ideological hegemony of neoliberal discourse on a global scale (Harvey, 2005), has structured the forms of political engagement in India no less intensely than in the developed North or other locations in the global South. Writing after the fall of the Berlin Wall, scholars such as Perry Anderson noted that the fate of classic forms of resistance to hegemonic economic and political formations could range from redemption to transvaluation, mutation, or oblivion (Anderson, 1992). In this political moment, deference to markets on all questions of policy and the dominance of rights talk in questions of justice color the very possibilities for critical engagement in historically specific yet not unfamiliar ways.

Seen in this light, human rights education (HRE) has grown in popularity since its first mention in the Universal Declaration of Human Rights in 1948 (Ramirez, Suarez, & Meyer, 2007). International declarations, conferences, and myriad nongovernmental efforts globally have worked toward educating individuals and communities about rights and guarantees. In India, HRE is a framework that has engaged public discourse, policy, and the work of nongovernmental organizations (NGOs) extensively, though in very different ways.

In India, the shift from Gandhian values and Nehruvian socialism toward more market-oriented understandings of individual rights—alongside India's adoption of neoliberal economic policies from the mid 1980s and early 1990s onward—has not gone uncontested. Indeed, there are many versions of HRE that correspond to a range of worldviews (Bajaj, 2011a); a variety of individual and institutional actors, from grassroots left activists and nonaffiliated educators to political parties and national-level policymakers, have all tried to mediate and direct the forms that local adoption of global human rights discourse might take.[1] These interplays and contestations are significant and mark the limits and possibilities of 'rights talk,' and education about rights in India.[2]

This chapter explores the rise of HRE in global discourse and Indian educational policy. We argue that HRE, though not without its limitations, offers surprisingly productive ways of engaging the minds and addressing the worst forms of oppression of some of the most marginalized communities and constituencies in the country. Political engagement is messy. No one form of political practice should be expected to be a panacea to all social ills on its own. Indeed, as Indian activist and writer Arundhati Roy suggests, the diversity of forms of resistance to the inequalities and injustices produced by contemporary forms of social organization offer hope and the possibility of more just futures in their very diversity. HRE, as some Indian activists and organizations have structured it, offers one important set of tools to these ends. The following sections explore the terrain of Indian education, the rise of HRE in policy and practice, as well as some of the limits and possibilities of this educational practice as it both enabled and constrained in distinct moments by neoliberal policies and discourse.

Indian Education: From Human Capital to Human Rights

Education has figured prominently in discussions of growth, progress, and national development since independence, influenced by Mahatma Gandhi's vision for schooling in a sovereign India.[3] The nation's first Prime Minister, Jawaharlal Nehru, was faced with a largely illiterate populace—only 16.7 percent of all Indians and 7.9 percent of women could read or write basic texts at the time. As such, Nehru placed great emphasis on education. Indeed, education is enshrined in the first Constitution (1950) as a directive principle, guiding the central and state governments in formulating policy (Premi, 2002). The prioritization of education resulted in massive school construction, village enrollment drives, free basic education for children, and the development of vocational education and literacy campaigns for adults. Inspired by the belief that an educated citizenry would drive economic growth, national cohesion, and self-reliance, the emphasis on primary, secondary, tertiary, and adult education was a fundamental part of Nehruvian socialism and resonated with global discourses of schooling as an integral factor in human capital development (Becker, 1964).

After Nehru's tenure (1947–1964), subsequent governments presided over growth in enrollment rates throughout the 1970s and 1980s. Schooling was a state responsibility in the years following independence, though in 1976, a constitutional amendment made education a concurrent responsibility of states and the central or national government. In 1986, the National Policy on Education (NPE) produced various initiatives that sought to utilize technology and equip all schools with the basic classroom materials needed for teaching (e.g., Operation Blackboard). The National Literacy Mission was also launched to combat adult illiteracy, particularly of women, nationwide. Some states in India had been providing midday meals to children at schools since the 1960s, though nationwide adoption of the program began only after a landmark 2001 Supreme Court decision provided a legal entitlement to the right to food in primary schools (Asia-Pacific Human Rights Network, 2002).

Globally, the right to education, first referenced in United Nations (UN) documents in 1948, began to be discussed as a basic human right in international meetings and conferences in the 1990s and 2000s. Drawing on international agreement around accomplishing universal primary enrollment, notably the consensus achieved in the Millennium Development Goals and Education for All conferences (1990 and 2000), India's domestic *Sarva Shiksha Abhiyan* (SSA) program, first announced in 2000, has sought to eradicate all obstacles to primary school access (Iyengar, 2010). Significant activities under this campaign have included expanded teacher training, the creation of district resource centers, the distribution of free materials and supplies to marginalized children, the construction of new classrooms, and in some states, the recruitment of para-professional teachers (UNESCO, 2004). In 2010, the Right to Education (RTE) Act came into effect. Access to education changed from a nonbinding directive principle to an enforceable fundamental right in Indian constitutional law. Specifically, the RTE provides all children aged 6–14 the right to a free and compulsory education in a school within one to three kilometers of their home. The facet of RTE that has been the most controversial among Indian elites has been the provision that requires that all private schools set aside 25 percent of their seats for low-income students free of cost; this piece of the Act suggests the potential for policy to interrupt social reproduction through schooling.

Despite these advances in educational enrollment and attainment in India, problems related to access, quality, and equal opportunity remain. India leads the world in the number of illiterate adults at 270 million and in the number of out-of-school children at 8 million (UN, 2010). India's high absentee rate in schools means that on any given day, an average of 24.8 percent of teachers are absent (Kingdon & Banerji, 2009; Kremer et al., 2005). Perhaps unsurprisingly, a recent study found that just over half of fifth standard (or grade) students across India could read a standard two-level story (ASER, 2010).

Nationwide, literacy rates differ significantly by gender across India's 1.21 billion residents. According to India's most recent census (GOI, 2011), the male literacy rate was 82.1 percent, while for women it was 65.5 percent. The high dropout rate of young women, especially as they reach secondary school, may contribute to this sizeable differential between male and female literacy rates. For example, insufficient or nonexistent latrines, particularly significant as girls hit puberty, is one cause of drop out. Notably, UNICEF reported that just 54 percent of schools across India had a separate girls' toilet that was usable for children in standards one through eight (UNICEF, 2010).

Additional school-based human rights issues include the still-common practices of corporal punishment, discrimination based on caste or gender, and corruption in schools (Nambissan, 1995; Nambissan & Sedwal, 2002; NCPCR, 2008). Corporal punishment was outlawed at the national level under the National Policy on Education and the Right to Education Act. Still, many states are not in significant compliance with these laws despite considerable efforts, such as those by the National Commission for Protection of Child Rights. Students interviewed in this study repeatedly mentioned forms of corruption, such as the extraction of money by teachers and headmasters, the siphoning off of government-allotted funds intended for students' midday meals and/or uniforms by headmasters and teachers, and sexual abuse in schools without report or sanction.

Additionally, absent significant financial resources for securing fee-based extra lessons ('coaching' or 'tuitions'), textbooks and exams often proved difficult and/or irrelevant for low-income, low-caste, and rural students in India. Scholar Prema Clarke (1997) has noted the "significant presence of the 'high culture' of the center and a concomitant absence of the physical and sociocultural world of the periphery within textbooks" (p. 134). Textbooks and exams are often normed to middle-class, urban students and fail to consider the realities of students living outside these conditions. Clarke argues that these situations limit the interest of marginalized children in schooling as well as the ability of their parents to appreciate the relevance and benefit of education.

In the 1990s, in line with the UN Decade for Human Rights Education (1995–2004) and subsequent international efforts, the government of India began to develop a plan of action to integrate HRE into schools nationwide, with the support of high-level officials such as the then-president, K. R. Narayan, and in more recent years, several national-level entities and authorities. While HRE is not an officially mandated or required subject of the Indian education system at any level, the subsections that follow detail national efforts in teacher training, NGO programs, and the variety of meanings ascribed to HRE (Bajaj, 2011c).

National-level Initiatives on Human Rights Education

Over the past three decades, nearly every national body charged with education and human rights in India has engaged with the concept of HRE at some point. Moreover, recent legislative victories around education and governance (such as the Right to Education Act and the Right to Information Bill)[4] as well as discussions of curricular reform have all been framed in human rights terms. National initiatives of government institutions related to human rights, we argue, are largely a product of a closer integration of India into the international community (and its normative, political, and discursive emphasis on individual rights). Social movements and NGOs often utilize human rights discourse as a strategy to frame diverse issues in ways that resonate globally. The distinct uses of human rights terms and concepts, including HRE, reflect what noted Indian legal scholar Upendra Baxi (2006) terms the different "languages and logics of human rights" (p. 119). The definitions of human rights in India range from market-based understandings of individual, and sometimes consumer, rights to broader notions of solidarity with social movements working toward greater equity and justice. It thus becomes important while noting the rise in rights talk, to parse out what underlying understandings and motives exist.

At the policy level, the National Council for Teacher Education (NCTE) has been discussing human rights, in some way, since the late 1980s. NCTE was established in 1973 as an advisory body for the national/central and state governments on teacher education, but it expanded to become a statutory body that regulated teacher education institutions nationwide in 1995 (NCTE, 2010). While not a curricular development body per se, the NCTE oversees and sets broad frameworks for the pre- and in-service training of India's six million teachers and more than 2,500 teacher-training institutions and university departments of education (NCTE, 2010; Panda, 2001).

NCTE issues a National Curriculum Framework for Teacher Education approximately every decade (Table 8.1) to emphasize the values, skills,

Table 8.1 Excerpts from National Curriculum Frameworks for Teacher Education (1978, 1988, 1998, & 2009; emphasis added)

1978: "[The purposes of teacher education are] (i) to develop *Gandhian values* of education such as *non-violence, truthfulness, self-discipline, self-reliance, dignity of labor* . . . [and] (ii) to develop an understanding of the objectives of school education in the Indian context and awareness of the role of the school in achieving the goals of *building up a democratic, secular and socialist society*."	1988: "[The objectives of teacher education are] (i) to develop in students qualities of *democratic citizenship, tolerance, concern for others, cooperation, responsibility, commitment to social justice*; (ii) To promote *environmental consciousness, scientific temper*; and (iii) To understand social, cultural and moral values oriented towards the *unity and integration of our people – democracy, secularism, . . . civic responsibility*."	1988: "[The objectives of teacher education are] (i) to promote capabilities for inculcating national values enshrined in the Constitution of India; (ii) To sensitize teachers towards the promotion of social cohesion, international understanding and protection of human rights and child rights; (iii) To sensitize teachers and teacher educators about emerging issues such as environment, ecology, population, gender equality, etc."	2009: "[In terms of teacher education], we need to reconceptualise citizenship training in terms of *human rights* and approaches of *critical pedagogy*; emphasize *environment and its protection, living in harmony with oneself and with natural and social environment*; promote *peace, democratic way of life, constitutional values of equality, justice, liberty, fraternity, secularism, caring values* . . . and *zeal for social reconstruction*."

methods, and approaches teachers should be equipped with through their education. In recent decades, human rights, equality, and social action have been highlighted as key priority areas.

In the 1970s, a time characterized by protectionism and extensive central government regulation of private industry, secular and Gandhian values were emphasized in educational policy. While many values, such as civic responsibility and national unity persisted across the decades, the way such issues are framed have changed to include more rights-friendly language. In the 1990s and 2000s, policy documents included environmental awareness, gender equality, and human rights as key objectives of national education. This shift toward greater emphasis on human rights emerged around the time of India's integration into the global economy starting with trade liberalization as early as the mid 1980s and in full force after 1991. Globally, the adoption of human rights language in policy and textbooks increased after the end of the Cold War when civil and political rights were prioritized in narrating the demise of communist rule in the Soviet Union and Eastern Europe (Ramirez, Suarez, & Meyer, 2007; Meyer, Bromley-Martin, & Ramirez,

2010). Still, despite the integration of human rights concepts and terms into policy documents and textbooks in India, significant variation exists in terms of what is taught under the banner of HRE. The discursive emphasis in policy documents on rights talk provides the space in which more radical interpretations—those that critique neoliberalism and seek to improve the lives of those most adversely impacted by widening socioeconomic disparities—can emerge.

The Possibilities of Human Rights Education in India

Data for this chapter come from 13 months of fieldwork in India from 2008 to 2010, utilizing primarily qualitative methods (observation, document review, interviews, and focus groups) with over 700 respondents (students, teachers, headmasters, activists, and policymakers). Representative themes were culled from the data after the fieldwork period, informed by grounded theory and an inductive approach to data analysis. The larger study involved a review of the HRE initiatives of a number of NGOs operating in 18 states, notably the Madurai-based Institute of Human Rights Education. The following is a partial and summary distillation of some of the trends observed there.

The Institute of Human Rights Education is part of the larger Indian NGO, People's Watch, an organization working against caste discrimination, police abuse, and violations of a range of civil, political, and economic rights. Their educational program, which operates in nearly 4,000 educational institutions, has textbooks in state languages and trains teachers to offer HRE twice a week in government-run schools (at the sixth, seventh, and eighth standard levels). An analysis of textbook content shows that the most common topic is economic disparities, the right to development, women's rights, and the rights of marginalized social groups (e.g., Dalits and Adivasis) (Bajaj 2011c).

Student reaction to this curriculum (across schools and states) came primarily in four areas as indicated by analysis of the data; action and intervention in an ongoing abuse was the most common (though not always the most effective) response by students. Students, typically from the most marginalized communities in the country, repeatedly related experiences in interviews and focus groups indicating the impact of instruction in human rights on their lives. Teachers and parents also corroborated these accounts. The specific impacts that HRE offered students, by their own telling, were (1) intervening in situations of abuse; (2) reporting or threatening to report abuse; (3) spreading awareness of human rights; and (4) attitudinal and behavioral shifts at home or in school that were more aligned with human rights principles and learnings. Although these categories were determined through inductive methods, they broadly correspond with scholars' articulations of what HRE should consist of, namely, a combination of information, values/behavioral changes, and active responses.

The first category of impact involved students intervening in situations of abuse to assist or advocate for victims, whether household or community members. Examples included trying to convince a peer involved in full-time remunerated work to return to school and visiting a family in the neighborhood to convince them not to kill a female baby (female infanticide was a common practice in many of the communities in which this study was carried out). For example, a group of students reported the following initiative they took after learning about human rights through the textbooks provided by the Institute of Human Rights Education operating in their school in Tamil Nadu:

> After reading human rights education in 6th, I overheard in my area that a neighbor was planning to kill their newborn girl baby. I formed a group of classmates and we went to their home. We explained to the lady [that this is wrong], but the father didn't accept. He scolded us and slapped us. We told [him] that the child also has a right to life, you should not kill the child. We said, 'If you are going to kill the child, we will complain to the police, we won't move from this area. We will stand here and watch what you are doing with this child.' Often we used to go to that home and watch that child. But now that child is older and is even studying in school.
>
> (Focus group, May 22, 2009)

Indeed, collective action was reported to be a more effective approach than individual actions given students' limited status (whether because of age, caste, income-level, or gender). Several students also mentioned trying to stop the practice of early marriage of their classmates, in which adolescent girls' marriages were arranged soon after they hit puberty. Students, again from the some of the most marginalized communities, asserted that this impeded their right to education.

The second category of impact consisted of students who identified, reported, or, equally effectively, threatened to report abuses to an authority, such as a headmaster, village level leader, or the police. Child labor, marriage under the age of 18, and female infanticide are all illegal practices. Often students sought an intermediary with (or at least with the specter of) greater authority to induce changed behavior on the part of those they identified as violating rights; perhaps a more strategic move given the ages (11–15) and (low) caste of the students in the study receiving HRE.

The third category of impact was more preventative. This included educating others or spreading awareness in some way about human rights based on what was learned at school. Students reported sharing their HRE textbooks or learning with parents, siblings, neighbors, and/or friends. Students also reported seeking out venues that their parents belonged to, to teach about human rights; many were community self-help groups (often organized around micro-finance). For example, several students discussed sharing information or taking their human rights textbooks to community settings to disseminate their new learnings. Students who were slightly more affluent or socially privileged engaged in a greater proportion of awareness raising, though some marginalized youth did so as well if abuses were not immediately visible in their households or communities.

The fourth category of impact related to personal changes or shifts in behaviors or attitudes at home or in school that resulted in greater respect for human rights. Students discussed renegotiating household mores related to gender, caste and/or religion. A boy in the seventh standard, for example, noted that he cleaned his own plate after eating rather than having his sister wash all the dishes, as was previously done. Students interacted with classmates of different backgrounds more readily than before HRE. This was a notable phenomenon given caste strictures against 'impurity' and contact with members of lower castes, even if it meant discontent on the part of parents, grandparents, or neighbors. Many villages in rural India are still largely segregated residentially by caste, subcaste, and religion.

The high number of both boys and girls claiming to act in the face of injustices suggests that students, through HRE, developed a sense of agency to intervene and confront violations (Bajaj & Pathmarajah, 2011). All four types of impact were noted at household, school, and community levels. Additionally, marginalized youth inspired by HRE often had to strategize how to intervene collectively or with an adult since their limited social status could frustrate their attempts at intervention or lead to unanticipated retaliation (Bajaj, 2011c).

The Limits of Indian Human Rights Education

Political engagement, by its own terms, can also involve cooptation, dilution, or a rearticulation of the original goals and aims of a particular project. The very fact of dialogue with state actors or representatives of social formations with different values or ideological references offers the possibility of transvaluation or mutation of the targets of a given initiative. Here, the programs reviewed all had to secure cooperation and formal permissions to offer their courses and trainings in HRE from various officials of the Indian state; local state Tribal Welfare Ministries, District Collectors, or local state Education Ministers as well as individual headmasters and teachers. These interactions, by definition, mediated the quality and character of these interventions.

In particular, HRE faced a variety of limits. Prior central governments sought to spiritualize education, a fraught and problematic endeavor given recent and past histories of communal violence in regions across the country. Some teachers and headmasters appeared to simply misunderstand, or perhaps not look too closely at the content of given HRE programs and initiatives. In India's resource-rich 'Red Belt,' NGOs focused narrowly on health and hygiene in seeming obliviousness to a low-level state of war and massive militarization of life for Adivasi (tribal or rural indigenous) communities living outside contemporary Indian consumer capitalism.

For example, during the Hindu nationalist Bharatiya Janata Party's time in national office (1998–2004), values or duties education was emphasized and the previous National Curriculum Framework issued in 2000–2001 sought to "Indianize, nationalize, and spiritualize" education nationwide according to Hindu fundamentalist doctrines (as cited in Lall, 2005, p. 5).[5] While none of the textbooks or programs scrutinized in this study contained any references to Hindu religious tenets and generally aligned more with common understandings of human rights, the nature of the reception of these efforts by particular state actors, at classroom or broader policy levels, sometimes mediated the particular instruction offered.

Several participants, who were offering or receiving human rights instruction through NGO programs, conflated HRE with concepts found in public discourses about Hindu morality. While some concepts perhaps overlap, teachers and students sometimes misunderstood human rights as a character-building exercise that sought to instill respect for elders and good behavior. For example, a district-level official charged with overseeing HRE in schools under her jurisdiction, related the following about why she supported the program:

> Human rights education is necessary because some children don't have any moral instruction at home.... Students should be taught what is good for them and what is bad for them. All of these bad things, like anger and jealousy, have not been given by God but have been created by humans. We have to teach children and give them some practices like meditation; they have to do it at least 10 minutes per day... So gradually, if we teach them spirituality and also human rights, they will become good citizens.
> (Interview, February 2009 as cited in Bajaj 2011c)

In no human rights textbook reviewed was meditation considered a part of rights framework; this official, and some others interviewed, attributed whatever they believed to be important to their understanding of human rights without having examined the curricular materials provided by NGOs.

To use a different set of examples, development efforts in rural communities, particularly those serving Adivasi communities, have long focused on health, hygiene, and sanitation. Getting children to school is still a considerable challenge in many of these communities, and once there, teachers and NGOs often utilize their presence to impart lessons related to public health. This includes education on matters such as adopting hygienic practices and preventing infectious diseases. Health data provides the rationale why Adivasi communities are targeted for such messages: the mortality rate in Adivasi communities for children under five is much higher (96 per 1000) than the rest of India (74), while the incidence of long-term malnutrition among Adivasi children is notably greater when compared to other Indian children (55 versus 42 percent) (Das et al., 2010).

As such, several teachers and students conflated HRE with these other programs, like hygiene campaigns, also present in their schools. In residential schools serving Adivasi children in Tamil Nadu and Orissa, a multi-year HRE course had been implemented in all the schools (by the NGO, the Institute of Human Rights Education), which sought to boost the dismal rates of post-primary education among Adivasi youth (just 23 percent compared to nearly double that for the rest of India). One teacher in Tamil Nadu stated the following with regard to Adivasi students' realities:

> The children come from a very remote area and they have no idea about how to clean their room and sanitation. They also don't know how to interact with other children. After imparting this human rights education, they understand what discipline is and why it is necessary to maintain hygiene.
> (Teacher focus group, February 2009 as cited in Bajaj, 2011c)

Another teacher in Orissa similarly noted that one of the outcomes of the human rights camps (that some students were selected to attend during summer holidays and operated by the same Institute) was that "students gained confidence and also learned about cleanliness" (interview, July 2009 as cited in Bajaj, 2011c). While HRE textbooks developed by the Institute of Human Rights Education did not contain messages about hygiene specifically, there were topics on the right to clean water and development that may have aligned with other initiatives. Alternatively, teachers receiving a variety of programs to implement may have assumed that they were all connected despite different trainings, materials, and curricular content.

Yet a larger factor for students in Orissa and nearby states was the Maoist armed insurgency or Naxalite movement that claims significant support from Adivasi communities across the 'Red Belt,' comprised of parts of India's poorest states of Bihar, Jharkhand, Chhattisgarh, Andhra Pradesh, Orissa, and

West Bengal. Students and teachers reported that members of these groups sometimes slept in their schools at night, fleeing state forces. Human rights reports have noted how these groups "are targeting and blowing up state-run schools. At the same time, police and paramilitary forces are disrupting education for long periods by occupying schools as part of anti-Naxalite operations" (HRW, 2009, p. 1). Many Adivasi communities are sympathetic to the Naxals because they attempt to resist—albeit through violent means—the usurpation of collectively held forestlands by mining companies who seek to extract natural resources.

As a result, students witnessed conflicts between their own indigenous communities, armed insurgents (from within and outside of their community), and police and state-aided paramilitaries who have been responsible for abuses ranging from damaging property to rape and killing of suspected Naxalite sympathizers (HRW, 2008). Anand,[6] a seventh standard student in Orissa, highlighted the following in relation to questions about his human rights learning: "Killing is a violation of our right to life. That happened here. A boy from this school was killed by the police during the firing on villagers nearby here" (focus group, July 2009 as cited in Bajaj, 2011c). Anand was relating an incident that happened a few years prior when community members occupied land that the government was trying to buy for less than market value in order for a steel plant to be built. In this case, the police fired on protestors and a student walking home from school was killed in the crossfire. Students were trying to interpret how the state's obligation to protect their rights matched with the day-to-day realities they witnessed in a complex and brutal sociopolitical environment that included the charged dealings of state forces, armed insurgents, large corporations, and nonviolent community activists.

The politics of communalism and the Maoist insurgency in India's Red Belt are, obviously, large, complex issues that are beyond the scope of this chapter. Needless to say, no given strategy for social betterment will be value neutral or apolitical and any given initiative, however it may be presented rhetorically, will be mediated by the social formations of which it is a part.

Conclusions

This chapter has worked from within and argued for the position that the conditions of possibility for political engagement in India (as elsewhere) are colored by the hegemony of neoliberal ideology, particularly the dominance of rights talk in questions of justice. The rise in prominence of human rights discourse, alongside India's processes of economic liberalization, has been mediated by a variety of actors on a range of levels, from national- and local-level policy actors, international institutions and foreign funders, to grassroots activists and NGOs. Nonetheless, an initial survey of HRE programs in 18 states involving observation, document review, interviews, and focus groups with over 700 students, teachers, headmasters, activists, and policymakers suggests that grassroots initiatives to promote appreciation of basic human rights in Dalit, Adivasi, and other marginalized constituencies in the country have had significant success measured in various ways (Bajaj, 2011c). In particular, these initiatives have been successful in both stopping actual instances of, and changing attitudinal norms around practices such as female infanticide, caste discrimination, child labor, and child marriage that are notable in their own right.

These initiatives are not without their limits. Attempts to promote awareness of human rights on local levels are sometimes met with indifference or coopted into other agendas. Additionally, rights talk foregrounds a narrow vision of justice in (often resource rich) communities subjected to the militarization of everyday life, extreme deprivation and some of the worst forms of degradation in the world.

Indeed, political engagement is messy. The very process of working with state officials and institutions grounded in sometimes largely different norms may also mean dilution and cooptation of agendas. Yet, the diversity of forms of resistance to the inequalities and injustices produced by contemporary forms of social organization—be it in the name of human rights, social justice, or other discursive frames—offer hope and possibility for more just futures. HRE as conceptualized locally offers one important set of tools, however qualified, to these ends.

Notes

1. This chapter contains excerpts from the book, *Schooling for Social Change: The Rise and Impact of Human Rights Education in India* (Bajaj, 2011c). This study involved many non-governmental programs working on HRE, though most of the data were collected from one school-based HRE program operating in 18 states. This initiative was operated by the Madurai-based Institute of Human Rights Education, an educational wing of the larger human rights organization People's Watch that has been offering HRE since 1997. For more information on the specific rise and nature of this program, please see: Bajaj (2011a, 2011b, and 2011c).
2. Tyack and Cuban (1995) note the distinction between policy talk, policy action, and implementation of change in U.S. discussions of educational policy. Similarly, rights talk does not necessarily imply action or implementation of policies, but a discursive engagement with human rights terms and concepts.
3. Leading independence leader Mohandas "Mahatma" Gandhi's ideas on education also shaped the early and continuing directions of rural schooling (Gandhi, 1932

as cited in Rajput, 1998). Gandhi promoted an education system called Basic Education, which focused on vocational education and the use of local vernacular as the medium of instruction. He emphasized manual labor and hands-on training in addition to intellectual pursuits to provide holistic development as well as skills. According to him, education should be provided for free and special attention should be paid to character building. One of the main components of Basic Education was religious education (in students' own religions), which, according to Gandhi, was synonymous with the concepts of truth and non-violence. He promoted education as a social good, emphasizing social responsibility, rather than having students view and use their educational qualifications solely for personal gains. Gandhi also advocated for a program of New Education, which emphasized through practice the values of self-reliance, living within a community, and oneness with nature.

4. The RTI Act was passed in 2005 and gives individuals the right to "to secure access to information under the control of public authorities, in order to promote transparency and accountability in the working of every public authority". In practice, RTI has forced public agencies (including those administering education) to become more responsive and accountable to citizen demands due to penalties associated with failure to comply with RTI requests for information. Human rights activists and groups have been instrumental in seeking passage of RTI and in filing requests for information related to cases of mismanagement, corruption, and abuses (Mander & Joshi, n.d.).
5. For greater textbook analysis of HRE programs in India, please see Bajaj (2011c).
6. All names have been changed to ensure confidentiality.

References

Anderson, P. (1992). *A zone of engagement.* London: Verso.
ASER (2010). *Annual status of education report.* New Delhi: Pratham.
Asia-Pacific Human Rights Network (2002). Right to food: The Indian experience. *Human rights features.* Retrieved from http://www.hrdc.net/sahrdc/hrfeatures/HRF58.htm
Bajaj, M. (2011a). Human rights education: Ideology, location, and approaches. *Human Rights Quarterly, 33,* 481–508.
Bajaj, M. (2011b). Teaching to transform, transforming to teach: Exploring the role of teachers in human rights education in India. *Educational Research, 53*(2), 207–221.
Bajaj, M. (2011c). *Schooling for social change: The rise and impact of human rights education in India.* New York: Continuum Publishing.
Bajaj, M. & Pathmarajah, M. (2011). En'gender'ing agency: The differentiated impact of educational initiatives in Zambia and India. *Feminist Formations, 23*(3).
Bag, K. (2011). Red Bengal's rise and fall. *New Left Review, 70* (July-August), 69–98.
Baxi, U. (2006). Human rights and human rights education: Arriving at the truth. In *Human rights learning: A people's report* (pp. 117–136). New York: People's Movement for Human Rights Learning.

Becker, G. (1964). *Human capital.* Chicago: University of Chicago Press.
Clarke, P. (1997). School curriculum in the periphery: The case of South India. In H. D. Nielsen & W. K. Cummings (Eds.), *Quality education for all: Community oriented approaches* (pp. 123–138). New York and London: Garland Publishing.
Das, M., Hall, G., Kapoor, S., & Nikitin, D. (2010). India: The scheduled tribes. In G. Hall & H. Patrinos (Eds.), *Indigenous peoples, poverty and development.* Washington, D.C.: The World Bank.
Elsbach, K. D., & Sutton, R. I. (1992). Acquiring organizational legitimacy through illegitimate actions: A marriage of institutional and impression management theories. *Academy of Management Journal, 35,* 699–738.
GOI (Government of India). (2011). Census of India 2011. Retrieved from http://censusindia.gov.in/
Harvey, D. (2005). *A brief history of neoliberalism.* New York: Oxford University Press.
HRW. (2008). *"Being neutral is our biggest crime": Government, vigilante, and naxalite abuses in India's Chhattisgarh State.* New York: Human Rights Watch.
HRW. (2009). *Sabotaged schooling: Naxalite attacks and police occupation of Schools in India's Bihar and Jharkhand States.* New York: Human Rights Watch.
Iyengar, R. (2010). Different implementation pproaches to a Common Goal: Education for All in the Indian Context. *Society of International Education Journal, 6*(1), (pp. 1–27).
Kingdon, G., & Banerji, R. (2009). *Addressing school quality: Some policy pointers from rural north India.* Cambridge, UK: Research Consortium on Educational Outcomes & Poverty.
Kremer, M., Muralidharan, K., Chaudhury, N., Hammer, J. R., & Rogers, F. H. (2005). Teacher Absence in India: A Snapshot. *Journal of the European Economic Association, 3*(2–3), (pp. 658–667).
Lall, M. (2005). *The challenges for India's education system.* London: Chatham House, The Royal Institute of International Affairs.
Mander, H., & Joshi, A. (n.d.). The Movements for Right to Information in India: People's Power for the Control of Corruption. *RTI Articles.* Retrieved from http://www.humanrightsinitiative.org/index.php?option= com_content&view= article&catid= 91%3Ashiva&id= 669%3Arti-india-articles&Itemid= 75
Meyer, J. W., Bromley-Martin, P., & Ramirez, F. O. (2010). Human Rights In Social Science Textbooks: Cross-National Analyses, 1970–2008. *Sociology of Education, 83*(2), (pp. 111–134).
Meyer, J. W., & Rowan, B. (1978). The structure of educational organizations. In J. W. Meyer, B. Rowan & W. R. Scott (Eds.), *Organizations and environments* (pp. 217–225). San Francisco: Jossey Bass.
Nambissan, G. (1995, April). Human rights education and Dalit children. *PUCL Bulletin.*
Nambissan, G., & Sedwal, M. (2002). Education for all: The situation of Dalit children in India. In R. Govinda (Ed.), *India Education Report* (pp. 72–86). Oxford: Oxford University Press.

NCPCR (2008). *Protection of Children against Corporal punishment in Schools and Institutions*. New Delhi: National Commission for the Protection of Child Rights.

NCTE (2010). NCTE at a Glance. Retrieved from http://www.ncte-india.org/theintro.asp

Panda, P. (2001). Human rights education in Indian Schools: Curriculum development. In: *Human rights education in Asian Schools Volume IV* (pp. 85–96). Osaka: Asia-Pacific Human Rights Information Center.

Prasad, S. N. (1998). Development of peace education in India (since Independence). *Peace Education Mini Prints, No. 95,* 1–14.

Premi, M. (2002). India's literacy Panorama. *Seminar on progress of literacy in India*. Retrieved from http://www.educationforallinindia.com/page172.html

Rajput, J. (1998). Gandhi on education. *National council on teacher education*. Retrieved from http://www.ncte- in.org/pub/gandhi/gandhi_0.htm

Ramirez, F., Suarez, D., & Meyer, J. (2007). The worldwide rise of human rights education. In A. Benavot, C. Braslavsky, & N. Truong (Eds.), *School knowledge in comparative and historical perspective* (pp. 35–52). Netherlands: Springer.

Roy, A. (2011). *Walking with the Comrades*. New York: Penguin Books.

Strang, D., & Lee, C. K. (2006). The international diffusion of public-sector downsizing: Network emulation and theory driven learning. *International Organization, 60,* 883–909.

Tyack, D., & Cuban, L. (1995). *Tinkering toward Utopia: A century of public school reform* Cambridge: Harvard University Press.

UN (2010). *Human development index*. New York: United Nations.

UNESCO (2004). *Para teachers in India: A review*. Paris: UNESCO.

UNICEF (2010). India: Education. Retrieved from http://www.unicef.org/india/education.html

Vanaik, A. (2011). Subcontinental strategies. *New Left Review, 70* (July-August), 100–114.

PART II

Globalization, Culture, and Education: Rural Priorities and Perspectives and Other Educational Contexts

CHAPTER 9

The Barua Community, Globalization, and Colonial Education: The Quest for Sociocultural Identity in Bangladesh

Bijoy P. Barua

Introduction

This chapter explores how the Barua community has perceived and sustained its social, cultural, political, and ethnic identity[1] in the face of colonial education, westernization, and neoliberal globalization in rural Bangladesh. The community has been trapped in a process of assimilation in the country through the simulation of western-centric culture and materialism (Barua, 2004). However, despite this assimilation into the culture of the colonial past and the culture of the Bengali community, the Barua community has not been able to participate in or represent the politics of the nation-state. In fact, the community has been unable to integrate with the political maneuverings of *adivasi* (ethnic minority) politics in Bangladesh. Despite its acceptance of colonial education and the regeneration of Theravada[2] Buddhism, it has failed to uphold its own community rights within the political space of the country. As a result, its ethnic/cultural/political identity is in an ambiguous position: members of the Barua community frequently shift between identifying themselves as Buddhist and Bengali. This is because inadequate attention is given to understanding notions of ethnicity/indigeneity and cultural heritage in learning processes in the country.

The chapter is based on my life experiences, my field observations, and narratives from my research in Bangladesh, as well as a review of existing literature. Here, I discuss the historical, social formation of the

Barua community's cultural/ethnic identity, in light of globalization, through the lens of anticolonialism. An anticolonial approach recognizes the value and merit of cultural heritage, local knowledge, and the realistic/pragmatic experiences of people. It rejects the notions of cultural domination, imposition, and domestication. In addition, this approach argues that local people have the intellectual ability for transformative learning and liberation (Dei & Asgharzadeh, 2001; Freire, 1970, 1973, 1985). In other words, an anticolonial approach emphasizes people's knowledge, their indigeneity, and decolonization processes, which highlight the distinct culture of a community (Barua, 2011; Kapoor, 2010). However, rediscovery of a distinct culture, or indigeneity, does not inevitably demand a return to the precolonial era (Thuen, 2006). Rather, indigeneity reflects a search for self-identification, distinctiveness, and social justice in a society (Kapoor & Shiza, 2010) by supporting a culturally appropriate social dynamics for collective living in a society. Additionally, it encourages people to uphold dignity and creativity in order to establish their cultural identity through shared social values and solidarity in the land (Barua, 2010a).

On the other hand, neocolonial education and neoliberal globalization have been used as political tools to delink and displace indigenous, minority communities from their social roots through the practice of mimicry, or didactic learning, in the subcontinent (Barua, 2004, 2010b; Kapoor, 2011). In other words, learning processes have tended to dislocate cultural heritage, indigenous knowledge, customary law, and local economics through the infiltration of the market economy and the global commoditization of education and western knowledge (Bowers, 1997; Kapoor, 2011; Norberg-Hodge, 1991), leading to the detribalization of ancestral lands. Neoliberal globalization is linked to the power of capital and corporate culture that tends to control others (Barua, 2011; Kapoor, 2011); 'Others' are seen as backward, inferior, and substandard by the proponents of modernization and globalization (Bowers, 1997). Over the years, colonial education has also created an inequality between urban and rural communities. In addition, it has tended to exclude and marginalize indigenous ways of knowing. In other words, this form of education has opted to obliterate collective learning and identities and historical memories in order to impose a new economic order upon others (Smith, 1999). I will use the terms neocolonialism, globalization, neoliberalism, market economy, and modernization interchangeably in this chapter. Here, I discuss the Barua community's cultural heritage and the construction of its social identity in light of colonial education, the revival of Theravada Buddhism, and the community's representation and participation in national politics.

The Barua Community and Cultural Heritage

Cultural heritage is transmitted from generation to generation and marks the distinct identity of a community and is in harmony with the community's traditions, customs, and practices. It is important to recognize and reclaim cultural heritage for the sociopolitical emancipation and decolonization of a community (Smith, 1999). Cultural heritage is not simply "a collection of objects (substances), stories and ceremonies, but a complete knowledge system with its own concepts of epistemology, philosophy, and scientific and logical validity" (Daes, cited in Battiste & Henderson, 2000, p. 221). The cultural heritage of the Barua community has yet to be explored in light of the cultural imposition and domination of the neoliberal agenda. Within the Barua community in Bangladesh, new business groups have become dominant and tend to be located in monasteries. However, they demonstrate no understanding of the community's cultural heritage and history. In other words, these business groups are in a position to use and control the monasteries for their own power and profit. As a result, these centers of collective learning and democracy have been eroded due to the infusion of market-driven agendas and materialistic values of the new business groups.

Undeniably, the Barua community retains a very distinct social and cultural identity within the villages it inhabits. The community mostly lives in the greater Chittagong[3] district of the country. There are several thousand Baruas in the Chittagong Hill Tracts.[4] Their appearance is usually different from the mainstream population of Bangladesh. They believe that their ancestors were in power in the ancient kingdom of Samatata (Chaudhuri, 1982; Khan, 1977). Traditionally, the Baruas believe that their ancestors took shelter in the hills and forest areas of the greater Chittagong district to protect themselves from the oppression and persecution of several successive rulers of the subcontinent. It is also assumed that the Baruas settled in the region during the sixth and seventh centuries.

The term "Barua" originated from the word *Boyoya*. In the past, the title Barua was probably not used by community members. Since the people of Bengal were unable to pronounce Arkanese or Burmese words, it is assumed that the word *Boyoya* was replaced by the word Barua. It seems that the community members started using this title more in the last quarter of the eighteenth century to obscure their social/ethnic identity in order to avoid political persecution and social discrimination from King Bodoipaya of Burma, who destroyed the kingdom of Arakan in 1785. While obscuring their ethnic identity, they also tried to connect themselves to the roots of royal blood or the great Aryan race[5] (Barua, 2004; Chaudhuri, 1982; Khan, 1977). In the words of Arthur P. Phayre (1863):

> [Their name] is given to them by the people of Bengal, and also to a class of people now found mostly in the district of Chittagong, who call themselves Rajbansi. The latter claim to be of the same race as one dynasty of the kings of Arakan, and hence the name they have themselves assumed. They are Buddhists in religion; their language now is Bengali of the Chittagong dialect; and they have a distinctive physiognomy.... I was formerly of the opinion that these people were a mixed race, the descendents of Arakanese, who, when their kings held Chittagong during the seventeenth century, had married Bengali wives.... It is very probable that one of the foreign dynasties of Arakan came from Southern Bihar, though... the fact has been concealed by Arakanese chroniclers.
>
> (pp. 47–48)

Hunter (1876) further argued that the Baruas are typically believed to be of mixed origin, with the blood of diverse ethnic groups such as the Aryans, Arakanese, Burmese, and Portuguese. He contended that they might have originated as a result of matrimonial alliances between Arakanese men and women of the lower castes of Bengal. The Baruas also adopted many Hindu customs and rituals as well as the Bengali language (Hunter, 1876; Risely, 1891). Nonetheless, some scholars from the Barua community have refuted this notion and claimed that the Barua *Maghs* are of *Kashtriya* (warrior/Aryan) origin and try to connect their descent with the ruling race of Bihar, India. In this view, the term "Barua" is derived from the Vajji tribe of Vaisali and comes from *batuk,* a Sanskrit word that means superior. There is a conventional belief that the Baruas are the descendents of the *Bara-Arya,* which means great Aryan (Chaudhuri, 1982; Khan, 1977). It is also argued that the Baruas of present day Bangladesh came from Magadha (now Bihar in India) and were forced to leave their homeland due to either the oppression of Brahmanism or persecution from the Mughals. They came through Assam, crossing hilly terrains and forests, to take shelter in the kingdom of Arakan (Chaudhuri, 1982; Khan, 1977).

Furthermore, it is believed that the Baruas belong to old Arakanese stock. Based on this, present day Arakanese identify the Barua as *maramma-gr,* which means elder (Chaudhuri, 1982; Khan, 1977; Thera, 1936). Indeed, in the past, most of the family names (e.g., Fhul Thoanja, Mulaim, Roaja, Keja, Annakka Phungi, and Thanja) and personal names (e.g., Mam-pru, Toaila-pru, and Cailapru) of the Barua community were akin to those of the Arakanese. Even today, community members use many Arakanese words in their daily life, such as *phara* (the Buddha), *ataim-mang* (Bengali *pansalla,* or meeting), *phang* (invitation to the monk), *choyaim* (offering food), *khiong* (temple), *chadam, chabaik* (eating pot), *wa* (rainy retreat), and *waik* and *gheing* (ordination place) (B. M. Barua, 1923; Khan, 1977).

Traditionally, the Baruas followed the *Maghi* (measure of time) era, instead of the Bengali era *(San)* or the Christian era, similar to the people of Arakan. This tradition began around 639–640 A.D. The *Maghi* era, or *Maghavda,* is popularly known as *Maghi San* among the Barua of Chittagong district (Chaudhuri, 1982). Religious festivals and ceremonies of the Barua community are deeply centered on the *purnima* (full moon), which is connected to the life of the Buddha (R. B. Barua, 1963, 1965; Khan, 1977). Besides these religious festivals, the *Biu-paraw*[6] is the most popular cultural festival among the Baruas of Bangladesh. *Biu-paraw* is celebrated on the last two days of *Caitra,* the last month of the Bengali calendar year (R. B. Barua, 1978; Chaudhuri, 1982; Khan, 1977). However, this rich cultural diversity and tradition of the community has been undermined due to the expansion and imposition of colonial education in the subcontinent. In other words, colonial education ignored the Baruas' cultural knowledge and customs in the interest of economic growth and profit.

Colonial Education and Social Identity

Colonial education was psychosocial indoctrination into an alien culture and value system that intended to mold learners through a process of rote learning in order to change the social and ethical practices of the people in the subcontinent (Barua, 2007). The colonial educational policies were formulated through the means of constitutional legislation to promote colonial political ideology in the country (Barua, 2007; Khatun, 1992). Specifically, this colonial education was introduced in the greater Bengal through the establishment of the Committee of Public Instruction in 1823 (Bandapaday, 1989) in order to expand capitalism and the international market in the subcontinent (Barua, 2007). This process was further "intensified when, in 1885, Queen Victoria declared that hiring by the British government would be based on English language skill. It would not be based on caste position and criteria" (Barua, 2007, p. 63). This policy eventually became a device for the creation of a new local elite group in the country. The Barua community embraced the colonial form of education in the later part of the nineteenth century in order to establish its sociopolitical identity in British India. In fact, this education was adopted as a survival strategy by the community. The acceptance of western education allowed the community to liberate itself from the psychosocial domination and cultural discrimination of the dominant groups (Barua, 2004). To this end, in 1868 the Barua community established English

Model Schools in the villages of the greater Chittagong district of Bangladesh. Although the Barua community established these schools, they were open to students of any community, regardless of their cultural or religious identity. All of these English-medium institutions were established close to the monasteries under the guidance of the local monks (Chaudhuri, 1982; Khan, 1977). This expansion of English education within the Barua community was more of a political strategy to claim and establish Buddhist cultural identity within the colonial system of British India (Barua, 2007). While claiming this, the Barua community always rejected the notion of an *upajati* (subclass/outcaste) as a sociopolitical identity in order to avoid social discrimination within the caste-based society of the subcontinent (Barua, 2004). In most cases, the Barua community utilized the western form of education as a tool with which to negotiate with the colonial administration about their cultural rights in India. Perhaps the Barua community also felt that political domination and social discrimination of the colonial agents would be less harsh than that of the local dominant groups due to the more distant geographic setting (Barua, 2007). Over time, these conditions favored the Baruas, who sought higher education in order to find jobs in the civil administration of British India. As Chaudhuri (1982) described,

> [t]he touch of modern [colonial] education gave them [the Barua and Chakma] a broad outlook and an undaunted zeal to upgrade their standard of living as well as a means of livelihood, so they could prove themselves worthy of participating in the present rally for the survival of the fittest. One will not find among the Baruas and Chakmas only farmers and cultivators, but also scores of distinguished doctors, engineers, professors, school teachers, respectable service holders, advocates, judges, businessmen and the like. This has been possible within a period of less than a century. Being a minority community, this achievement is, no doubt, commendable. Even female members of the community are not backward nowadays.
>
> (pp. 59–60)

This statement indicates that the community neglected its cultural identity and heritage as it was lured toward colonial education. Although this created a new space for the community of the greater Bengal, it also shaped members' patterns of life and traditions by promoting cultural dependency. Rona, a member of the Barua community, expressed the following:

> Presently, our people are more inclined toward degrees and certificates through modern [colonial] education. However, these degree holders are quite ignorant

of human quality and cultural traditions. They do not pay any respect to the elders and traditions.

(Cited in Barua, 2009, p. 144)

The formalized model of colonial education reallocated the community from the rural life to the urban hub. Over the years, this has weakened the collective life of the community in the villages and displaced it from its ancestral lands. Although a united power of the community has not been able to protect and establish its cultural rights and ethnic identity in the country, there have been instances of nonviolent activism (through the mobilization of *vipassana* meditation and other cultural events) in the villages (Barua, 2007, 2009).

Revival of Theravada Buddhism and Buddhist Identity Construction: Challenges

The Barua community (along with the Chakma, Marma, and Rakhaine communities) was socially, culturally, and politically empowered and mobilized through the revival of Theravada Buddhism in 1864 in Bengal. At that time, Buddhist education was included in the school curriculum in order to eradicate non-Buddhist rituals, practices, and magical manipulations from the community. This religious movement allowed the Barua community to protect their sociopolitical rights against the sociocultural oppression within society. Simultaneously, such socioreligious movements were geared up in Burma and Sri Lanka in order to establish a Buddhist cultural identity regardless of race, culture, and geographical distance (R. B. Barua, 1978; Chaudhuri, 1982; Khan, 1977; Tambiah, 1992). In this social movement, the monks and the people were united by their shared Buddhist ideology rather than by any national or ethnic identity. This effort was not only limited to the Buddhist monasteries, but also spread into the larger communities. In this process, the Barua community was mobilized and educated through organizations, such as the *Shanga Shammalani* (Assembly or Association), the *Chattagaram Bauddha Samity* (Chittagong Buddhist Association in Chittagong), the *Bauddha Dharmankar Sabha* (Bengal Buddhist Association in Kolkata), and the *Bauddha Mission* (Buddhist Mission in Burma), which nurtured a cultural identity based on Buddhist ethics and values. These organizations realized that the true meaning of Theravada Buddhism would not be reflected within society if the monks were not educated and trained properly. In this endeavor, Buddhist villages used the monasteries as centers of learning, social transformation, and development without any discrimination toward sect or race within society (Barua, 2004, 2007). Subsequently, the organizers of this movement officially gave a representation in 1887 to the British government in order to establish a separate identity for themselves in Bengal, as well as in greater India. Since then, the Barua, Chakma, Marma, and Rakhaine communities were recognized as distinct cultural/religious groups within the political context of the subcontinent (Barua, 2007).

Despite this, the cultural identity based on Buddhist values is in a critical state due to the changing political and economic conditions in the country. It is a fact that the survival of the minority community is determined through the politics of exclusion and isolation. This notion of exclusion and isolation has also spread into the thinking of the rural people of Bangladesh. It is mostly confined to the realm of the Muslim and Hindu communities, which want to maintain their power and authority in the region. If a group is geographically scattered, it is more difficult to preserve or nurture its ethnic identity. For example, the Barua community lives on the plains of Bangladesh within the social space of the mainstream community. However, as the partition of the subcontinent created a space for both the Hindu and Muslim communities by the colonial authority, the identities of smaller ethnic groups were threatened. This divide-and-rule policy weakened the Buddhist identity movement, although it was more visible from the nineteenth century to the middle of the twentieth century in greater Bengal. In fact, this socioreligious movement was active until the later part of the 1960s in Bangladesh. Buddhist organizations were often used by the successive governments of Bangladesh to connect with Buddhist countries in Asia for political and economic gains. Despite this political maneuvering, the Buddhist identity movement did not mobilize as expected; rather, it helped a few English-educated middle-class leaders of Buddhist communities keep up political ties within the country and abroad (Barua, 2004). Moreover, the Buddhist identity movement was unable to retain its momentum in the country as the political movement of Bengali nationalism emerged against the repression of Pakistani ruler. This political movement was grounded in the notion of secularism in Bangladesh (Barua, 2004). The social solidarity among the greater Buddhist communities further declined due to the rise of the ethnic social movement in the hills of the southeastern part of the country. Additionally, contradictions among the Barua Buddhists based on ideological differences or conflicts among sects *(nikaya)* also became apparent, posing a challenge to collective endeavors. Furthermore, social movements based on indigenous culture and *adivasi* identity have now become an issue in Bangladeshi politics. For example, the Chakma, the Marma, and the Rakhaine communities have been engaged in establishing their distinct identities or *adivasi* culture in the country. On the other hand, the Barua community has been trapped into the politics of isolation and alienation as its representation for cultural identity was not mobilized and activated in the country or in global politics (Barua, 2004).

Representation and Participation of the Barua Community in National Politics

Both representation and participation of the Baruas in national politics in Bangladesh is almost negligible. As a result, the community has not been able to mobilize any political agenda, or any social movement to establish its social, cultural, and political rights. Over the years, the Barua community has always attempted to develop its identity on the basis of either religion or Bengaliness. For example, the members of the Barua community have often identified themselves with the Bengali identity as they speak Bengali, which has associated them with the basics tenets of Hindu law in Bangladesh (Barua, 2004). Although the colonial authority officially recognized the Baruas (along with the Chakma, Marma, and Rakhaine) as Buddhists, it never attempted to enact a Buddhist law for them. In fact, the colonial power forced the Barua community to live in the country without having any true ethnic identity. Moreover, the English educated Baruas of Bangladesh were also diffused and emulated by the Bengali Renaissance[7] since they had established a social network with the *bhadralok* (educated upper-middle classes) of the Bengali community. Perhaps this behavioral assimilation (Gordon, 1971) was embraced in order to avoid social discrimination within the rigid *varna* (caste) system of the subcontinent (Barua, 2004). Consequently, the community has lost its own cultural identity. In other words, the community has yet to determine its political/cultural/ethnic identity in Bangladesh. In recent years, the community was neither identified as an ethnic community nor included as an *adivasi* group in Bangladesh, although 45 categories of ethnic groups were classified in the country (Rahman, 1996; Sagar & Poulson, 2003). Despite this, there is minimal political activism by the Barua community at the national level for their social rights and ethnic identity in the country. A community member, Kiran, expressed the following:

> The Barua community does not have any political identity in this country. Although we are fewer people, we have several organizations and we are champions in this regard. For example, we have the *Kristi Prachar Sangha, Bouddha Samity,* and *Buddhist Federation.* In such a situation, we see more conflicts, contradictions, and differences within our community. Interestingly, when even five Baruas meet, we seem to begin an organization. Because of the conflict

in the community, we are quite disorganized within ourselves. We live in a noncooperative environment, without any collective efforts in the country.

(Interview notes, 2011)

Similarly, Roni—another Barua—stated,

> Frankly speaking, the monastery was once the center for learning, meeting, and development. But now it has become a place of *nabbha dhani* (nouveau riche), who go there to do politics and to create divisions within the community. These people try to control simple living people through deceptive tricks and money. They disregard the collective lives of the people for their own personal gain. The monastery should not be used as a commercial commodity and it is not the place to legitimize the corporate or business culture. Because of this, our community cannot be united to establish its cultural rights in the country.
>
> (Interview, 2011)

Obviously, this has made it very difficult for the community to establish its rights in a democratic environment. In a free market economy, the spiritual and cultural heritage and collective living of the community have been neglected in order to expand consumer culture. I believe that the members of the Barua community need to emphasize critical understanding and contemplation of mind *(citta sikkha)* in order to free themselves from the clutches of materialism, since they claim to be Buddhists (Barua, 2007). In fact, the Buddha was a critical thinker and pragmatic idealist who denounced the caste system in his time. In reality, the Buddha "did not take life out of the context of its social, political and economic background; he looked at it as a whole, in all its social, economic and political rights" (Rahula, 1994, p. 24). Most importantly, social rights and justice can be established only if the voice of the community is expressed through collective efforts. These rights could be established from the social and cultural position of the community in light of the Universal Declaration of Human Rights of 1948. Members of the Barua community may attempt to establish cultural rights within the framework of rights of indigenous ethnic minorities or indigenous communities as they maintain a cultural identity distinct from the dominant society (World Bank, 1991).

Over the years, the Barua community has experienced cultural alienation from its own roots and origin within the political context of the country, due to social, cultural, and political assimilation into the mainstream society. However, the sociocultural and political uniqueness of the community must be identified in order for the community to re/discover its distinctiveness and political/ethnic identity through nonviolent activism in the country. For this, a collective learning practice needs to be initiated in order to create a space for social transformation without any imposition and domestication in the national politics.

Concluding Reflections

In this chapter, I used an anticolonial lens to examine issues of cultural/ethnic identity/social formation of the Barua community within the processes of colonial education and globalization. Over the years, although the community has attempted to construct and consolidate its sociopolitical identity through links either to Buddhism or Bengali in order to avoid social discrimination, it has not been able to determine its true ethnic identity due to the colonial learning processes and the domination of the market economy. In fact, this learning displaced the community from its cultural roots and land. In other words, colonial education weakened the collective life of the community in the villages and cities. Although the community has constantly encountered challenges to its identity within the nation-state, there are instances of nonviolent cultural resistance through the mobilization of *vipassana* mediation and other cultural events at the local level.

However, there is no visible political participation or social movement by the community at the national level. In addition, contention has developed among the members of the community because of their lack of acquaintance with their cultural heritage in the national curriculum. Another challenge is that members of the community are more confined to local contexts, meaning that their leaders have extremely limited access to national and international social movements. Thus, although the Baruas maintain a distinct and unique cultural identity, they have no clear understanding of the notion of indigeneity. To remedy this, the community needs to reflect on and project its sociocultural perspectives through collaborative and contemplative learning practices in order to establish a cultural/ethnic identity within the political context of the country. In other words, it is important for the Barua community to re/discover its cultural history so that it can express its cultural heritage and identity in the greater context of global politics. Re/discovery of indigeneity does not necessarily contend a return to a primitive or a colonial era; rather it invites a search for self-identification and liberation for collective living and dignity in the contemporary global world.

Notes

1. Ethnic identity is a sociocultural, political, and psychological construction. Most social scientists will agree that the Barua community maintains a distinct identity based on common cultural traits and values.

2. In *Pali, thera* means elders and *veda* refers to doctrine or teaching. In South and Southeast Asia, Theravada Buddhism is considered to be the oldest of the Buddhist sects. It is believed that the Buddha founded this immediately after his enlightenment at the foot of the Bo-tree at Bodhgaya.
3. Chittagong or *Chattagram* (in Bengali) did not exist until the middle of the tenth century. Over the centuries, various rulers, scholars, and visitors have identified Chittagong by various names. The present English name "Chittagong" was given by the British colonial administration when it occupied Chittagong in 1760 (Chowdhury, 1988).
4. This district was created by the British colonial administration in 1860 as a non-regulated tribal area with the goal to use the forests and natural resources. The district of Chittagong Hill Tracts was divided into three major circles: Chakma Circle, Bomang Circle, and Mang Circle (B. P. Barua, 2001).
5. This ideology is especially prevalent among the western-educated individuals. Although western-educated Baruas assimilated into the higher classes of Bengal and Assam, they are considered a *scheduled tribe,* which allows them to enjoy minority quotas and facilities in India.
6. The boys and girls of the Barua community in the northeast part of Chittagong go to the forest to collect *Biu fhul* (wildflowers collected for *Biu*) before sunrise. While engaged in this, first they collect and then they perform a ritual by setting fires in the courtyards of their houses and singing a song for the welfare of their families and their village (Khan, 1977). This type of cultural ritual of worshiping nature and mother earth is seen among Native Canadians such as Inuit and Métis.
7. This concept was basically endorsed and promoted by the British colonial power through the Fort William College in Bengal. It has also been observed that the educated Baruas tend to speak Bengali rather than the local language even in the villages.

References

Bandapaday, K. (1989). Jatiya Shikha [National Education]. In H. B. Chowdhury (Ed.), *Dr. B. M. Barua centenary commemoration volume* (pp. 44–50). Calcutta, India: Bauddha Dharmankar Sabha [Bengal Buddhist Association].

Barua, B. (2004). *Western education and modernization in a Buddhist village of Bangladesh: A case of the Barua community.* Unpublished doctoral dissertation, Department of Sociology and Equity Studies in Education, Ontario Institute for Studies in Education, University of Toronto.

Barua, B. (2007). Colonialism, education and rural Buddhist communities in Bangladesh. *International Education, 57*(1), (pp. 60–76).

Barua, B. (2009). Nonformal education, economic growth and development: Challenges for rural Buddhists in Bangladesh. In A. Abdi & D. Kapoor (Eds.), *Global perspective on adult education* (pp. 125–140). New York: Palgrave Macmillan.

Barua, B. (2010a). Ethnic minorities, indigenous knowledge, and livelihoods: Struggle for survival in southeastern Bangladesh. In D. Kapoor & E. Shiza (Eds.), *Indigenous*

knowledge and learning in Asia/Pacific and Africa: Perspectives on development, education, and culture (pp. 63–79). New York: Palgrave Macmillan
Barua, B. (2010b). Development intervention and ethnic communities in Bangladesh and Thailand: A critique. *Journal of Alternative Perspectives in the Social Sciences, 2*(1), 372–400.
Barua, B. (2011). Critical perspectives on development and learning in community action in Bangladesh and Thailand. In D. Kapoor (Ed.), *Critical perspectives on neoliberal globalization, development and education in Africa and Asia/Pacific* (pp. 171–186). Rotterdam: Sense Publishers.
Barua, B. M. (1923). *Bauddha parinaya paddhati* [Buddhist method of marriage]. Calcutta, India: Chowdhury and Barua.
Barua, B. P. (2001). *Ethnicity and national integration in Bangladesh: A study of the Chittagong Hill Tracts*. New Delhi, India: Har-Anand Publications Pvt. Ltd.
Barua, R. B. (1963). Rituals and festivals of the Buddhists of East Pakistan. *Journal of Asiatic Society of Pakistan, VIII*(1), 13–25.
Barua, R. B. (1965). Some important festivals of the Buddhists in East Pakistan. *Journal of Asiatic Society of Pakistan, X*(1), 15–34.
Barua, R. B. (1978). *The Theravada sangha*. Dhaka, Bangladesh: The Asiatic Society of Bangladesh.
Battiste, M. & Henderson, J. Y. (2000). *Protecting indigenous knowledge and heritage*. Saskatoon, Canada: Purich Publishing Ltd.
Bowers, C. A. (1997). *The culture of denial: Why the environmental movement needs a strategy for reforming universities and public schools*. Albany, New York: State University of New York Press.
Chaudhuri, S. (1982). *Contemporary Buddhism in Bangladesh*. Calcutta, India: Atisha Memorial Publishing Society.
Chowdhury, A. H. (1988). *Chattagramer samaj-o-sanskritir ruprekha* [An outline of socio-cultural history of Chittagong]. Dhaka, Bangladesh: Bangla Academy.
Dei, G. J. S., & Asgharzadeh, A. (2001). The power of social theory: The anti-colonial discursive framework. *Journal of Education Thought, 35*(3), 297–323.
Freire, P. (1970). *Cultural action for freedom*. Cambridge, MA: Harvard Education Review and Center for the Study of Development and Social Change.
Freire, P. (1973). *Education for critical consciousness*. New York: Continuum and Seabury Press.
Freire, P. (1985). *The politics of education, culture, power, and liberation*. New York: Bergin & Garvey.
Gordon, M. M. (1971). Assimilation in America: Theory and reality. In N. R. Yetman & C. H. Steele (Eds.), *Majority and minority: The dynamics of racial and ethnic relations* (pp. 261–283). Boston: Allyn and Bacon.
Hunter, W. W. (1876). *A statistical account of Bengal* (Vol. VI). London: Trubner & Co.
Kapoor, D. (2010). Learning from Adivasi (original dweller) political-ecological expositions of development: Claims on forests, land and place in India. In D. Kapoor & E. Shiza (Eds.), *Indigenous knowledge and learning in Asia/Pacific and Africa:*

Perspectives on development, education, and culture (pp. 17–33). New York: Palgrave Macmillan.

Kapoor, D. & Shiza, E. (2010). Introduction. In D. Kapoor & E. Shiza (Eds.), *Indigenous knowledge and learning in Asia/Pacific and Africa: Perspectives on development, education, and culture* (pp. 1–13). New York: Palgrave Macmillan.

Kapoor, D. (2011). Neoliberal globalization, saffron fundamentalism and dalit poverty and educational prospects in India. In D. Kapoor (Ed.), *Critical perspectives on neoliberal globalization, development and education in Africa and Asia/Pacific* (pp. 69–86). Rotterdam: Sense Publishers.

Khatun, S. (1992). *Development of primary education policy in Bangladesh.* Dhaka, Bangladesh: University of Dhaka.

Khan, A. M. (1977). *The Buddhists in Bangladesh: A socio-cultural study,* Unpublished Master's Thesis. Jahangirnagar University, Dhaka, Bangladesh.

Norberg-Hodge, H. (1991). *Ancient futures: Learning from Ladakh.* San Francisco: Sierra Club Books.

Phayre, A. P. (1863). *History of Burma including Burma proper, Pegu, Taungu, Tenasserim and Arakan.* London: Susil Gupta.

Rahman, K. M. L. (1996). Minorities of Bangladesh and their alienation: Causes and implication. *Journal of Asiatic Society of Bangladesh, 41*(2), 299–314.

Rahula, W. (1994). Buddhism in the real world. In C. Whitemyer (Ed.), *Mindfulness and meaningful work: Explorations in right livelihood* (pp. 23–270). Berkeley, CA: Parallax press.

Risely, H. R. (1891). *Tribes and castes of Bengal.* Calcutta: The Bengal Secretariat.

Sagar, T. & Poulson, N. (2003). *Education for indigenous children: The BRAC model.* Retrieved from http://www.sil.org/asia/ldc.parallel_papers/sagar_and_poulson.pdf_microsoft.

Smith, L. T. (1999). *Decolonizing methodologies: Research and indigenous peoples.* London: Zed Books.

Tambiah, S. J. (1992) *Buddhism betrayed? Religion, politics, and violence in Sri Lanka.* Chicago: The University of Chicago Press.

Thera, D. (1936). *Saddharma ratnakar: Boddha mission granthmala.* Rangoon, Burma: Boddha Mission.

Thuen, T. (2006). Discussion: The concept of indigeneity. *Social Anthropology, 14*(1), 24–25.

World Bank. (1991). Indigenous peoples. In *The World Bank operational Manuel* (pp. 1–6). Washington, DC: The World Bank.

CHAPTER 10

Performing and Politicizing Education in West Bengal, India[1]

Dia Da Costa

Introduction

In an essay that combines life, organizational, and social history, Jana Sanskriti (JS) activist Renuka Das wrote this about a fellow JS activist:

> Pradeep gave a speech in front of Amartya Sen. This would not have been possible without his presence in JS and the JS commitment to give him a space to freely pursue his talents. I have seen a lot of organizations who have used people from the lower classes as workers to fulfill their mandate. What our organization wants is that the more people recognize things, learn things, the more they will understand things
>
> (Das, 2010, p. 58).[2]

Jana Sanskriti (JS) was formed in 1985 and it is a political theater organization of Bengali agricultural laborers working in a regional context of progressive land reforms, political decentralization, and consecutive electoral success for the political Left from 1977 to 2011. JS is composed of two urban, middle-class members, and over 1,000 agricultural and wage laborers in West Bengal. JS's rural members come from landless to middle-class and low- to middle-caste families. Two out of ten people in the central coordinating committee of JS are from urban backgrounds. All central committee members, including Pradeep Sardar, have had affiliations with a range of regional political parties. Five out of 10 coordinating team members are women. JS also has nine all-women theater teams across West Bengal. Since 1985, JS has grown in other districts in West Bengal, and has built theater teams in alliance with mass movements in 12 other states across India. By recent estimates, their theater reaches an audience of over 250,000 people. The purpose of their theater thus ranges from mobilizing around local social problems to distributing the means of intellectual debate and political action to building broader struggles across linguistic and provincial divides within and beyond India.

As Renuka's words highlight, it was a matter of great pride for members of JS that one of their own, Pradeep Sardar, presented his views on the state of rural education in West Bengal to an audience of academics, practitioners, and policymakers that included Amartya Sen, among other notables, in Kolkata. In part, this pride came from the fact that Pradeep dropped out of school in grade four and came from a landless household of six. In the common sense imagination and everyday experience of hierarchy in India, Pradeep would be viewed as an illiterate villager—one whose view is rarely heard or valued by the *bada aadmi* (big person) or *bhadralok* (gentleman of the cultural and political intelligentsia) he was addressing (Sarangapani, 2003). This pride also came from the fact that JS's everyday pedagogical work accounted for Pradeep's pursuits and accomplishments in political learning. Through JS's work, people like him have come to believe in their right to access education, and have also learned to debate the purposes, meanings, and processes of education.

In this chapter, I draw out some of the modes and processes of JS's alternative space of pedagogy and political society compared to education for all (EFA) premises and structures. I highlight JS's relation to and epistemological distinction from dominant policy enthusiasm for EFA as articulated in human development models, world education conferences, and the millennium development goals. I argue that EFA is a model that accommodates to a civil society model of democracy, in Partha Chatterjee's (2004) sense of the term. In contrast, JS's members work and live with a pedagogy defined by its commitment to constructing an alternative political society, which, I argue, demands a more complicated view than Partha Chatterjee's (2004) neat distinction between civil and political society.

Partha Chatterjee's account rests on a Gramscian distinction between civil society and political society, operationalized through a Foucauldian lens of governmentality. In postcolonial societies where socioeconomic policies of the developmental state combat poverty and 'backwardness', citizens are first and foremost enumerated as various population groups on governmental surveys (landless, squatters, jobless, refugees, below-the-poverty-line card holders, etc.). Civil society, founded on ideas of popular sovereignty, equality, free entrance and exit, contract, deliberative procedures, and rights and duties, is limited to those "culturally equipped citizens" who have the privilege to realize idealized equal citizenship (Chatterjee, 2004, p. 41). The rest of the population, particularly the urban and rural poor, are only "tenuously, and even then ambiguously and contextually, rights-bearing citizens" (p. 38). Outside civil society proper, yet enumerated and living within national territory, they are subject to control and potential claimants on state welfare and rights. These citizens are routinely pushed toward criminal and illegal action as a result of government inability to reconcile private property rights with the mandate of welfare for all citizens.

In the first section of this chapter, I question the unmitigated enthusiasm for education within (human) development thinking, policy, and practice. I highlight the material and representational inequalities that limit the benefits of education to some citizens, rather than making it available for disenfranchised populations. I argue that despite the human rights, development, and capabilities approach that informs the EFA commitment to inclusive and diverse education, both rhetoric and strategy have shaped education in alignment with liberal democracy, which relies on market participation and civil society organizations competing for private sources of welfare funding. In the second section, I demarcate aspects of JS pedagogy and theater that make it the kind of education that disenfranchised populations have reason to value. In the third section, I trace the legacy, contours, and processes of JS practices to Paulo Friere's (1970) pedagogy of the oppressed and Augusto Boal's (1979) theater of the oppressed. In the fourth section, I distinguish JS work from the proliferation of co-opted forms of theater *for* development, while further distinguishing JS's alternative practice in the fifth section by identifying their activists as what I call 'spect-actors of history'.[3] Ultimately, in this chapter, I conclude that contrary to dominant *conceptions* of education as intrinsically and instrumentally valuable in human development models that elide questions of inequality and power, JS practice places a *political value* on education—one that is committed to resisting material and representational inequality within existing frameworks of development, governance, and education.

"Education for All": Material and Representational Inequalities

In 1990, 1,500 delegates from 155 countries and representatives from 150 NGOs gathered at the World Conference on Education for All (EFA) in Jomtien, Thailand, to call for the universalization of primary education and reduction of illiteracy before the turn of the millennium. The Dakar Framework for Action (2000) echoed the Jomtien Declaration and Millennium development aim of achieving universal primary education for all as one of eight fundamental goals of education. Research, policy, and governance institutions at global, state, and civil society levels have been working on implementing these goals to varying degrees, constructing complex educational regimes that at once overlap with and override colonial and national developmentalist legacies.

Critics suggest a number of structural hindrances likely to impede the realization of EFA's goals and strategies: (1) despite the overall financial affordability of achieving the EFA goal of universal primary education by 2015, critics note declining political will and contributions for overseas development assistance, especially for education (Delamonica, Mehrotra, & Vandemoortele, 2004; see also Nussbaum, 2004); (2) the debilitating effects of growth-oriented policies and structural adjustment programs on public spending on education (Drèze & Sen 1997; Samoff & Caroll, 2007); (3) the rhetorical commitment to human rights and development contradicted by an overemphasis on meeting numerical quotas, management strategies, and increased financial dependence on bilateral and multilateral funding (Tamatea, 2005); (4) the formation of multitiered, uneven education systems as a result of intensifying civil society involvement in provisioning education (recommended by the Dakar Framework), which reinforces already existing hierarchies in society (Balagopalan, 2005); and (5) a global, national, and local intensification of the assumption that "education is unproblematic and intrinsically positive" in discursive and policy frameworks (Jeffery, 2005, p. 15).

Critical theorists of education have long since articulated the ways in which education is situated in material and representational inequalities. Some scholars have pointed out that education ought not to be viewed as a silver bullet panacea for development goals such as population control and girls' education. After all, education is itself often a site and mode of reproducing inequality (Bourdieu, 2007; Bourdieu & Passeron, 1977). However, the popularity of the human development and capabilities approach since the 1990s makes less definitive critiques of education. Amartya Sen, for example, points to the constitutive role of education in shaping development in terms of the "intrinsic importance of human freedom" (Sen, 1999, p. 37) and the instrumental value of education in enabling political freedoms, economic facilities, social opportunities, transparency guarantees, and protective security. While Sen argued that development should be understood in terms of enabling people to value what they have reason to value, EFA implementation is far too comfortably aligned with the dominant structures and policies of neoliberal development, which stress participation in the market-oriented economy, leaving much less room for maneuver than Sen's theories might suggest.

For example, Karuna Morarji (2010) has asked, '*what kinds of lives do people have reason to value?*' (p. 52, italics in the original). In her study of rural India, Morarji questioned the assumption that villagers want to leave behind their farms and fields in pursuit of consumer lifestyles and urban livelihoods. This is a pervasive claim that has in fact been actively produced by neoliberal agricultural policies that have made an already debt-ridden smallholder agriculture even more unviable since the 1990s in India. These policies also reinforce a general urban middle-class disregard for the very possibility of cultural preferences for living rural futures (Da Costa, 2010a; Morarji, 2010). As such, educating villagers can place them at a structural disadvantage because an education biased toward urban futures implies that villagers neither aspire to agrarian livelihoods, nor do they possess the cultural, social, and economic capital to fit into the competitive job environment of the cities. Thus, Morarji's (2010) question, "where does the rural educated fit?" (p. 50) problematizes what counts as relevant education (i.e., education that one has reason to value) within an unequal political economic environment where people are hardly free to pursue what they have reason to value.

In other words, in the climate of market oriented futures, people are not free to value small farming as a viable option for their futures. Indeed, Sen himself was explicitly critical of peasant resistance to land acquisition for industrialization in West Bengal. Sen viewed dispossession of fertile agricultural land next to West Bengal's water systems as justified if it encouraged industrialization because "industrial production could generate many times more than the value of the product produced by agriculture. The locations of great industry, be it Manchester or Lancashire, these were all on heavily fertile land" (Saha with Sen, 2007).

While industry wins in this competition, it wins through a circular logic, holding European developments as ideal and through a definition of current value that is captive to a market episteme. Other values and substantive freedoms such as rural livelihoods, skills, and futures apparently do not seem to matter. Indeed, this judgment about rural unviability is pervasive in the culturally equipped voice of civil society and academic leaders such as Amartya Sen. The point is that reigning political economic policies and realities foreclose freedom even as Sen's conceptual vocabulary promises development in and as freedom.

Considering the degree to which EFA policy builds on human development, rights, and capabilities discourse to bolster its rhetorical commitment to education, it is noteworthy that EFA strategies are couched in terms of making educational systems accountable, professional, predictable, and well-integrated (UNESCO, 2000). Despite the rhetorical commitment to the "most vulnerable and disadvantaged children" and to participatory educational governance (pp. 8–9), EFA strategies of time-bound action and midterm reviews through select performance-indicators are far more in line with the mandates of civil society organizations than with rural villagers' dilemma of pursuing educational aspirations in an environment that actively constructs agrarian futures as materially and representationally unviable. The distance between the EFA document and the dilemmas and position of the most disadvantaged children suggests that theorizing education as inculcating a freedom to value what one has reason to value is a theory that fits the already well-positioned and culturally equipped citizen, rather than a disenfranchised population.

In contrast to Sen's seemingly inclusive view, Pierre Bourdieu (2007) addressed the relation between instrumental and intrinsic value. He argued that a "class of practices whose explicit purpose is to maximize monetary profit" needs to construct another class of human engagement that can be characterized more in terms of "purposeless finality," that is, the "gratuitous activities" of cultural and artistic practices and their products (pp. 83–84). In this view, instrumental and intrinsic values are ideological designations necessary for the sustenance of an overall system within which "priceless things have a price" (p. 84). Education is not viewed as a straightforward means of increasing national productivity by maximizing the talents of people, as policy makers tend to assume. Rather, education is a means of reproducing the unequal transmission of material and representational inequality. Similarly attentive to intractable forms of power, Michel Foucault (1977) theorized the ways in which modern institutions (among them the prison and the school) involve architectural and disciplinary regimes of hierarchical observation through which people learn how to belong to given positions within a spectrum of normality and morality. In these perspectives, the educated person is not the freed individual of the liberal imagination, but more likely one whose power and place is produced in and through being subject to and subject of institutional discipline and inequality.

As I argue, JS places political value on education in order to contest the disciplinary regimes and inequalities embedded in rural education. Although JS might view political voice and action as the priceless or intrinsic value of education, they underscore rather than elide the forms of inequality and power within which learning takes place. Moreover, my focus on alternative spaces and forms of education places equal importance on the political imagination with which actors respond to structural delimitations and inequalities. Using JS as one example of such political imagination and action, in the next section I ask, What constitutes Jana Sanskriti as a space of learning? What are the defining features and goals of education as it is provided in Jana Sanskriti? And finally, how should we think about such spaces of learning in light of the dominant policy call for delivering EFA?

An Education that JS has Reason to Value

While Sen's position as expert and member of an educated class with economic, cultural, and social capital is clear, it is not as clear where on the spectrum of value, civil society, and political society to place Pradeep Sardar. The latter has little education, land, or cultural capital. Nonetheless, he morally and politically invests in the possibility of small-holder agrarian futures that have little contemporary cache. What exactly can be said about Pradeep Sardar's positionality and sphere of legitimacy and how did he come to have an encounter with Amartya Sen? I argue in this section that despite Pradeep's lack of academic credentials, it is important to recognize the epistemologically distinct legacy and processes through which Jana Sanskriti nurtured an education that Pradeep has reason to value. By accepting Pradeep as educated, I am talking about education constructed *by* all, rather than education for all. This is akin to the distinction made by Gayatri Chakravorty Spivak between the model of human rights, which she views as the "burden of the fittest," and the model of "subordinate cultures of responsibility" through which marginalized groups rework dormant ethical scripts and knowledges to construct postcolonial pedagogies and futures (Spivak, 2008, p. 36).

At the same time, it is important to recognize the contemporary alliances between critical pedagogy legacies and recent theater *for* development trends that support neoliberal development policy and practice. No doubt neoliberal development practice can co-opt sanitized versions of critical theater into participatory governance strategies. However, understanding JS as an alternative space of pedagogy and political society entails recognizing that JS has constructed education as politically valuable insofar as it enables critical thinking, play, and action. Thus, when I say education by all, this should not conjure up some kind of utopic, equal society. Among JS activists and members, there is an acute recognition of the inequalities and hierarchies that mark any participatory action *by* the oppressed. No political activism or educational intervention by all can be bereft of power relations. Indeed the point in JS work is not so much to excise power relations as to ensure that participatory practices neither elide their existence nor shy away from addressing them.

Permanent Liberation and Permanent Critique

JS work must be placed within the legacy of Paulo Freire's and Augusto Boal's philosophical and political theories. Writing in the context of military dictatorships and postcolonial inequalities in Brazil, Freire (1970) drew on liberation theology to develop a pedagogy that would actively fight the banking concept of education where students are conceived as passive receptacles of information servicing a capitalist society. According to Freire's pedagogy of the oppressed, much of modern education assumes that teachers are sources of authoritative and uncontestable information to be deposited into students. The test of knowledge in this system is determined by students' ability to repeat information acquired in monologue-driven learning, acquire credentials based on retention and regurgitation, and cash in on the rewards in a job market that is well-calibrated to this form of knowledge production. The product of this education system is a student who can retain but not critically think about the information that they hold.

By contrast, Freire redefined literacy not as reading the word, but as acquiring the critical capacity to read the world. Freire proposed an education process that would rely on praxis, or critical thinking and critical action that emerges from a vision of students (and teachers) as engaged actors and teachers (and students) as responsive listeners. Rather than a reversal of roles, Freire's goal was to place dialogue at the heart of any educational process so as to recognize debate and conflict as germane to social relations and therefore to the knowledge produced in it. Freire's model was not just meant for the classroom but for any context of learning where some people assume a leadership role and others assume a passive listener's role. From adult education to social movements, Freire's philosophical approach has been extensively applied to contexts across the world.

Freire emphasized the notion of permanent liberation, the second of two stages of liberation. In the first stage of Freire's humanist pedagogy, "the oppressed unveil the world of oppression and through the praxis commit themselves to its transformation. In the second stage, in which the reality of oppression has already been transformed, this pedagogy ceases to belong to the oppressed and becomes a pedagogy for all people in the process of permanent liberation" (Freire, 1970, p. 54). Freire believed in the possibility of a pedagogy of the oppressed that transforms all selves within society in an ongoing way to produce a permanent liberation from oppression.

JS practices 'theater of the oppressed', which is Augusto Boal's innovative translation of pedagogy of the oppressed into a theatrical vocabulary. Similar to Freire, Boal wrote *Theater of the Oppressed* in the 1970s in the context of combating military dictatorship and neocolonialism in Brazil. Friere's and Boal's conceptions of pedagogy drew on Marxist theories of capitalist society, while rejecting and reimagining ideas about the political vanguard. Among Boal's techniques used commonly by JS, Forum Theater refers to the process of scripting plays by weaving together images portraying daily experiences enacted by participants in theater workshops. Often Sanjoy Ganguly, the artistic director of JS and the increasingly nonurban middle-class actors, weave these stories told during workshops into a short play on given social issues (e.g., dowry, local government corruption, rural livelihoods, liquor production, or rural education). The themes of plays build upon the political concerns and campaigns in any given time and context. The play is performed for an audience. A second enactment of the play uses a joker who prompts the audience to rescript the play at any given stage of its telling. In the Forum Theater format, audience members are encouraged to step onstage to rescript roles, norms, and taken-for-granted interactions of daily life that lead to the extraordinary social issues being discussed.

Boal's signal contribution—the spect-actor—nurtures and brings the creative powers and critical thinking of audience members onstage into a process of rescripting a play. A spect-actor gives theatrical form to Freire's engaged student who is no longer a passive receptacle in knowledge production. I have on occasion witnessed ten-minute first enactments of JS plays turn into three hours of discussion with scores of interventions from the audience. With these routine debates witnessed publicly, JS aims to generate debate on alternate social norms and possibilities and make imagined possibilities daily material realities.

In addition to the intellectual alienation that Freire's pedagogy attempted to combat, Boal's theatrical methods aim to combat the "muscular alienation" of oppressed bodies that serve capital accumulation (Boal, 1979, p. 127). In so far as the "body is an accumulation strategy" within capitalism (Harvey, 2000, p. 97), it is crucial in the Boalian view that both body and mind are placed at the centre of processes and techniques for learning. Moreover, this attitude to muscular alienation has been a crucial ingredient of a critical pedagogy among agricultural laborers in India because it allows the participant and leader to question their own assumptions about what and whether (agricultural) knowledge and work counts in the urban, middle-class cultural orientation of capitalist modernity, development, and globalization in India.

To be sure, scholars such as Philip Auslander have rightly questioned whether it is possible for the body to exist outside ideological encoding (Auslander, 1994). However, the body is perpetually in movement in Boalian theatrical practice, where the goal is to try on different masks, different ideological encodings (Auslander, 1994). In JS practice the goal of trying on different masks is not multicultural inclusion, but rather to nurture critical and collective embodied thinking. Engagement in theater of the oppressed becomes a mode of questioning and problematizing one's muscular alienation and ideological encoding. In this sense, JS pedagogical practice lies somewhere between nurturing a belief in permanent liberation while using Boalian and Freirian techniques to effect permanent critique.

Co-opting Critical Pedagogy for Development

Freirian forms of education and Boalian forms of theater, especially Forum Theater, became increasingly popular through the 1980s and 1990s all over the world. The last two decades have witnessed a dramatic increase in funding for civil society organizations that use theater for development, especially in the field of HIV/AIDS education. Ironically, a democratic mode of political education and action can also become a tool for delivering pre-scripted development messages among preliterate audiences. In this form, the ideal of dialogical education and praxis is entirely corrupted as it is incorporated into a system of accumulating credentials and satisfying funding agency goals by formally including the voices of the poor and hitherto excluded illiterate populations into ultimately pre-scripted visions of development, liberal democracy, and capitalist society (Ahmed, 2002; Kerr, 2003; Plastow, 1998). The cooperation between political activism, theater, and neoliberal development gives community-based governance the added cache of being innovative, creative, citizen participation in human development. Used in this way, critical pedagogy, and the place of theater in it, becomes one more part that legitimizes an antipolitics machine. The latter is James Ferguson's (1994) term for the depoliticizing institutional and discursive apparatus of development policy and practice.

One result of this collaboration between theater and depoliticized notions of development is that it contributes to declaring political theater dead since such action is no longer seen as capable of challenging status quo and constructing alternative political society, but merely reinforcing a liberal model of better, more creative forms of civil participation within existing political economic structures and inequalities. Considering that mainstream development practices are adept at co-opting the very methods developed to resist capitalist development to further their own legitimacy, the challenge as I see it is to consider how to identify political theater and political action. While recognizing the politicizing possibilities that can and do exist within cultural practices in an increasing commodified world, like any intervention or system of education, it is important not to treat liberatory systems as pure or autonomous historical, pedagogical, or transformative forces. By implication, it is important to study the Boalian stage and JS work offstage not just as a *vehicle* of transformation but as *lens* on and *space* of political economy—a task to which I turn in the next section.

Spect-actors of History

With the term spect-actor of history, I seek to question the dominant modes of seeing political theater as creative political action in times of repression (the safety-valve model) and the view of political theater as a default site of resistance (Da Costa, 2010a). I argue that theater is both a lens on and a space of political economy. It is a culture of responsibility that constructs a pedagogy with no guarantees (Spivak, 2008). Seeing JS activists as spect-actors of history highlights the dilemmas they encounter in the process of consciousness raising by and among the oppressed. After all, raising consciousness through practices such as spect-acting in Forum Theater has to constantly confront the inequalities, complexities, and ambiguities *within* categories such as the oppressed and oppressors that are not stable or undifferentiated positions, identities, or subjectivities. JS performances and political actions bear the traces of this difficult work of unifying a struggle that cannot count on a unified category of the oppressed. Rather than a narrative of the oppressed being liberated through the use of a critical technique and pedagogy, I am arguing for a less linear, more complex view of learning and social struggle in which processes of intervention, engagement, representation, and any transformation is ridden with inequalities. With this term, I also qualify Augusto Boal's term 'spect-actor' (for engaged and active spectators) in light of JS commitment to make acting *onstage* and political activism *offstage* constantly feed each other.

One telling example of a spect-actor of history appears in the words and actions of one JS activist, Pradeep Haldar, who recounted how villagers began to draw on lines, critiques, and cues learned from the JS play BPL (Below the Poverty Line) in order to make life hell for government ration dealers in the increasingly defunct and corrupted public distribution system (Haldar, 2010). Despite numerous examples of offstage audience activism following JS performances, JS activists do not harbor an inflated sense of their work. Pradeep Haldar's account of the effect of the play BPL on villagers is marked by doubt: " 'Now someone might ask, 'How do you know it is the result of your play that is making people demand all of this?' " (Haldar, 2010, p. 82). Pradeep's response to this commonly asked question is simply brilliant:

> Well, that ration dealer is a man from our village. He comes to us every day and says 'Brother what kind of play have you started? People come to me daily and give me such a hard time.' We asked him in turn, 'How do you know they are coming to you as a result of our play.' He said, 'Well, because nobody asked us these questions before.' After your plays, every day people come and say any number of things. If you're not leading them to this, then you tell me who is?' We asked him, 'Are the questions people are asking valid or not? Are we showing incorrect things in the plays?' He responded, 'Well, you may be showing the correct things in your play, but how can I give a real receipt for the rations when every other dealer scribbles things on a chit of paper. In any case, who gives the correct amount of rice and wheat to people? And if they don't

give less, how would it be sustainable as a shop?' We said, 'Why are you saying all of this to us? Why don't you try to respond in this way to the ones who are coming to you?' When we said this, the dealer's face lost all colour and he left.

(Haldar, 2010, pp. 82–3)

Pradeep Haldar is a spect-actor of history, one who engages in constant critical play on *and* offstage by upsetting the assumed boundaries between fiction and reality in order to construct social change. This spect-actor of history takes the limits of becoming a spect-actor in performances seriously, not in order to generate apathy in the face of the complexity of real life, but to rejuvenate political struggle. He places the general skepticism about the real life efficacy of Forum Theater right back into the lap of the offstage oppressor. Pradeep asks the actual ration dealer *himself* (the source of immediate oppression in the play) how he knows that JS plays are causing all this trouble for him. The ration dealer disregards the supposed boundaries between fiction and reality by admitting that he was not harassed about accountability, receipts, and his corruption before the JS play. As far he is concerned, the absence of accountability for corruption made being a ration dealer (an ostensibly state enterprise) a profitable business! Moreover, the JS play has created trouble by creating a norm of seeking accountability at the ration shop. Rather than allow the ration dealer to have the last word on harassment, Pradeep forces recognition of who is harassing whom by asking the ration dealer to confront the public with the rationale that honesty and accountability will sink his business.

Here, learning does not stop onstage, and therefore the stage cannot be seen as a mere fictional safety valve that does nothing to alter everyday political economic or normative structures. Moreover, this form of learning is not dependent on the kind of financial structures and bureaucratic reviews to which EFA initiatives will no doubt be subject. Yet, accountability and poverty alleviation lies at the heart of this learning process. Its sources and processes of legitimacy and accountability are realized one performance, one day, one issue, and one audience member at a time. Here, villagers vote on the quality and efficacy of their education through their individual and collective political action at the ration store.

Another JS activist, Satyaranjan Pal, spoke of the effects of a JS play entitled Sarva Shikhsa Abhiyan (Education for All) that was extensively performed by various village theater teams on education:

> Village intellectuals such as teachers, doctors, retired teachers, and such are now mobilizing to protest the condition of education and health in the villages. They now hold regular discussions with local JS members. Earlier these

village intellectuals would see us as a theater group in the village. But today we are an important political constituency that needs to be involved with debate and discussions about situations in the village. For example, there is now a debate about whether the midday meal should accompany the teaching process in ICDS [Integrated Child Development Services] or whether it should be a separate element of village development schemes. This question came up through our forum theater discussions where people questioned the corruption in food allocation and the time it took away from children's education. Now there is a widespread debate around this issue in which village intellectuals communicate using examples that they have seen expressed in our forum theater performances and in JS discussions. In other words, the nodes of our activity have led to people questioning systems previously taken for granted and tolerated. Today, the questions and problems people are raising through forum theater have become an integral basis for discussions in the village. The intellectuals have had to take us seriously as much more than a theater group.
(Pal, 2010, pp. 196–7)

It is striking that village intellectuals, who have the respected status of being educated intelligentsia (like Amartya Sen), have come to rely on JS performances not just as a site of political theater or even public debate, but as a source of reliable research and information about practices and problems in rural schooling and child development services. The JS stage is not one where power relations and inequalities disappear, but neither are they elided and obscured. Finally, JS is an alternative space of education, in light of a highly divisive context of rural party politics in West Bengal. JS has been able to construct vibrant political debate and action that is not dependent on seeking accountability on a partisan basis or on civil society organizations and their funding and review cycles. These are the different ways in which JS as a space of alternative education takes on political value compared with EFA initiatives and structures.

Thus, JS theater enables an ongoing critical and collective debate about issues in ways that do not treat welfare as a claim that becomes a divisive and criminalizing force among the rural and urban poor, which is Chatterjee's construction of political society. Rather, JS theater and critical education shows that the poor have the political imagination to construct alternative political society in order to enable better collective access to provisioning welfare and education than the processes conceived of by state and NGO officials. In this construction of an alternative political society, JS spect-actors of history are crucial because they ensure that the relationship between the stage and society is never obscured. That is, what appears onstage refuses the designation of fiction even while relying on the safety of fiction to voice difficult critiques. Learning onstage is not assumed to be real learning till it finds expression offstage. And power relations and inequalities offstage are assumed to mark the engagements and ideas that appear onstage. The ideological boundaries that separate the space of art and the space of political economy are deliberately muddied in order to construct this alternative space of learning.

Conclusion

While it is clear that EFA policies are deeply embedded within material and representational inequalities, they also deploy strategies that have suspect political economic efficacy, despite the lofty rhetoric and goal of universal primary education for all by 2015. Comfortably aligned with human rights, development, and capabilities thinking, management-guided performance review strategies, and civic participation by culturally equipped citizens, EFA epistemologically and politically ties education to a market economy and a depoliticized civil society model of democracy. In contrast, JS draws on a legacy, theory, and pedagogy that give education a fundamentally political value. Here, the idea is to set the curriculum of learning on collectively determined social needs for reading the world, as Freire imagined popular education. The idea is also to set a course of political action in a given social context based on collectively debated problems and ideas for restructuring a world of institutions and norms.

My goal in this chapter has been to capture various contours of the JS space of learning to highlight that absent educational credentials that EFA policies clamor to rectify are ultimately an impoverished measure of the complex and ambiguous value and meaning of education. Not only does the EFA model have the capacity to reinforce representational and material inequality, it trades in and relies on beneficiaries *not* dwelling on the political and transformative values of education. While theater for development could easily be co-opted into an EFA agenda, an epistemologically alternative space of education and political society such as JS is constituted by its capacity to give the knowledge and education of Amartya Sen and Pradeep Sardar equal value, to give the village intellectual and the critical voice on the Forum Theater stage equal place in reshaping knowledge production, access to resources, and structures that enable belonging within society.

Notes

1. With the pedagogical elements of Jana Sanskriti's practice being the primary focus, this chapter extends some key ideas from my book, *Development Dramas:*

Reimagining Rural Political Action in Eastern India (2010a) and the edited volume, *Scripting Power: Jana Sanskriti On and Offstage* (2010b).
2. Renuka's essay was an outcome of a writing workshop and oral interview process that I conducted with a range of Jana Sanskriti (JS) activists over a two-year period starting in 2009. The preliminary responses were then discussed and edited by JS activists and published in time for their 25 year anniversary celebrations in December 2010. All the activists' words quoted in this chapter are extracted from that edited volume entitled *Scripting Power: Jana Sanskriti On and Offstage*.
3. Spect-actor is Augusto Boal's term for active, engaged spectators in theater of the oppressed performances (Boal, 1979).

References

Ahmed, S. J. (2002). Wishing for a World without "Theater for Development": Demystifying the case of Bangladesh. *Research in Drama Education, 7*(2), 207–219.

Auslander, P. (1994). Boal-Blau-Brecht: The body. In Jan Cohen-Cruz & Mady Schutzman (Eds.), *Playing Boal* (pp. 124–33). New York: Routledge.

Balagopalan, S. (2005). An ideal School and a Schooled ideal: Education at the Margins. In R. Chopra & P. M. Jeffery (Eds.), *Educational regimes in contemporary India* (pp. 83–98). New Delhi: Sage.

Boal, A. (1979). *The theater of the oppressed.* New York: Urizen Books.

Bourdieu, P. (2007). Forms of Capital. In A. Sadovnik (Ed.), *Sociology of education: A critical reader* (pp. 83–95). New York: Routledge.

Bourdieu P., & J.-C. Passeron (1977). *Reproduction in education, society, and culture.* London, Thousand Oaks, CA, and New Delhi: Sage Publications.

Chatterjee, P. (2004). *The politics of the governed.* New Delhi: Permanent Black.

Da Costa, D. (2010a). *Development dramas: Reimagining rural political action in Eastern India.* New Delhi: Routledge.

Da Costa, D. (Ed). (2010b). *Scripting power: Jana Sanskriti on and offstage.* Kolkata: Camp Publishers.

Das, R. (2010). My dream palace, will it stay together? In D. Da Costa (Ed.), *Scripting power* (pp. 46–59). Kolkata: Camp Publishers.

Delamonica, E, Santosh, M., & Vandemoortele, J. (2004). Education for all: How much will it cost? *Development and Change, 35*(1), 3–30.

Drèze, J., & Sen, A. (Eds.) (1997). *Indian development: Selected regional perspectives.* New Delhi: Oxford University Press.

Ferguson, J. (1994). *The anti-politics machine: "Development", depoliticization, and bureaucratic power in Lesotho.* Minneapolis: University of Minnesota Press.

Foucault, M. (1977). *Discipline and punish: The birth of the prison.* London: Penguin.

Freire, P. (1970). *Pedagogy of the oppressed.* NY: Continuum.

Haldar, P. (2010). A rock cannot ultimately stop the momentum of water. In D. Da Costa (Ed.), *Scripting power* (pp. 76–87). Kolkata: Camp Publishers.

Harvey, D. (2000). *Spaces of hope.* Berkeley: University of California.

Jeffery, P. (2005). Introduction: Hearts, minds, and pockets. In R. Chopra & P. M. Jeffery (Eds.), *Educational regimes in contemporary India* (pp. 13–38). New Delhi: Sage.

Kerr, D. (2003). Art as tool, weapon or shield? Arts for development seminar, Harare. In B. Jeyifo (Ed.), *Modern African drama* (pp. 486–493). New York: W. W. Norton.

Morarji, K. (2010). Where does the rural educated person fit? Negotiating social reproduction in contemporary India. In P. McMichael (Ed.), *Contesting development: Critical struggles for social change* (pp. 50–63). London: Routledge.

Nussbaum, M. (2004). Women's education: A global challenge. *Signs: A Journal of Women and Culture, 29*(2), 325–355.

Pal, S. (2010). The market is like a Hungry Shark. In D. Da Costa (Ed.) *Scripting power* (pp. 184–197). Kolkata: Camp Publishers.

Plastow, J. (1998). Uses and abuses of theater for development: Political struggle and development theater in the Ethiopia-Eritrea war. In K. Salhi (Ed.), *African theater for development: Art for self-determination* (pp. 97–113). Exeter: Intellect.

Samoff, J. with Bidemi C. (2007). Education for all in Africa: Still a distant dream. In *Comparative education: The dialectic of the global and the local* (pp. 257–288). Plymouth: Rowman and Littlefield.

Saha, S. (2007, July 23). Prohibiting the use of agricultural land for industries is ultimately self-defeating. Interview with Amartya Sen. *The Telegraph*. Retrieved from, http://www.telegraphindia.com/1070723/asp/nation/story_8094453.asp

Sarangapani, P. (2003). *Constructing school knowledge: An ethnography of learning in an Indian Village*. New Delhi: Sage.

Sen, A. (1999). *Development as freedom*. New York: Knopf.

Spivak, G. C. (2008). *Other Asias*. Oxford: Blackwell Publishing.

Tamatea, L. (2005). The Dakar framework: Constructing and deconstructing the global neo-liberal matrix. *Globalisation, Societies, and Education, 3*(3), 311–334.

United Nations Educational Scientific and Cultural Organization (UNESCO) (2000). *The Dakar Framework for action: Education for all. Meeting our collective commitments*. Retrieved from, http://unesdoc.unesco.org/images/0012/001211/121147e.pdf

CHAPTER 11

Colonization and Decolonization: Resistances and Assaults on Traditional Agriculture in Pakistan

Azra Talat Sayeed

Introduction

Pakistan has been experiencing the impact of neoliberal agriculture policies since the introduction of Green Revolution technologies in the 1960s. The liberalization of the seed sector in the 1990s was a hallmark of the capitalist onslaught on Pakistani agriculture. The impact of agriculture-based privatization, deregulation, and trade liberalization has been immense. The country's food security has been seriously threatened, with the small and landless farmers directly bearing the impact. And although the consumer market has reached the villages directly, these farmers are having increasing difficulty accessing food and shelter. At the same time Pakistan has faced numerous 'natural disasters', most of which could be blamed on either global warming and/or faulty 'development projects' (e.g., the Left Bank Outfall Drain, or LBOD, a drain built on faulty designs and weak embankments) that have caused immense economic, social, and ecological loss to the country in general, and rural populations in particular.

The increasing poverty, hunger, livelihood insecurity, and migration in the rural economy are a result of the neoliberal globalization (globalization of capitalism) of agriculture. This has advanced the hegemonic control of agrochemical transnational corporations (TNCs), consolidating their relationship with the feudal, military, and bureaucratic elite in Pakistan. For instance, one of the major thrusts of the agrochemical TNCs has been the induction of genetically engineered (GE) seeds and crops. It is believed that 70 percent of all cotton being produced in the country is now transgenic cotton (personal communication with A. Ali, October, 2011), with both big and small farmers sowing Bt Cotton seeds. In this chapter, I discuss Roots for Equity[1] and small farmer-led campaigns, and related learning in social action to address TNC-led neoliberal globalization and the continued capitalist colonization of agriculture in Pakistan.

Colonialism and the Green Revolution

The Green Revolution was introduced near the end of the colonial period in Asia and there are numerous reasons why Pakistan so readily accepted it. Third World countries that had recently gained independence were still deep in the grip of a colonial mindset that was etched with the idea that all that is 'white' is better. As a result, the Green Revolution in Pakistan was easily accepted and in just over 40 years, the entire system of agricultural production that had been practiced for at least 7,000 years was overridden. At the time of independence (1947), strong alliances were sought with the United States and the United Kingdom. These were reinforced through the presence of Pakistani bureaucrats who had strong roots in the British Raj administration, which "reflected the limited depth of administrative and political talent in the Muslim League hierarchy" (Kux, 2001, p. 20). Civil servants who had been trained by and served under the British *Raj* had long been used to accepting and believing in the dictates of their colonial masters. In addition, they believed that their own did not have the potential to seek development paths using their own systems or traditional knowledge (Barber, 1974) and that people in the former colonies had to follow the technologies and skills left by the colonialists. Indeed, at present, much of the legal framework regarding land reforms is still based on the laws enacted in the 1800s during the British Raj. Written by the feudal class, it advocated against sharecroppers having the right of permanent land tenure (Naqvi, 1987).

In addition, after independence in 1947, there remained a massive presence of British technology. It continued to be considered the finest of the era (Kibria, 1998) and this influenced the easy acceptance of the Green Revolution. Visible technology, such as the irrigation canal system and the Sukkhur Barrage built in the 1930s, coupled with the country's inferiority complex, made it easy for Pakistan to accept foreign technologies, such as the high yielding variety seeds (HYVs) of the Green Revolution. Because of the high productivity of HYVs, especially in the very first round of planting, feudal lords, with hundreds of acres of land, reaped very high profits. For small farmers and sharecroppers, the bounties gained by rich landlords were a high incentive to follow suit in sowing these miracle seeds.

In the 1960s-1970s, there was also a great deal of pressure to adopt Green Revolution (GR) technologies coming from the government and a wide network of agricultural extension service workers who visited small farmers to convince them of the benefits of these new farming approaches. The older generation of farmers across the country has many stories about how the entire government mechanism ensured that farmers would adopt the new technologies. For instance, farmers in Shikarpur district had urea bags dumped in their fields by agricultural department personnel. This direct application of urea on farmers' fields yielded abundant harvests, resulting in increased income; this helped convince farmers to switch to a new technology that had as yet not stood the test of time. Similar stories are heard throughout the canal-irrigated areas of Sindh and Punjab.

GR technology is enshrined in the philosophy of capitalism; that is, it is concerned only with production and profits. The production paradigm, though ostensibly focused on the need for providing food for a growing population, is no doubt based on ensuring markets for agricultural inputs, which are produced by capitalist industry in the United States. In addition, surplus production also provided another avenue for imperialist policies (Stavrianos, 1981). Overall, there is ample reason to believe that Green Revolution was not only a policy instrument for increased food production, but also an agenda for a subtle form of coercion over countries in the process of breaking the shackles of colonialism.

Colonial Continuities: The Emergence of the TNC-Led Model of Industrial Agriculture and its Socioeconomic Implications

In the past 20 years or so, there has been a vast expansion of agrochemical TNCs in agricultural production. Although race dynamics may still play a critical role in the advancement of northern technologies in Pakistani research institutions, market policies now drive changing research dynamics. The interventions of GR technologies increased the potential for higher profits for the feudal elite class of Pakistan and, in the era of globalization, have influenced adopting technologies that continue to provide profitable harvests.

Monopolizing Academic Research and the Media: Legitimization through Questionable Science and Propaganda

TNCs have been able to gain hold in the market through deliberate intervention in the research agendas of public research institutions in the North and South. Neoliberal policies have allowed TNCs in the field of agricultural biotechnology to advance certain types of knowledge, which allowed innovation to be used for commodification and marketing of resulting research-based technologies (Peekhaus, 2010). Critical policy changes in federal government funding to institutions of higher learning have resulted in public research universities losing their independence in setting research agendas. Consequently, there has been a massive increase in technology transfer offices, which allow for the commercialization of research outputs. In genetic engineering, for example, there is a trend toward technology-based research rather than the science-led research. As a result, there is "a near absence of interest in funding research that considers possible adverse affects of genetic engineering" (Peekhaus, 2010, p. 418). Apart from tilting research in agricultural biotechnology in favor of industry, there has also been a marked tendency to disregard the work of social scientists, who have highlighted diverse social and economic issues faced by rural communities (Pritchard, 2005).

As the entire Green Revolution technology was based on information and knowledge generated in northern universities and other institutions, the roots of the so-called science have remained firmly embedded in the North. Roots for Equity visited the University of Agriculture, Faisalabad (UAF) in October 2011 to understand the position of agricultural universities in the country on the issues surrounding GE. The Roots for Equity team had a meeting with the Office of Research, Innovation, and Commercialization (ORIC). The international funders at ORIC include the World Bank, Asian Development Bank, and Rockefeller Foundation. The neoliberal policy agenda of these institutions is clear and it needs no reminding that the biggest pushers of Green Revolution in the 1950s were the Rockefeller Foundation and the World Bank. The agenda of ORIC is clear and close to the philosophy being pursued in northern universities, where the emphasis is on quick transfer of technology-based research into marketable goods and services (Islam, 2011; Zafar, 2011).

To date, no GE food crops have been produced in Pakistan; that is, they are all imported. Although Pakistan drafted a Plant Breeders Rights' Act years ago, it still awaits parliamentary approval. At the ORIC meeting, it was noted that this delay was due to the interventions of national self-interest groups that are connected to those who are able to benefit from multiplying Bt Cotton seeds locally and are able to locally distribute the seeds. Regulatory mechanisms would destroy the competition between these groups. In the meeting, there was a strong sense of nationalism, which advocated researching and marketing local GE seeds. This is apparent in the local news as well, where seed deals made with multinationals are seen as annihilating "national seed companies, besides causing huge financial burden on the national treasury" (Bokhari, 2011).

The positions of research scientists on genetically modified seeds were not based on opposing antimarket forces or the ethics of patenting life forms, but on ensuring that national research institutions could maintain their primary position in providing GE seeds to the national market. This is because in Pakistan, Monsanto, a multinational agricultural company, has not been able to market its Bt Cotton seed; however, for the past decade, it has been coming illegally into Pakistan from India and Australia. In 2009, the government of Punjab approved some varieties of Bt Cotton developed by Pakistani research institutions. Recently, however, Monsanto got approval to field test Bt Corn, which has raised alarm in certain quarters of Pakistani society. The Bt Corn approval process has been riddled with scandal and Monsanto acknowledges that the report on the outcomes of the trial was prepared by its own staff. Not surprisingly, it clearly recommended that "GM corn seed be allowed for commercial release" (*The News,* 2011). Another significant change has been the range of 'informative' TV programs and promotional advertisements that reinforce the supremacy of chemical-industrial agriculture. The tentacles are so deep that even the intra-rural bus services emphasize the magic of chemical fertilizers, promising to transform poor farmers from rags to riches over the next generation.

Socioeconomic Impact of TNC-led Industrial Agriculture: Culture and Class Inequality

The Green Revolution was not only a shift in technology with respect to agriculture and food production; it was a paradigm shift in how societies started viewing themselves in the context of food production and consumption. Before Green Revolution seeds were adopted so widely, food production and consumption was viewed in the context of nutrition, taste, and cultural norms of family sharing. Women in rural communities would raise *desi* (traditional) hens for eggs and chicks, used for *yakhni* (chicken broth) for family members. Cow, goat, and buffalo milk were used for a number of food products of immense nutritional value and cultural affinity at the local community level. With few ready-made food stuffs available in the market, hospitality and cultural exchanges were based on the sharing of homemade food (wheat, corn, rice, milk, butter, and vegetables).[2] However, this cultural value of food sharing in rural communities has eroded given the increased penetration of the capitalist valuation of individualism.

The impact of technology on culture has exacerbated class disparities (Reddy, as cited in Stavrianos, 1981). The abundant harvests being reaped through Bt Cotton, especially in the first few years, has led farmers to believe that Bt Cotton seed cannot fail. Pro-Bt Cotton farmers are invariably those with larger land holdings (15–30 acres of land) who can make larger profits. In the days of conventional cotton, farmers would start clearing their land by mid-October to prepare for wheat sowing. But with high yields of Bt Cotton, farmers with large land holdings commonly ignore the wheat season and continue with the cotton harvest until January since cotton yields higher profits than wheat. Small farmers with five acres of land or less do not have this choice, as they cannot compromise their own food security. Maula Bux Lahsari, a farmer with 29 acres of land and ten sharecroppers, said in an interview with Roots for Equity that he keeps the cotton crops for as long as possible, but he then has to clear his fields to sow wheat. He is able to reap nearly 900 *maunds* (1 *maund* = 40 kilograms) of wheat from his land and he has to share half of this with his sharecroppers. He believes that it is not only critical for his own family to have at least 300 *maunds* of wheat for annual consumption, but also for his sharecroppers, who require wheat as food security. If he had additional land for wheat, then he could allow his cotton fields to stand longer, leading to greater earnings since the wholesale rate of cotton per *maund* is highest at the end of the season. Big landlords, with 100 acres or more of land at their disposal, are able to reap huge profits. They keep some land available for wheat production for their families as well as their sharecroppers, and can keep a Bt Cotton crop up until January.

Furthermore, the economic (capitalist) paradigm has convinced farmers that urea and other chemical inputs will reap the most production and that more production is most beneficial. Interestingly, however, with the food and economic crisis of the recent years, especially in 2008 and 2011, small farmers are now unable to access the chemical inputs due to their astronomical prices. In just a few years, urea bags have gone from Rs 500 to Rs 1800; there has been a similar jump in cost for a chemical 'nutrient' called DAP (Di-ammonium Phosphate). These increases have led small farmers to seek alternatives and once again to experiment with traditional forms of agricultural production. Needless to say, rich peasantry and feudal landlords show no such tendencies, especially in the context of commercial production. However, it is common practice for them to grow chemical and fertilizer free wheat for domestic consumption; these are considered to taste better and to make better quality traditional bread (*chapatti/roti*).

This overbearing economic paradigm has immensely impacted the cultural values of rural communities. Initially, cultural change based on capitalist modernization was felt only in the urban centers. But the migration of rural-based workers (being made redundant through mechanized farming) to urban centers has had a great impact on feudal values, norms, and practices. Today, the values of collective living and sharing have weakened. Farmers are following suit in adopting mechanisms for making and showing off wealth, using a combination of village-based norms as well as more urban value patterns. For example, rich peasants cultivating Bt Cotton are increasing their social standing by spending money to build bigger *autaq* (public male guesthouses in Sindhi rural communities). Generally, in rural communities in Pakistan, there are strict segregation norms and males are not allowed to visit family quarters that do not belong to the same caste. In order to maintain segregation, families have separate visiting areas for men. The richer households maintain an ostentatious *autaq,* which reflects the status of the landlord class. Thus, the profit associated with Bt Cotton seed has had an immediate influence on class dynamics in rural societies.

It is important to note that although sharecroppers' earnings are just one tenth of the big landlords, they bear the extra cost of the higher quantities of chemical fertilizers. Though their earnings are higher than those of small farmers, they have to pay a higher production cost per acre. Such dynamics offer landlords the space to continue their exploitative practices, such as putting a higher cost on inputs than the market rate since the poor peasant can only pay for his input cost after harvest. At the same time, landlords have a tendency to give their sharecroppers their share of the harvest at a lower rate than the one set by the market. The Green Revolution has allowed such practices to be used widely against sharecroppers. The so-called Gene Revolution is allowing further space for cost shifting toward the sharecropper by the landholding class.

There is no doubt that the burden of work is much higher for the sharecroppers of the rich farmer than those of other small farmers. The rich farmer I interviewed has his sharecroppers spray pesticides at least once a week. In addition, he is saving his own seeds and has done so for the past five years. This additional work is done by the sharecroppers; that is, labor exploitation is reserved more for poor farmers than it is for the rich peasantry. The small farmer, with no sharecroppers, was not saving Bt Cotton seeds (as shared in interviews), as it entailed extra work that he was not able to carry out on his own.

NGO and Small Farmer Campaigns and the TNC-Led Agro-Industrial Model: Learning in Social Action

Since 1997, when it was formed, Roots for Equity has been working with small and landless farmers to popularize the negative impact of neoliberal (capitalist) agriculture on rural communities. From 2009 to 2011, Roots for Equity and the Pakistan Kissan Mazdoor Tehreek (PKMT), an alliance of small and landless farmers, has held many information sharing seminars, rallies, and mass-based dissemination discussions on the impact of GE crops, specifically Bt Cotton, in Pakistan.

Radio Programs and Community Learning

As part of the anti-Bt Campaign, PKMT and Roots for Equity aired eight radio programs on issues related to seed ownership. The programs were broadcasted from an FM Channel in Multan, Punjab, and Khairpur, Sindh, in 2011. The programs resulted in a number of interactions with small farmers on the issue of GE. However, it has also become evident that the transnational corporate sector is actively keeping any eye on such NGO-farmer educational initiatives. For instance, after a particular radio program that highlighted ethical and technical issues with GE seeds and their negative impact on small farmers, a person, who identified himself with the transnational agrochemical corporation Syngenta, called the program anchor. He challenged the information being provided about Bt Cotton as well as the debate on GE seeds that was presented in the radio program. He asked to see the research that supported what was being provided in the program. Such open questioning is indeed ironic, given the biased research carried out in public research institutions across the continents already discussed here.

The radio programs raised several issues. First, they examined GR technologies and made the link to the first wave of commercialization of seeds, which has eroded the presence of traditional seeds. It also opened the debate on farmers' collective ownership of seeds and the ethical issues with respect to GE. Third, the programs debated the technical claims made by Bt Cotton advocates. Though it is not possible to gauge the total impact of the program, there was considerable feedback from farmers calling in to express their concern on the three issues. It also became clear that there is little information available to farmers regarding the biological leap that GE has made in the development of transgenic seeds and its ongoing ramifications, especially for small farmers.

Signature Campaigns

PKMT and Roots for Equity carried out a signature campaign against Bt Cotton in the early part of 2011. Various information-sharing events were held in small town markets, villages, and government schools in five districts of Sindh, and two districts of Punjab. There was consistent feedback that Bt Cotton shows splendid results. Farmers or youth had no information on the quantum leap that has been made in the context of breeding differences between high yielding varieties and transgenic seed. All farmers believed that Bt Cotton seed was just another variety of cotton seed. In other words, they were unaware of the biological difference between conventional and transgenic seeds and the genetic tampering at play. This lack of information is a clear indication of imperialist control of agrochemical TNCs and the collusion of various elite classes and sectors in the country, including academia, industry, and the feudal class.

Awareness Raising and Organizing: PKMT, Political Education, and Food Sovereignty Modules

Roots for Equity has been working on antiglobalization issues since its inception in 1997. Based on its work with landless farmers in lower Sindh, many of whom were Hindu minorities, the organization came to two key realizations: First, working within one province could not really lead to any real change in society; and second, there was no peasant platform that represented the issues of the most marginalized of the small and landless farmers. Therefore, organizing farmers was a pointless task unless they were able to represent themselves through a specific platform. Based on this learning, Roots for Equity implemented a national political program for small and landless farmers. The basic idea was to bring farmers under the platform of food sovereignty, a concept that was first encouraged by La Via Campesina, an international farmers' organization. Much of the political and educational material was based on Food Sovereignty Modules developed by People's Coalition on Food Sovereignty and Pesticide Action Network Asia Pacific (Rosario-Malonzo, 2006), and Asia Pacific Forum on Women's Law and Development (APWLD) (Sayeed & Pasimio, 2006). These modules were written in English and were translated into Urdu (Sayeed & Pasimio, 2007; Rosario-Malonzo, 2007). A national alliance called Pakistan Kissan Mazdoor Tehreek (PKMT) was formed and it has been actively advocating against Green Revolution technologies, especially chemical inputs, GE seeds, and land grabbing, and advocating for sustainable agriculture and for the development of traditional seeds banks.

The Food Sovereignty Module for Women produced by APWLD was a collaborative effort of support organizations for farmers and fishers across five countries from South and Southeast Asia. These organizations were working with women fisher folk, small and landless farmers, and other subsectors involved in food and agriculture related production. APWLD produced this manual to help organize and mobilize the grassroots being impacted by the World Trade Organization (WTO) and its neoliberal agreements. However, WTO agreements are written in technical language and in English. Much of the discourse is also in mainstream languages, which are not necessarily read, spoken, or understood by village communities. So the task was to present the technical details and the political debate to the grassroots across Asia. The manual was aimed at literate women activists at the grassroots who could use the modules for their organizing work in the villages. The 'master' version of the module was produced in English, the lingua franca among women across Asia, and it was initially translated into five languages and later into three more. Urdu was among these languages since Roots for Equity was part of the group responsible for the development and writing of the module.

There were many issues that needed to be addressed in developing the module. Language was of course one of them. Another issue was making sure that the modules, which are used by rural activists and created for rural communities, would not be too heavily dependent on the written word. The solution was to use many graphic and pictorial representations addressing significant topics.

Three sub-modules were developed around two to three educational sessions. Each session is based on specific objectives and possible activities. They also include guiding questions and a possible concluding synthesis. In addition, each session provides simple reading material as well as numerous visual representations pertaining to the session topics. The modules covered four main areas: (i) a rural woman's everyday life, including her social and economic life; (ii) various internal and external actors and factors affecting her social, economic, and political life, with emphasis on the current globalization policies and politics; (iii) the history of rural women's lives, with emphasis on the colonial background of the countries and its impact on the lives of rural women and their responses historically; and finally (iv) rural women's present day struggles to achieve food sovereignty.

The People's Coalition on Food Sovereignty developed another critical manual for organizing and mobilizing rural communities across Asia. This module is also based on four subsections: (i) the socioeconomic and political framework of the food sovereignty debate in the context of the rural people; and (ii) a detailed outline for food sovereignty policy development. This section of the manual provides specific policy directed inputs for agriculture and food production, consumption, health and nutrition, and food sovereignty demands in the context of natural disasters; (iii) policy advocacy targets for people's food sovereignty; and (iv) a guide for building policy advocacy campaigns by people's organizations.

Roots for Equity has also translated this module into Urdu. This organization developed a political education curriculum based on the input from these two manuals. This curriculum combines global, regional, and national colonial history; post colonial state-led agricultural development policies and programs; people's analyses of the socioeconomic and political situations of their own lives; and options for fighting their way out of current multiple crises, including the steady decline of decent livelihood, mounting hunger and deprivation, and the overwhelming impact of climate change.

The basic blueprint of the manuals was immensely useful in creating a framework for discussion in rural communities. These were guided with audio-visual materials, including specially produced flashcards that reflect the socioeconomic realities of people in rural communities. The connections to the colonial past, especially in the context of present day feudalism, and now the imposition of imperialist corporate agriculture were clearly etched out. The very poor quality of formal education in rural communities was a constant hurdle as rural communities have little historical and geographical knowledge. Though these were difficult barriers to bridge, they were not necessarily insurmountable thanks to visual aid tools that people could relate to. For instance, the geopolitical mapping of colonial powers and its continuation and linkage to the current imperialist nations was easy to show on a globe map.

The most critical point of analysis in the discussions concerned the impact of the Green Revolution on the lives of small and landless peasants. The economics of present day agricultural production and dependence on agrochemical TNCs were the easiest issues for farmers to grasp and the modules provided them with tools for analyzing the impact of the WTO and its agreements.

The quick affiliation of farmers with the analysis being presented and specifically against the Green Revolution, is indicative of the real hardship that farmers are facing, especially in the aftermath of the food price increases in 2008 and 2011. The inability of small farmers to buy external inputs such as urea, potassium, and nitrates is one reason that farmers are willing to join a platform such as PKMT. Farmers are actively seeking for alternatives that would set them free from the 'bondage' of urea and Di-ammonium Phosphate (DAP). For every acre of land, farmers need Rs 9,000 (100USD) worth of urea and DAP for profitable yields of wheat. However, the land now 'requires' these fertilizers and agricultural production has become fertilizer-dependent; yet the extremely high cost of these chemical fertilizers is driving farmers to debt, hunger, and poverty, resulting in increased migration from their lands to urban areas as well to foreign countries in search of a decent livelihood.

Another fertile ground for political mobilizing of communities concerns the impact of feudal structures and practices on rural livelihoods. However, it was easier to organize and mobilize peasants on issues around corporate agriculture than feudalism, as the latter is a current class force that would retaliate immediately against popular mass action. This has been a core reason that farmer alliances in general, and PKMT in particular, have been much more active with respect to seed-based politics than on issues related to land reforms and land grabbing.

Production-based success stories that appear in the news with respect to Bt Cotton (e.g., Syed, 2011) are a matter of serious concern for those campaigning against genetically engineered seeds and crops. And now with the approval of field trials for GM corn, a wider and more intense response is even more likely. The obvious economic prosperity associated with GE seeds has made the work of social and political activists and social movements very difficult. While rich farmers are able to show stunning profits, there are countless stories of small and landless farmers who are victims of debt encouraged by the high prices of inorganic fertilizers and increasing food prices, all phenomena that receive little official publicity.

Landless farmers are being forced to work for increasingly meager wages and they face evictions, or other more exploitative threats, if they try to resist their decreasing wages. This is especially the case for farmers who are organizing themselves, for example, as PKMT members. For instance, a small Hindu village in Tando Mohammad Khan with many PKMT members worked to get a primary school approved for their village; however, the local landlord has been able to get a stay order for the school. The entire village is now fighting and resisting the landlord's attempt to put a stop to the school; consequently, they face the constant pressure of eviction. Such incidences are increasingly becoming the norm due to increasing pressures on land use and landlords' rebuttal of any form of political organizing of the landless for land.

The primary learning that Roots for Equity gained through the signature campaign was that a moral discussion has far more immediate impact on the recognition of issues around GE than other aspects, such as the monopoly control of seeds by TNCs, or even potential health impact of GE seeds. The village-based discussion sessions on GE, with particular emphasis on Bt Cotton, yielded three different forms of learning. First, farmers were particularly concerned about the moral dimensions of GE. In one village in Janpur, Rajanpur district, farmers gave up sowing Bt Cotton entirely based on the moral issues related to using transgenic seeds. Follow-up visits in the past months (November 2010 to August 2011) have shown their determination not to go back to Bt Cotton. Second, there is a dilemma related to using religion as a basis for changing societal values since similar values have proven to be very anti-people in the context of religious minorities and for women's space in society. The norms of an already negligible secular culture are further eroded when a religious value argument is emphasized. Finally, neither the media nor national academia is providing information on three critical aspects of transgenic crops: (i) ecological harm; (ii) moral values embedded in the transgenic organism; and (iii) intellectual property over living organisms and the total appropriation over seed ownership by agrochemical TNCs. The bulk of this responsibility has fallen to social movements and NGO activists that are trying to raise these issues in both urban and rural sectors and in national academia. Also, given the rigid conservative religious base of Pakistani society, religious forces have also failed to engage in the debate.

These points of fragmentation and division are of critical concern to social movements as well as social and political activists. It is ironic that although corporate propaganda has no qualms in using patriarchy and other religious norms in advancing its products into the rural economic systems and cultural norms, a more people-oriented approach based on genuine democracy makes the path of social and political activists much more difficult.

Concluding Reflections

There is a critical need to deepen the political and cultural discourse on the so-called genetic revolution to be able to counter the increasing penetration of GM seeds in Third World agriculture. The losses faced by rural societies and the ecological harm caused by the Green Revolution and TNC-led capitalist agriculture have escalated poverty and hunger in the Third World. The ecological crisis is now rocking these communities further, as witnessed in two recent and recurrent massive floods in Pakistan. However, the panacea offered is still through a northern capitalist science.

Social movements will need to utilize various streams of engagement to enable sociopolitical change in relation to rural agriculture. Apart from political organizing of small and landless farmers, it is critical to encourage, develop, and implement traditional sustainable agricultural systems. Much of this science and art is lost to the current farming community and there is deep distrust and skepticism attached to adopting traditional agricultural practices. Roots for Equity, in its learning through working with PKMT, has come to the realization that farmers do engage these concerns on political/moral and technical platforms. This ensures a reasonable livelihood and food security for themselves and their families. For successful engagement with farmers, both of these aspects have to be addressed. A viable model of sustainable agriculture would not only utilize more productive seeds but also employ organic fertilizers to improve yields.

These learnings are gleaned from the various positions that have been advocated by the PKMT platform. Different members of PKMT tend to take different positions and interestingly they all fall in the sphere of food sovereignty. Farmers tend to advocate for different positions based on their own realities. Landless and small farmers, who are facing evictions either due to landlord-directed evictions or land grabbing, have come to understand the critical importance of organizing themselves as well as aligning with all chapters of PKMT to seek active solidarity and build alliances.

Others, especially those who are reeling under the skyrocketing agriculture input prices are seeking practical measures to reduce their production costs and move toward more sustainable production systems. Many at the PKMT mass meetings have voiced the importance of reviving traditional and more nutritious foods.

In short, there is now a slow and gradual understanding of the neocolonial hold that agrochemical TNCs and other capitalist forces have over the farmlands in Pakistan, aided and abetted by the feudal and bureaucracy elite of Pakistan. There is no doubt that only multiple levels of interventions, such as those identified in this chapter, will need to be engaged in order to resist, if not break the hold of the globalization of the TNC led agro-industrial model. These would include critical life style changes, which would regenerate traditional food intake practices and create resistance to and boycott of corporate foodstuffs. The ability to grow and exchange local traditional seeds, store and increase organic manure and fertilizers, and increase livestock are other forms of necessary and ongoing silent resistance to corporate dominance. Finally, strong political demands for land reforms, resisting land grabbing through constant street demonstrations and other forms of mass action are all necessary foundations for overcoming the collusion of the local, national, and global elite and the neoliberal globalization of agriculture and rural life.

Notes

1. Roots for Equity is an NGO that was formed in 1997. It is committed to highlighting the plight of the most vulnerable, marginalized communities which include religious minorities, women, and children in the rural and urban sectors, as well as providing interventions which could help them to increase their economic, social, and political rights to demand a standard of living considered appropriate by the International Human Rights Charter.
2. It is important to note that the bulk of the work for cooking such vast quantities of daily and stored food fell on women in the household. This additional contribution of women to the household budget as well as nutritionist needs not only to be acknowledged but also has a complex dimension in the context of women being pushed in the background and being given no recognition for their web of contributions in society.

References

Barber, S. (1974). *The United States aid to Pakistan: A case study of the influence of the donor country on the domestic and foreign policies of the recipient.* Karachi: Pakistan Institute of International Affairs.

Bokhari, A. (2011, June 23). Field trials of genetically modified corn. *The Daily Dawn.* Retrieved from, http://www.dawn.com/2011/06/20/field-trials-of-genetically-modified-corn.html

Islam, S. (2011, December 29). Agricultural university to set up exhibition zone. *Express Tribune.* Retrieved from, http://tribune.com.pk/story/313368/agricultural-university-to-set-up-exhibition-zone/

Kibria, G. (1998). *Technology acquisition in Pakistan: Story of a failed privileged class and a successful working class.* Karachi: City Press.

Kux, D. (2001). *The United States and Pakistan 1947–2000: Disenchanted Allies.* Karachi: Oxford University Press.

Naqvi, S. N. H., Khan, M. H., Chaudhary, M. G. (Eds.) (1987). *Land reforms in Pakistan: A historical perspective.* Islamabad: Pakistan Institute of Development Economics.

Peekhaus, W. (2010). The neoliberal university and agricultural biotechnology: Reports from the field. *Bulletin of Science Technology & Society, 30*(6), 415–429.

Pritchard, B. (2005). Implementing and maintaining neoliberal agriculture in Australia, Part II: Strategies for securing neoliberalism. *International Journal of Sociology and Agriculture and Food, 13*(2), 14p. Retrieved from, http://www.ijsaf.org/archive/13/2/pritchard2.pdf

Rosario-Malonzo, Jennifer Del (2006). *Modules on food sovereignty.* People's Coalition on Food Sovereignty and Pesticide Action Network Asia Pacific.

Rosario-Malonzo, Jennifer Del (2007). *Tarbiyati Kitabcha: Haq-e-khud iradiyat barae khurak.* [Modules on food sovereignty]. Karachi: Roots for Equity.

Sayeed, A. T. & Pasimio, J. (Eds.) (2006). *Women and food sovereignty kit.* Chiang Mai, Thailand: Asia Pacific Forum on Women Law and Development.

Sayeed, A. T. & Pasimio, J. (Eds.) (2007). *Aurat aur khorak ki khud mukhtari per aik tarbiyati kitab.* [Food sovereignty module for women]. Karachi: Roots for Equity.

Stavrianos, L. S. (1981). *Global rift: The Third World comes of age.* New York, NY: William Morrow and Company, Inc.

Syed, R. (2011, December 20). Cotton crop season 2011–12 to achieve more than 15m bales. *Daily Times.* Retrieved from, http://www.dailytimes.com.pk/default.asp?page= 2011%5C12%5C20%5Cstory_20-12-2011_pg5_8

The News. (2011, June 16). Foreign company speaks on GM corn field trials, *The News.* Retrieved from, http://www.thenews.com.pk/TodaysPrintDetail.aspx?ID= 6758&Cat= 13

Zafar, I. (2011). Golden jubilee celebrations: Changing mindset and building capacity for innovation and commercialization. Retrieved from, http://www.uaf.edu.pk/golden_jubilee/events/111029-2.html

CHAPTER 12

Globalizing Capitalism: Accumulation by Dispossession and the Specter of Subaltern Social Movement (SSM) Activism and Anticolonial Pedagogies in Rural India[1]

Dip Kapoor

Peasant movements like Chipko (northern India) and peasant protests reveal how policies of 'economic development' or 'modernization' formulated at the top levels of states, corporations, and international financial institutions are often experienced by peasants, rural women, and laborers—as exploitation. In the strategies of economic development, indigenous peoples, landless peasants, and women are expected to bear the brunt of industrialization; disease, social unrest, food insecurity, and land hunger testify to the impact of this process

(Guha, 1990, pp. 195–196)

There is no understanding of communities as the subjects of dislocation or ways of life that are destroyed. There is an abyss of incomprehension on the part of Indian elites toward rural and tribal communities. Ripping them out from lands that they have occupied for generations and transplanting them overnight into an alien setting (which is the best they can expect) is understood as rehabilitation and liberation from their backward ways of life.

(Menon & Nigam, 2007, pp. 72–73)

Thus the land question has become one of defending the right of peasants, including tribal peoples, to their land and livelihoods. Not only can it never be separated from the fight against imperialist globalization, this fight is a necessary condition for any advance on the land question. It is shameful that no resistance has been articulated by the liberal intelligentsia and political movements to the modification of ceiling laws or the permission for nonagriculturalists to acquire land, all for the benefit of corporations.

(Patnaik & Moyo, 2011, pp. 51–52)

Introduction

The Lok Adhikar Manch (LAM) (see Table 12.1) (Kapoor, 2011a, pp. 132–34) is a "trans-local alliance" (Da Costa, 2007, p. 315) of 13 SSM groups or a state/provincially based network in rural Orissa, India, that has been an emergent and growing formation since the lead movements initiated the process in the late 1990s. LAM's Manifesto states,

> At this crucial juncture, we resolve to work together to protect ourselves, our interests, our natural bases [*prakrutik adhar*] and fight against any unjust appropriation of our natural habitations by commercial and state development interests. The manner in which industrialization is taking place [especially mining and dam projects], displacing the sons and daughters of the soil, destroying our resource and life base, we collectively oppose it and resolve to stand together to oppose it in the future. We have nothing to gain from liberalization [*mukto bojaro*], privatization [*ghoroi korono*], and globalization [*jagothi korono*], which are talked about today. We want to live the way we know how to live among our forests, streams, hills and mountains and water bodies with our culture, traditions and whatever that is good in our society intact.

(LAM statement, fieldnotes, April 2009)

The above statement and formations like LAM can be better appreciated when contextualized in relation to the historical and current processes of *primitive accumulation* or the core elements of the process by which noncapitalist social formations are transformed into capitalist ones (e.g., land enclosures that dispossess Adivasis,[2] Dalits, and peasants—subalterns—and turn land into private property and capital) (Glassman, 2006) or *accumulation by dispossession* (Harvey, 2003). These processes have been gathering momentum in the state of Orissa and in the mineral-rich central-eastern region of India (including neighboring Chattisgarh, Jharkhand, and West Bengal and related movements at Singur and Nandigram or Jagdalpur) after the neoliberal turn (1991) in the Indian economy (Neeraj, 2007; Sanyal, 2010).

While Adivasis constitute 8 percent of the Indian population (or 80 million of more people belonging to some 612 Scheduled Tribes), they account for 40 percent of development displaced persons (DDP) (Rajagopal, 2003). In the state of Orissa (the context of the research base for this chapter), which is home to 62 groups numbering eight million or more people, where Adivasis make up 22 percent of the population, they account for 42 percent of DDPs (Fernandes, 2006; Hussain, 2008). According to some estimates, dams, mining, industries, and parks have displaced 21.3 million people between 1951–1990 (prior to the neoliberal turn and the establishment of Special Economic Zones, or SEZs, that have accelerated this process), of which 40 percent were Adivasi and 20 percent were Dalit (Scheduled Caste) peoples (Nag, 2001). The government of India acknowledged 15.5 million displaced persons when it finally drafted a national rehabilitation policy in 1994, of which 75 percent are/were still awaiting 'rehabilitation' (Bharati, 1999). Policies pursued by the CPI(M)-led Left Front (LF) government in West Bengal (who were unseated in the last election) have become virtually indistinguishable from those of other parties committed to the neoliberal agenda (Menon & Nigam, 2007) and according to one calculation, the acquisition of some 120,000 acres over the past five years of land reforms in the state has been accompanied by an increase of 2.5 million landless peasants (Banerjee, 2006). Such rural dispossession compels migration to already dense urban centers, leading to the proliferation of a 'planet of slums' (Davis, 2006) where subalterns are again compelled to take on urban-based struggles for space and livelihood (Harvey, 2009; Mookerjea, 2011).

This chapter considers these processes of primitive accumulation or accumulation by dispossession (capitalist colonizations) of Adivasis (original dwellers/Scheduled Tribes), Dalits (Scheduled Castes/the downtrodden) and landless peasants (together referenced as *subaltern* classes/groups in *political society*) in the state of Orissa, India as a consequence of the post-1991 neoliberal turn and the expansion of mining and agro/industrial development activities by a corporatized states and trans/national corporations. The simultaneous growth of subaltern social movement organizing and activism (trans/local) in the state is mapped as are the contours of an anticolonial pedagogy in relation to SSM mobilizations; an education that has been integral to shaping, sustaining and scaling up these dis/organized movements, contributing toward a *political society* anticolonial politics for material and cultural space by subaltern classes and communities in rural and forested regions. This discussion and related postulations/observations are based on episodic funded research engagements with subaltern social movement/struggle formations (like LAM and the Adivasi-Dalit Ektha Abhijan or ADEA, a 120 village region in South Orissa including some 20,000 Kondh Adivasi and Panos/Dalits member participants) between 2006 and 2010 in India on the eastern seaboard, a forested/rural and hilly region (eastern ghats) that is 130 kilometers away from the Gopalpur coast line (Kapoor, 2009b).

Contexts of Dispossession and SSM Formations in Political Society[3]

World systems theorists have long recognized that the history of capitalism begins with the transformation of land rights (Wallerstein, 2012). The modern concept of land rights denotes the establishment of bourgeois land rights in the countryside (leading to export-led commercial agriculture) and in the city (real estate). The massive social transformations that this has involved over centuries of struggles for and against the establishment of bourgeois property rights in land and it's usage has been considered in relation to a complex global history of the commodification of land in four historical periods (primitive accumulation; colonialism; developmentalism; and globalization) in terms of five features which include "the increasing privatization of the earth's surface through dispossession and displacement of peasants and indigenous populations" and "the destruction of nonmarket access to food and self-sustenance and creation of a mobile global proletariat that is massively concentrated in the urban centers of the world economy" (often living under a regime of forced underconsumption) (Araghi, 2010; Araghi & Karides, 2012, p. 1). Speaking to the current period of "neoliberal globalization," they observe that this is a period that

> has witnessed a vast expansion of bourgeois land rights at the expense of small/partial landholder remnants of the developmentalist era on the one hand and rise of powerful 'counter enclosure movements' on the other. Currently, a global land grab unprecedented since colonial times is underway as speculative investors—who now regard 'food as gold'—are acquiring millions of hectares of land in the global South (p. 3).

These land grabs often involve the eviction of local producers and forced expropriations under the rubric of confronting the global food and energy crisis (McMichael, 2012). According to an Oxfam study (2011), in developing countries, as many as 227 million hectares of land—an area the size of Western Europe—has been sold or leased since 2001, mostly to international investors with a bulk of these taking place over the past two years. In the African context alone, 125 million acres (roughly the equivalent of Sweden) have been grabbed by rich countries for outsourcing agriculture production to supply food to supermarkets in the West and to an emerging trans/national consumer elite in Asia the Gulf and pockets in Africa (Shivji, 2011).

Speaking to the Indian context, economist Utsa Patnaik suggests that "corporate subjugation of peasant production is nothing but the imperialist domination of our peasantry for the purposes of export production and it pauperizes the peasantry and labour" (2011, p. 51). According to Patnaik's analysis, giant corporations are increasingly entering Indian agriculture (made possible by liberalization of the sector) and tying peasants to contracts under debt by way of advances of high-tech genetically modified (GM) seeds and inputs (see the preceding chapter by *Azra Talat Sayeed* concerning same in Pakistan). The terms of the contracts "grind peasants down to subhuman levels of living because they ruthlessly seek to maximize corporate profits in a global commodities market where prices remain unpredictable" (p. 51). The end result has been the post 1998 phenomenon of indebtedness-driven mass peasant suicides, some thing that has not happened in India prior to 1991, a toll that has reached 198,000 recorded farmer suicides between 1998 and 2008, 60,000 being more clearly attributed to being debt driven (Patnaik & Moyo, 2011).

The historical roots of these processes in India go back to the days of British colonialism in the 1880s and the de-tribalizaion and de-peasantization or restrictions of tribal/subaltern rights over land and forests through the various Indian Forest Rights Acts for instance, wherein "British colonialism distorted the land structure, ecology, forest resources and flora and fauna with grave implications for the Adivasis" (Behura & Panigrahi, 2006, p. 35), reducing them to encroachers on their own territories. This trend continues into the postindependence period via the Forest Policy of 1952, the Forest Conservation Act (1980) and the (2006) version which is now being critiqued after the initial euphoria around same (Ramdas, 2009), the Wild Life Protection Act (1972), and the Land Acquisition Act whereby eviction for an undefined larger public interest has been regularized (in recognition of the *eminent domain* power of the state). Some 500,000 people have been displaced by state-corporate development in Orissa between 1951 and 1995 (Behura & Panigrahi, 2006). The neoliberal turn has exacerbated this trend through policies promoting reservation; leasing of state land to industrialists (the intended creation of over 300 Special Economic Zones/SEZs or free zones is the latest in an unfolding pattern of state-corporate industrial land grabs, with invasive implications for rural subalterns/Adivasi in Orissa given that the state boasts 70 percent of India's bauxite reserves located mostly in Scheduled Areas/allegedly protected areas for Adivasi worth more than twice India's GDP at 2004 prices); the activation of a Wild Life Protection Act that defines the tribal as the enemy of ecology; and demarcation of land/forests for sanctuaries and national parks that exclude tribals (Pimple & Sethi, 2005).

For instance, under the Indian Forest Act (1927) and the Forest Conservation Act (1980), cultivable lands that existed prior to both Acts are being categorized as encroachment areas. As a result of this, for example, 148,000 people (mainly Adivasi) occupying 184,000 hectares of land in forest areas in the state of Madhya Pradesh suddenly became encroachers on 24 October 1980 and this liable to eviction (ACHR, 2005). Even under the current and relatively more subaltern-friendly Forest Rights Act (FRA) of 2006, production for food (subsistence) as opposed to commercial/market production for exports while laboring for corporate-controlled agriculture, is being interpreted by Forest Departments as encroachment and is being met with considerable aggression to evict Adivasi/subalterns from their lands across the country (see World Rainforest Movement bulletin 135, October 2008, for a disturbing analysis of atrocities committed by state agents against Adivasi/Dalit women, while allegedly implementing the FRA). In Orissa alone forest diversion (state euphemism for industrial/development land grabs) in the neoliberal era has doubled between 1991 and 2004, while 26 percent of forest land cleared since 1980 has been after the introduction of the FRA (2006) (Wani & Kothari, 2008). Despite Constitutional provisions in the 5th and 6th Schedules that recognize tribal ownership rights over land and forests in Scheduled/Protected Areas (reaffirmed in the FRA, 2006), "people do not have the right to question the decision of the government on forceable evictions" (ACHR, 2005, p. 9).

When it comes to mining development alone, under the new National Mining Policy (2006) the corporatized-state has leased one billion tons (of India's estimated 1.6 billion) of bauxite to trans/national corporations through MOUs (Memorandums of Understanding) (Indian People's Tribunal on Environment and Human Rights [IPTEHR], 2006). The single largest foreign direct investment (FDI) in Indian commercial history is in coal and iron in the state of Orissa (by Posco Ltd. of South Korea, with Citibank as a major shareholder), a US$12 billion project that is being held up by betel leaf farmers and the *Posco Pratirodh Manch,* which includes significant Adivasi/Dalit participation [for more on mining development, see Felix Padel and Samarendra Das, 2010, who provide a detailed historical and contemporary look at trans/national state-corporate mining encroachments (specifically bauxite/Aluminium) and related dam development and its ecological, cultural and political-economic ramifications for subalterns and Adivasi in particular and related subaltern resistances, in Orissa in their magnum opus, *Out of this Earth: East India Adivasis and the Aluminium Cartel*).

Despite these repeated postcolonial colonizations, SSM assertions continue to "deflect globalizations reinvention of colonial processes" while being "within, besides and against colonization" (Barker, 2005, p. 20) and "continuing to exist vigorously and even develop new forms" (Ludden, 2005, p. 100). SSM struggles in India today clearly continue to proliferate (Baviskar, 2005; Da Costa, 2007; Ghosh, 2006; McMichael, 2010; Menon & Nigam, 2007; Mookerjea, 2010, 2011; Oliver-Smith, 2010; Padel & Das, 2010; Rajagopal, 2003) in conjunction with the penetrations of a colonial trans/national capitalist development (agricultural and industrial). SSMs are distinguished from other social movement formations (Kapoor, 2009c) along several dimensions, including for instance, their possible socio-cartographic location in political society (see end note 3) or the fact that these agents are motivated by direct and immediate material impacts of colonial developmentalist and globalist displacements and dispossession from land, water and forests and are being subsequently subjected to the loss of the means to produce their material existence and all the related implications for subaltern cultures/ways and modes of meaning making too. SSMs engaged in an anticolonial politics that seeks to address these incursions rely on pedagogies of mobilization, which imbue education with political value (see *Da Costa's* chapter in this collection around same).

Anticolonial Pedagogies and SSM Mobilizations

Relatively well-publicized political society SSMs and resistance to dispossession in the eastern regions include those at Singur (Bengal), Nandigram (Bengal), Lalgarh (Bengal), Kashipur (Orissa), Lanjigarh (Orissa), Kalinganagar (Orissa), Earasama/Dhinkia (Orissa), Keonjhar (Orissa), Jagdalpur (Chattisgarh), and so on, against a growing number of state-corporate trans/national industrial ventures involving various partners at different points in time, including TATA, Jindal, Birla, Ambani, Mittal, Vedanta, Posco, Salim, Norsk Hydro, ALCAN etc. and several lesser known or documented subaltern resistances that are scaling up their actions through a trans-local coalitional politics (such as LAM, Table 12.1) (Kapoor, 2011a, pp. 132–34).

SSM learning (Kapoor, 2007; 2009a) is integral for initial and ongoing framing of movement purpose/directionality, collective motivation, organizational solidarity/building, movement expansion, action and pacification/healing in times of loss, for example, in response to several experiences with state-corporate violence as in the case of the Kalinganagar January 2nd, 2006 repression where 20 Adivasi died and 3 bodies were returned to the community minus their hands post anti-TATA demonstrations (see www.countercurrents.org/ People's version of Kalinganagar firing, January 6, 2006) and for movement continuity (enabling learning experiences).

Table 12.1 Lok Adhikar Manch (LAM)

Movement participant (year established)	Location/operational area	Social groups engaged	Key issues being addressed
1. Kalinga Matchyajivi Sangathana (Kalinga fisher people's organization) (early 1980s)	Gopalpur-on-sea (center) including coastal Orissa, from Gopalpur in Ganjam district to Chandrabhaga and Astaranga coast in Puri district	Fisher people (mainly Dalits) originally from the state of Andhra Pradesh called Nolias and Orissa state fisher people or Keuta/Kaivartas	• Trawler fishing, fish stock depletion and enforcement of coastal regulations/zones (Trans/national Corporate—TNC—investments) • Occupation of coastal land by defense installations (e.g., missile bases) • Hotel/tourism industry developments along coast (TNC investment) • Special economic zones (SEZ) and major port projects for mining exports (TNC investment) • Pollution of beaches and oceans • Displacement of fisher communities related to such developments
2. Prakritik Sampad Suraksha Parishad (PSSP) (late 1980s)	Kashipur, Lakhimpur, Dasmantpur and adjacent blocks in Rayagada district of Orissa Approximately 200 movement villages	Adivasis including Jhodias, Kondhs and Parajas and Pano/Domb Dalits	• Bauxite mining (alumina) (TNC investments) • Industrialization, deforestation and land alienation/ displacement • Peoples rights over "their own ways and systems"
3. Jana Suraksha Manch (2007)	Adava region of Mohana block, Gajapati district including sixty or more villages	Saura and Kondh Adivasis and Panos (Dalits)	• Government/local corruption • Police brutality/atrocities • Deforestation and plantation agriculture (NC investment)

4. Adivasi Dalit Adhikar Sangathan (2000)	Jaleswar, Bhograi and Bosta blocks in Balasore district and Boisinga and Rasagovindpur blocks in Mayurbhanj including over 100 villages	Dalits, Adivasis, fisher people and Other Backward Castes (OBCs)	• Dalit and Adivasi land rights and land alienation • Industrialization, port development and displacement of traditional fisher people (TNC investment)
5. Adivasi-Dalit Ekta Abhiyan (2000)	Twenty panchayats in Gajapati and Kandhmal districts including 200 plus villages (population of about 50,000)	Kondh and Saura Adivasis, Panos (Dalits) and OBCs	• Land and forest rights • Food • Sovereignty/plantation agriculture **(NC investment)** • Industrialization, modernization and protection of indigenous ways and systems • Communal harmony • Development of people's coalitions/forums (no state, NGO, corporate, "outsider," upper/middle castes participants)
6. Indravati Vistapita Lokmanch (late 1990s)	Thirty villages in the district of Nabarangapur	Several Adivasi, Dalit and OBC communities	• Dam displacement (Indravati irrigation and hydro-electric project) **(NC investment)** • Land and forest rights • Resettlement, rehabilitation and compensation for development displaced peoples (DDPs) • Industrialization and modern development and protection of peoples ways

Table 12.1 (Continued)

Movement participant (year established)	Location/operational area	Social groups engaged	Key issues being addressed
7. Orissa Adivasi Manch (1993–1994)	State level forum with an all-Orissa presence (all districts) with regional units in Keonjhar and Rayagada districts and district level units in each district	Well over forty different Adivasi communities	• Adivasi rights in the state • Tribal self rule, forest and land rights and industrialization (SEZs) (TNC investments)
8. Anchalik Janasuraksha Sangathan (2008)	Kidting, Mohana block of Gajapati district including some twenty villages	Kondh and Saura Adivasis and Panos (Dalits)	• Land and forest rights • Conflict resolution and communal harmony between Adivasis and Dalits over land and forest issues
9. Dalit Adivasi Bahujana Initiatives (DABI) (2000)	Five blocks in the Kandhmal district with ten participating local movements (networks)	Kondh Adivasis, Panos (Dalits) and OBCs	• Land and forest rights • Food sovereignty and livelihood issues • Communal harmony
10. Uppara Kolab Basachyuta Mahasangh (late 1990s)	Umerkote block, Koraput district (includes a thirty village population base displaced by the upper Kolab hydroelectric and irrigation reservoir)	Paraja Adivasis, Panos and Malis Dalits and OBCs	• Displacement due to the upper Kolab hydro-electricity and irrigation reservoir (NC investment) • Compensation, rehabilitation and basic amenities for DDP's • Land and forest rights

11. Jeevan Jivika Suraksha Sangathan (2006)	Three panchayats in the border areas of Kandhmal and Gajapati districts including fifty or more villages with a population of 12,000 people	Kondhs and Saura Adivasis and Panos (Dalits) and OBCs	• Land and forest rights/issues • Communal harmony • Food sovereignty and livelihood issues
12. Adivasi Pachua Dalit Adhikar Manch (APDAM) (2000)	Kalinga Nagar industrial belt in Jajpur district (twenty-five or more villages, along with several participants in the Kalinganagar township area)	Adivasis, Dalits and OBCs	• Industrialization and displacement (TNC investment) • Land and forest rights • Compensation and rehabilitation • Police atrocities/brutality • Protection of Adivasi-Dalit ways and forest-based cultures and community
13. Janajati Yuva Sangathan (2008)	Baliapal and Chandanesar block in Balasore district including thirty-two coastal villages being affected by mega port development (part of SEZ scheme).	Dalit fisher communities and OBCs.	• SEZs (TNC investments) • Industrialization and displacement • Land alienation and marine rights of traditional fisher communities

Kapoor (2011a, pp. 132–34).

Subaltern (mainly Adivasi/Dalit in the ADEA region or primary location for the research in South Orissa) social movement learning is an act of socio-spiritual relationship and solidarity, co-construction, constant connectivity (e.g., unity of time; unity of space; unity of lives/being; spirituality-political economy-culture-place-history; storying-narrative-witness-testimony-song-poetry-dance-music-ritual-feasting-grieving), consensus, deferrals (for settling outstanding disagreements), mutual recognition and strategizing/planning. The following attempt to provide a brief sense of SSM anticolonial learning/pedagogies is based on fieldnotes from several episodic engagements as a participant/observer and on occasion, participatory actor (Kapoor, 2009b) in ADEA village gatherings, regional and central level meetings and/or LAM congresses or SSM activism between 2006 and 2010. For heuristic purposes and brevity, dynamic processes and events are being distilled into four dimensions pertaining to anticolonial learning/pedagogies relevant to understanding movement learning – social action/politics connectivity in contexts of dispossession, a process that has been escalating since the neoliberal turn in 1991.

1. Our Ways Learning: Unities of Time-Space-Being and Colonial Relations

An elderly Kondh Adivasi woman sings (with a stringed instrument, *sarangi*), accompanied by three younger ladies:

> In olden times oh brothers and oh sisters
> In the time of the British rule, the Britishers used our grandparents like servants
>   and beat them severely to make them work
> During that period oh brothers and sisters, the revenue collectors came and took
>   the measurement of our lands and paddy fields
> They said, "you will be given land, paddy fields and dry land"
> We went to work even when we did not have anything to eat
> But when the work was done
> Our land, our paddy fields and dry land were transferred to the rich people and the
>   big people, the outsiders
> From then we lost our way, from then we are hopeless

An elderly man explains,

> The plain land has been taken away (fertile valley bottoms) and whatever is left has been marked by the *sarkar* (government) as grazing land or military land. The *sarkar* has hundreds of ways to reserve land for itself and keep people away. The flat land is no longer accessible to us. We the Adivasis, have access only to hilly land for cultivation to sustain us (stony land, sloping, and often degraded/waste land). The British prospered on our backs as their cultivators

and today they still exploit us like the British did by taking away our land. We are people of the land and forest and without them we are nothing. We sing this song because this is an expression of our *sangharsh* (struggle).

The song continues,

> This forest, this mountain and this land is ours
> Given by our Gods to our ancestors
> But people are destroying the forests, they are cutting the trees, they are lucking leaves and making them barren
> Is this now left as ours for name sake? How can we depend on it if everything is gone?
> Oh God of Sun (*Surjo devta*), oh Moon God (*Chandra devta*), why are you giving us sorrows? [call continues to several Gods including *Gungi* (forest Goddess), *Pahar devta* (mountain God), *Ghaso devta* (God of grass), *Dhuli devta* (God of dust), *Durga Pena* (rain God) etc.]

A Kondh woman leader explains,

> The *sarkar* (government) and their workers think that we Adivasis do not know anything and we are good for nothing, that we are weak and powerless and will not question them if they treat us unjustly. That is why they think they do not need to ask us anything before going ahead. To the government, we are of no significance (*sarkar amar prathi heyogyano karuchi*). They are selling our forests, they are selling our water and they are selling our land and may be they will sell us also.

An Adivasi leader of the ADEA adds to these explications around contemporary conceptions of the coloniality of power (and racism):

> Even today you will find there is not cultivable land available for our people because they have taken it away... They have the power of *dhana* (wealth) and *astro-shastro* (armaments). They have the power of *kruthrima ain* (of artificial laws and rules)—they created these laws just to maintain their own interests... and where we live, they call this area *adhusith* (or Adivasi-infested as in pest-infestation)... we are condemned to the life of *ananta paapi* (eternal sinners), as *colonkitha* (dirty/black/stained), as *ghruniya* (despised/hated).

An Adivasi elder, is quick to point out that despite these pressures, the value of "our ways" and must be recognized and embraced.

> Earlier all these forests and land area belonged to all the people who lived in the area. In the past, in the time of our grandparents, we (these two villages)

had one common graveyard, we had a common system of sharing (or bheda in the Saora language, in relation to sharing of fruits, benefits, forest products, meat and land/forest usage) and we had a collective contribution system to support each other. Land was not assigned to any particular person or family—it was a common claim that goes back to our ancestors. We were together in sorrows and joys. But since the government's revenue demarcation of land and forests, what belonged to all of us suddenly got divided into two moujas/areas of claim and people have started saying, "this is mine and this is mine." They (the Adivasis of the neighboring village) are now not allowing us to set foot in their mouja and they are saying that you should not cut our trees or bamboo for your use. And we are doing the same. This is not our way.

2. Critical Political-Analytical Knowledge/Learning

This type of knowledge and learning pertains to an analytical appreciation for the nature and process by which structured unequal relations of power (political-economic, cultural/racial/caste, of violence and multi-scalar sociopolitical interpolations) play out in relation to Adivasi/Dalit lived situations (e.g., the ability to read and expose the state-corporate-civil society nexus and assess its implications for political-practical purposes discussed below) (Kapoor, 2009a). For instance, in a focus group session (February, 2008) engaging 23 leaders of the ADEA, the following analysis was shared between several participants, each adding perspective to build a collective portrait of state-corporate collusions and developmental violence against Adivasis/Dalits:

> P1: The Dalit, the farmer, and fisherman are always forced to give up whatever we have, suffer and sacrifice for the sake of what they call development. Why should the government develop this country at the cost of our way of life? The government, the industrialists and their intellectuals accuse us of being obstacles in the process of development and as enemies of modernization, enemies of progress and enemies of Indian society.
>
> P2: What they mean is that we are in the way of their process of exploitation of natural resources for this development. With the help of the big companies and industrialists and multinationals, the central and state governments want to continue to exploit our natural resources to the maximum. And we know what this means for us... we have people here from Maikanch who know how the state police always act for the industrialists and their friends in government who want to see the bauxite mine go forward in Kashipur against our wishes, even if it meant shooting 3 of our brothers; we have people here from Kalinganagar... from Chilika who opposed TATA's shrimp culture... in all

these movements and struggles many people have been killed by the state and industrialist mafias.

P3: They are coming quietly to our forests and hills and in secrecy they are making plans to dig them up and destroy them (mining). Not only this, they are diverting our water to the towns for their use (dams). They are making dams and water reservoirs and our villages are submerged and we have to leave the land, leave the place and become landless and homeless. We have become silent spectators (*niravre dekhuchu*) to a repeated snatching away of our resources.

P4: It is time we seriously start to think about this destruction in the name of development... otherwise, like yesterday's children of nature, who never depended on anybody for their food security, we will have no option but to go for mass transition from self-sufficient cultivators and forest and fish gatherers to migratory labourers in far away places. After displacement we stand to lose our traditions, our culture and our own historical civilization.

P5: Who wants to go to the city to join the Oriyas and do business and open shops and be *shahari* (city/moderns) if they give you a chance or to do labour like donkeys to get one meal? Even if they teach us, we do not want to go to the cities—these are not the ways of the Adivasi. We can not leave our forests (*ame jangale chari paribo nahi*). The forest is our second home (after the huts). There is no distance between our homes and the forest. You just come out and you have everything you need... my friends and brothers, we are from the forests. That is why we use the small sticks of the *karanja* tree to brush our teeth—not tooth brushes.

In relation to NGO/civil society actors, leaders questioned the role played by NGOs in the state-corporate bid to foist development on Adivasis/Dalits. NGO tactics dissected and exposed included: (i) use of social development programs (e.g., in health or micro-credit) to bribe/soften resistance to mining projects; (ii) exploiting their role as "brokers" (between the state-corporate nexus and movements) to secure themselves; (iii) derailing movements and direct action by persuading leaders to channel their disagreements into legal avenues (recourse) which then slowed down actions and activism as the court system is inundated (plus NGOs actively delayed legal proceedings themselves); (iv) under recent Constitutional changes, decision-making authority has been shifted to the Gram Sabhas/village level and NGOs have tried to

> channel public protest aimed at the company, to this nonsense about activating and working through Gram Sabha process which is subject to all kinds of manipulations by state-corporate people. So like this they are controlling the force of the movement.

Leaders also recognized the dangers in accepting funding from NGOs given that they felt NGOs were trying to

> make us into program managers and statisticians concerned with funding accountability and the management of our people for the NGO. They expected us to work with village development committees (VDCs) run by a small group when we are engaged in an *andolan* (movement struggle) and not a donor-focused program.

3. Political-Practical Knowledge/Learning

Critical political analytical knowledge/learning informs political-practical knowledge/learning or strategic, tactical and informational learning (Kapoor, 2009a). Strategic learning refers to the knowledge and learning crucial for the development of a movement position (e.g., developing an experiential and tacit sense of why it would be beneficial to take one broad approach, such as outright anticolonial resistance to development dispossession, than another). Tactical learning refers to the development of specific ideas and learning to select from a host of possibilities in relation to specific manoeuvres that the movement organization would need to consider in relation to it's strategic orientation (e.g., choosing when to initiate or escalate pressure or stay quiet; when to use blockades, *gheraos*/encirclement, letter campaigns, rallies, *dharnas*/sit downs, etc.). Informational learning refers to the acquisition of new/emergent facts necessary to inform tactical, strategic or critical learning/analysis and usually means learning new information or outsider/alien constructs such as human rights or Constitutional provisions and other modernist categories that Adivasi/Dalits have 'bumped into'. Both, LAM and ADEA formations have prepared materials around such information to share in village gatherings, regional events and during demonstrations/political action (e.g., Scheduled Caste/Scheduled Tribe Atrocities Act or Fifth Schedule Constitutional provisions around protections for forest dwellers and Scheduled Areas vis-à-vis land/forest rights)—information that is shared in a more didactic fashion than other knowledge/learning engagements (e.g., in relation to "our ways learning").

In relation to strategic and tactical knowledge and learning, for instance, various leaders and member villages have recognized the importance of collective tactical action (e.g., preemptive land occupations) and political learning for anticolonial movement formations to address processes of accumulation by dispossession.

> P1: We developed land formulas for ourselves—we have seen what we can accomplish together. Water sources that were once defunct have now come

alive, just like we have. Through collective action we have secured house *pattas* (titles) for all hutments in our villages so that we cannot be evicted as encroachers and we are pressuring the state for land distribution and reclassification in our favor. We are giving importance to land occupation (*padar bari akthiar*) and land use (*chatriya chatri*). Before the government uses *anawadi* land to plant cashew, eucalyptus, or virtually gives the land to bauxite mining companies, we must encroach and occupy and put the land to use through our plantation activities and agricultural use.... this is like the opening of knowledge that was hidden to us for ages.

P2: When we sit together, discuss and find out proper ways together, much more is accomplished. Through collective pressure—and we have to go at them like water on stone... we get results and even the government gets afraid (*sarkar bhaiyo koruchi*) and work is done immediately (*sighro kajo kari hoichi*). We have big issues and that is why we will always need bigger unity (*bara ekta*) and a bigger federation (*sangha badha*).

P3: Most people today because of the ADEA action would challenge this idea of *bhagya* (destiny). We have to teach each other (*bujha-sujha*), explain to each and that is how education has happened and made things possible for us.... we organize workshops and gathering and have created a learning environment for all our people—I feel so happy and satisfied, I can not tell you—we have been creating a political education around land, forest and water issues and debating courses of action. We are expanding.

P4: As an activist of the ADEA I know we must continue to debate and create awareness on land and forest issues—it is a political awareness, an adult education about society (*samajik shiksha*)—a different kind of schooling perhaps?

4. Movement Motivation and Directions

Constant massaging around the central messages of the movement (purpose/aims and general direction) at various gatherings and events help to educate the broader community around the motivations behind and need for social action on a long term basis given the issues at stake. This deepens movement understanding and is part of a gradual process of foundation building that creates movement depth and width (together constituting strength) as the number of people with a better understanding of what needs doing and why can help to propel a movement further and sustain difficult political action for longer (staying power).

P1: The ADEA is there to fight collectively (*sangram*) to save (*raksha*) the forests and to protect our way of life. The ADEA is a means of collective struggle for the forest (*ame samastha mishi sangram o kariba*). Our struggle is around *khadyo, jamin, jalo, jangalo o ektha* (food, land, water, forest and unity).

P2: The government and the companies come and take away truckloads of bamboo and *pia sal*. The forests, which our ancestors nurtured (*banchaye chanti*) is getting destroyed by these *bahari ko lok* (outsiders). How can they say the Adivasis are destroying the forests when they are the ones doing this? When the Adivasi depends on the forest for their life, the *vyavasahi* (business people) and the government are destroying them for their own profit (*labho*).

P3: We are laying a claim on the government who is supposed to serve all the people in this land. We are demanding a place for ourselves—we are questioning the government and asking them to help us develop our land using our ways. ADEA's idea is that our livelihood should be protected and our traditional occupations and relationship to the land and forest be protected in the form of community control over land and forests in our areas and this is our understanding of our Constitutional rights too. There is no contradiction. Once this is understood, we can cooperate and when necessary, work with the government to take care of the land and forests. If they can help the *shaharis* (moderns/urban people) destroy the forests, then they can and should help us to protect it and listen to our story too.

P5: They are fighting against those who have everything and nothing to lose. We will persist and as long as they keep breaking their own laws—this is only makes it easier for us! That is why even after the police firing in Maikanch in 2000, over 10,000 of us showed up to oppose the UAIL project the very next month.

Prognosis: The Specter of SSM Politics in the Rural Belt

SSMs continue to make a conspicuous case for pluri-nationalism (and pluri-modalities of production and power) by exposing and resisting the machinations of trans/national colonial-capitalist dispossession in forest and rural spaces where 80 percent or more of Orissa's 36 million people reside in some 55,000 villages. The escalating decibel level of SSM challenges to compulsory modernization, agro/industrial development, and close/long distance colonial-capitalist penetrations (attempted globalization of capitalism and state-socialist variations of the same as in the case of West Bengal) being advanced by the state-market-civil society nexus are likely to continue to proliferate in India.

This is likely given, for instance (a) the demise of the party-political left formations in the 2009 elections which provided some recourse for addressing SSM suffocation/aspiration in formal institutional spaces; (b) the magnitude of displacement and dispossession being considered/undertaken in the densely populated rural/forested areas of the country/this region; and (c) the arguable significance and strength of the sense of place/rootedness of subaltern cultures expressed in movement/other learning (whether for historico-spiritual or pragmatic reasons) now being magnified through direct or vicarious experiences of neighbors being displaced and dispossessed of life, home and livelihoods as industrial road-kill. Unlike in the West where capitalist industrialization stabilized itself before facing democratic demands, India is having to deal with the compulsions of democracy and human rights while enforcing a capitalist transformation (Kaviraj, 1996) (accelerated development) thereby creating an opportunity structure for SSMs (other movements) in/directly seeking to address the rule of capital. SSMs in Orissa do not appear to be backing down from the task ahead, no matter the odds. To conclude with the words of an Adivasi leader of the ADEA:

> We have hope in our movement. We need to take strong action so that *shahari* (city) people and outside exploiters will not capture our land, forests, hills and water. ADEA will work to ensure that they have no clue as to how to continue this process of control. When the time is right, we will need to tie our knot (*samoyo thao thao ganthi bandhiba darkar*). The people will be activated so that the dominant groups cannot continue to shock us. We need to face those who look down on us as *neech* (beneath them) as one. It is a significant development to think that poor people who were just lying low for years are actively tightening their belts (*onta bhirunchanti*) and in our region, this has already happened and will continue to happen.

Notes

1. A term first coined by Antonio Gramsci (1971, p. 55, pp. 325–326) to refer to peasants and labouring poor/common people and a "subaltern consciousness" (a possible basis for a unifying peasant consciousness) in Italy, the term is being used here interchangeably with 'people' (and 'subaltern classes' where industrial/agrarian capitalism has *classed* subalterns), in keeping with Guha (1997) who acknowledges the historical specificity of this empirical judgment, wherein subaltern is loosely defined in the Indian context with all its ambiguities to refer to landless poor (migrant un/der employed labor), poor (small) peasants, pastoralists/nomads, Adivasis (original dwellers or Scheduled tribes in state parlance), Dalits ('untouchable castes' or Scheduled Castes), Other Backward Castes (OBCs) and development displaced peoples (DDPs) specifically from these former categories, including women in any of these groupings. Subalternity is also understood as a social location and in terms of the dialectics of super-ordination and subordination (between these groups and classes, caste, gender, urban and/or ethnically dominant/elite groups embedded in and across multiple modes of production) in global and national hierarchical social relations of exploitation (including but not restricted to those that reproduce capitalist property relations).
2. Adivasi is a claim to indigenous location as 'original dwellers' or first (*mulo nivasi* or 'root people' is the expression used by Kondh Adivasi research participants in

this study) inhabitants vis-à-vis later arrivals. In keeping with the UN and the Declaration of the Rights of Indigenous Peoples, self-definition is consistent with recognition for the self-determination of indigenous peoples and the usage in this chapter is in keeping with this understanding. Adivasi is also understood in terms of what may well be the common historical and contemporary experience of most indigenous peoples including: being original inhabitants of a land later colonized by others; non-dominant sectors of society with unique ethnic identities and cultures; strong ties to land and territory; experiences or threats of dispossession from ancestral territory; the experience of being subjected to culturally foreign governance and institutional structures; and the threat of assimilation and loss of identity vis-à-vis a dominant society (McNeish & Eversole, 2005). This being said, the designation in the Indian and Asian contexts (estimated to be the spatial container for 70 percent of the world's indigenous peoples) in general is vigorously contested given that: (1) governments in Asia (including India) do not recognize the category (with the exception of the Philippines); (2) indigenous could often mean prior rather than original peoples given the multiple waves of colonization and migration in Asia/India; (3) dissident ethnic/caste groups (e.g., Dalits/Scheduled castes in India) sandwiched between indigenous and non-indigenous peoples obscure such claims by demanding indigenous status as well (e.g., given the state-category/taxonomy for Adivasi in relation to a politics of exclusive governmentality – see Ghosh, 2006, for a critique of such ethnoracist state-craft); and (4) indigenous peoples of Asia (post colony) do not have the clarity of definition afforded to indigenous peoples of the settler colonies of North America, Australia, and New Zealand where the indigenous category came into existence with western European colonialism (Barnes, Gray, & Kingsbury, 1995). Archana Prasad (2003) refers to the "orginal peoples = forest dwelling" argument as a "creation myth of the original inhabitant" citing historical evidence/records to suggest that forest-dwelling status/location happened largely as a result of marginalization of tribals by caste Hindu peasants in central India and their sedentization into forests by the British land settlements" (p. 28); that is, the permanent settlement of agricultural and zamindari lands (feudal arrangements) by the British ensured that the movement of tribals between the highlands and plains was stopped forever. That said, in terms of the politics of representation, the Adivasi/indigenous category troubles the real and representational left-politics (Kamat, 2001; Prasad, 2004) of class struggle by disaggregating the preferred category of peasant (compels a peasantization of Adivasi—see Kapoor, 2011a for this discussion). Left-academic politics also obscures/dismisses (either as pure caricature/representational politics or as mere British colonial invention) Adivasi claims to being "original peoples" in the necessary interests of addressing the real politik of class struggle aimed at the very forces (including a conservative saffron politics that dismisses Adivasi as "jungle peoples" or, conversely, pragmatically enlists Adivasi in a divisive caste politics aimed at Scheduled castes/Dalits) that displace and dispossess Adivasi and/or peasant alike. Gandhian-environmentalist (Shiva & Bandopadhyay, 1990) politics of representation are also similarly critiqued by

Guha (1988) and others (Prasad, 2003; 2004) for their attempts to deploy the Adivasi (forest/original peoples positioning and *aranya sanskriti* or forest culture as embodying a living-critique of development) to set up an ideological counterpoint to development (caricaturing) which excludes the Adivasi as conscious subjects of their own history, while Alpa Shah (2010) refers to the same tendency as "eco-incarceration" (p. 130). This politics of representation adds to the complexity of definition and location of Adivasi (original dwellers) in India (Kapoor, in press).

3. According to Partha Chatterjee (2001), contrary to Gramsci's usage in relation to political parties/formal politics, *political society* refers to local spaces outside normal *civil society* and is constituted by populations (taxonomized/enumerated in state Schedules for instance) that are not bodies of citizens belonging to the lawfully constituted *civil society* but are populations in need and deserving of welfare and who are not proper citizens under the law, consequently having to make collective demands on the state founded on a violation of the law, or who survive by side-stepping the law. It is being suggested here that anti-colonial SSMs constitute and take root in *political society* as movements that are primarily located outside and against the state-market-civil society nexus (as suggested when discussing the "anatomy of dispossession" above) and the laws and institutions constructed and strategically deployed by this nexus (Kapoor, 2011b). Subsequently, SSMs as agents that are/from *political society*: (a) face unequal treatment under the law or are victims of the law, (b) are expendable through multiple and racial/ethnically-targeted dispossessions and subjected to other forms of violence if need be (since they are not lawfully constituted *civil society*) and are (c) compelled to resort to extra-legal collective activism through land occupations by stealth or uncivil activism and transgressions of laws that keep them out (see Kapoor, in press). Furthermore, SSM/*political society* constituents and politics is motivated by the direct and immediate impacts of colonial trans/national development displacements and dispossessions (e.g., dams and mining), as opposed to a New Social Movement (NSM) civil-societarian politics of identity and sympathetic environmentalism as these agents consume resources here while aiming to protect nature over there (Kapoor, 2011b).

References

Araghi, F. (2010). Accumulation by displacement: Global enclosures, food crisis and the ecological contradictions of capitalism. *Review: A Journal of Fernand Braudel Center, 34*(1), 113–146.

Araghi, F., & Karides, M. (2012). Land dispossession and global crisis: Introduction to the special section on land rights in the World System. *Journal of World-Systems Research on Land Rights, 18*(1), 1–5.

Asian Center for Human Rights [ACHR] (2005). *Promising picture or broken future? Commentary and recommendations on the Draft National Policy on Tribals of the Government of India.* New Delhi: ACHR.

Banerjee, P. (2006, November 18). West Bengal: Land acquisition and peasant resistance in Singur. *Economic and Political Weekly* (Kolkata), 4718–4720.

Barker, J. (2005). *Sovereignty matters: Locations of contestation and possibility in indigenous struggles for self-determination.* Lincoln: University of Nebraska Press.

Barnes, R., Gray, A., & Kingsbury, B. (Eds.). (1995). *Indigenous peoples of Asia.* Ann Arbor, MI: Association for Asian Studies.

Baviskar, A. (2005). Red in tooth and claw? Looking for class struggles over nature. In R. Ray & M. Katzenstein (Eds.), *Social movements in India: Poverty, power and politics* (pp. 161–178). Lanham, MD: Rowman & Littlefield.

Behura, N., & Panigrahi, N. (2006). *Tribals and the Indian Constitution: Functioning of the fifth schedule in Orissa.* New Delhi: Rawat Publications.

Bharati, S. (1999). Human rights and development projects in India. *The PRP Journal of Human Rights, 3*(4), 20.

Chatterjee, P. (2001). On civil and political society in post-colonial democracies. In S. Kaviraj & S. Khilnani (Eds.), *Civil society: History and possibilities* (pp. 165–178). Cambridge: Cambridge University Press.

Da Costa, D. (2007). Tensions of neoliberal-development: State discourse and dramatic oppositions in West Bengal. *Contributions to Indian Sociology, 41*(3), 287–320.

Davis, M. (2006). *Planet of slums.* London: Verso.

Fernandes, W. (2006). Development-related displacement and tribal women. In G. Rath (Ed.), *Tribal development in India: The contemporary debate* (pp. 112–132). New Delhi: Sage Publications.

Ghosh, K. (2006). Between global flows and local dams: Indigenousness, locality and the transnational sphere in Jharkhand, India. *Cultural Anthropology, 21*(4), 501–534.

Glassman, J. (2006). Primitive accumulation, accumulation by dispossession and accumulation by 'extra-economic' means. *Progress in Human Geography, 30*(5), 608–625.

Gramsci, A. (1971). *Selections from the prison notebooks.* London: Lawrence & Wishart.

Guha, R. (1988). Ideological trends in Indian environmentalism. *Economic and political weekly, 23*(49), 80–92.

Guha, R. (1990). *The unquiet woods.* Berkeley, CA: University of California Press.

Guha, R. (1997). *Dominance without hegemony: History and power in colonial India.* New York: Harvard University Press.

Harvey, D. (2003). *The new imperialism.* Oxford: Oxford University Press.

Harvey, D. (2009). *Social justice and the city.* Athens, GA: University of Georgia Press.

Hussain, M. (2008). *Interrogating development: State, displacement and popular resistance in North Eastern India.* New Delhi: Sage Publications.

Indian People's Tribunal on Environment and Human Rights [IPTEHR] (2006). *An inquiry into mining and human rights violations in Kashipur.* Mumbai, India: IPEHR publication.

Kapoor, D. (2007). Subaltern social movement learning and the decolonization of space in India. *International Education, 37*(1), 10–41

Kapoor, D. (2009a). Adivasis (original dwellers) "in the way of" state-corporate development: Development dispossession and learning in social action for land and forests in India. *McGill Journal of Education, 44*(1), 55–78.

Kapoor, D. (2009b). Participatory academic research (par) and People's Participatory Action Research (PAR): Research, politicization, and subaltern social movements in India. In D. Kapoor & S. Jordan (Eds.), *Education, participatory action research and social change* (pp. 29–44). New York: Palgrave Macmillan.

Kapoor, D. (2009c). Globalization, dispossession and subaltern social movement (SSM) learning in the South. In A. Abdi & D. Kapoor (Eds.), *Global perspectives on adult education* (pp. 71–92). New York: Palgrave Macmillan.

Kapoor, D. (2011a). Subaltern social movement (SSM) post-mortems of development in India: Locating trans-local activism and radicalism. *Journal of Asian and African Studies, 46*(2), 130–148.

Kapoor, D. (2011b). Adult learning in political (un-civil) society: Anti-colonial subaltern social movement (SSM) pedagogies of place. *Studies in the Education of Adults, 43*(2), 128–146.

Kapoor, D. (in press). Human rights as paradox and equivocation in contexts of Adivasi (original dweller) dispossession in India. *Journal of Asian and African Studies, 47*(4), (17 pages).

Kaviraj, S. (1996). Dilemmas of democratic development in India. In A. Leftwich (Ed.), *Democracy and development: Theory and practice*. Cambridge: Polity Press.

Ludden, D. (Ed.). (2005). *Reading subaltern studies: Critical history, contested meaning and the globalization of South Asia*. New Delhi: Pauls Press.

McMichael, P. (Ed.). (2010). *Contesting development: Critical struggles for social change*. New York: Routledge.

McMichael, P. (2012). *Development and social change: A global perspective*. Thousand Oaks, CA: Pine Forge Press.

McNeish, J., & Eversole, R. (2005). Overview: The right to self-determination. In R. Eversole, J. McNeish & A. Cimadamore (Eds.), *Indigenous peoples and poverty: An international perspective* (pp. 97–107). London: Zed.

Menon, N., & Nigam, A. (2007). *Power and contestation: India since 1989*. London: Zed Books.

Mookerjea, S. (2010). Autonomy and video mediation: Dalit Bahujan women's utopian knowledge production. In D. Kapoor & E. Shizha (Eds.), *Indigenous knowledge and learning in Asia/Pacific and Africa* (pp. 165–178). New York: Palgrave Macmillan.

Mookerjea, S. (2011). On learning how to liberate the common: Subaltern biopolitics and the endgame of neoliberalism. In D. Kapoor (Ed.), *Critical perspectives on neoliberal globalization, development and education in Africa and Asia* (pp. 51–68). Rotterdam: Sense Publishers.

Nag, S. (2001, March 1). Nationhood and displacement in the Indian subcontinent. *Economic and Political Weekly (Kolkata), 36*(51), 4753–4760.

Neeraj, J. (2007). *Globalization or re-colonization*. Pune, India: Lokayat Press.
Oliver-Smith, A. (2010). *Defying displacement: Grassroots resistance and the critique of development*. Austin: University of Texas Press.
Oxfam (2011). Land and power: The growing scandal surrounding the new wave of investments in land. Retrieved from www.oxfam.org/en/grow/policy/land
Padel, F., & Das, S. (2010). *Out of this earth: East India Adivasis and the aluminium cartel*. New Delhi: Orient Blackswan.
Patnaik, U., & Moyo, S. (2011). *The agrarian question and the neoliberal era: Primitive accumulation and the peasantry*. Cape Town, SA: Pambazuka Press.
Pimple, M, & Sethi, M. (2005). Occupation of land in India: Experiences and challenges. In S. Moyo & P. Years (Eds.), *Reclaiming land: The resurgence of rural movements in Africa, Asia and Latin America* (pp. 235–256). London: Zed.
Prasad, A. (2003). *Against ecological romanticism: Verrier Elwin and the making of an anti-modern tribal identity*. New Delhi: Three Essays Collective.
Prasad, A. (2004). *Environmentalism and the left: Contemporary debates and the future agendas in tribal areas*. New Delhi: Left Word Books.
Rajagopal, B. (2003). *International law from below: Development, social movements and Third World resistance*. Cambridge: Cambridge University Press.
Ramdas, S. (2009). Women, forest spaces and the law: Transgressing the boundaries. *Economic and Political Weekly, 64*(44), 65–73.
Sanyal, K. (2010). *Rethinking capitalist development: Primitive accumulation, governmentality and post-colonial capitalism*. New Delhi: Routledge.
Shah, A. (2010). *In the shadows of the state: Indigenous politics, environmentalism, and insurgency in Jharkhand, India*. Durham, NC: Duke University Press.
Shiva, V., & Bandyopadhyay, J. (1990). Asia's forests and Asia's cultures. In S. Head & R. Hienzman (Eds.), *Lessons of the rainforest* (pp. 66–). San Francisco, CA: Sierra Club Books, 66–74.
Shivji, I. (2011). Preface. In U. Patnaik & S. Moyo, *The agrarian question in the neoliberal era: Primitive accumulation and the peasantry* (pp. 1–6). Cape town, SA: Pambazuka Press.
Wallerstein, I. (2012). Land, space and people: Constraints of the capitalist world-economy. *18*(1), 6–14.
Wani, M., & Kothari, A. (2008, September 13). Globalization v. India's forests. *Economic and Political Weekly*, 19–22.

Author Bios

Sajid Ali is Assistant Professor at the Aga Khan University's Institute for Educational Development, Karachi. He has a PhD in policy studies from the University of Edinburgh, an MEd in leadership and policy from Monash University, and a master's in sociology from the University of Karachi. Dr. Ali is the recipient of various awards, including the A. R. Kiyani Gold Medal (1997), Australian Development Scholarship (2003), Commonwealth Youth Leadership Award (2003), Edinburgh Research Scholarship (2006), and South Asian Visiting Fellowship at Oxford (2011). Dr. Ali has also taught at Hamdard University, Karachi University, and the University of Edinburgh. He is the current General Secretary of the Pakistan Association for Research in Education (PARE). His research interests include globalization and education policy, new forms of educational governance, policy networks, education reforms, and the role of knowledge resources in shaping policy.

Monisha Bajaj is Assistant Professor of international and comparative education at Teachers College, Columbia University. Her research and teaching interests focus on education as a force for social transformation in the global South. In addition to authoring numerous articles, she also is the editor of the *Encyclopedia of Peace Education* (2008), and the author of a teacher-training manual on human rights education (UNESCO, 2003) as well as a recent book entitled, *Schooling for Social Change: The Rise and Impact of Human Rights Education in India* (Continuum, 2011). Dr. Bajaj has developed curriculum—particularly related to the incorporation of peace education, human rights, and sustainable development—for nonprofit educational service providers and intergovernmental organizations such as the UNICEF. She is also an Honorary Visiting Professor at the Indian Institute of Dalit Studies in New Delhi, India.

Bijoy P. Barua is Associate Professor of the Department of Social Sciences at East West University, Dhaka, Bangladesh. He offers courses at graduate and undergraduate levels in the areas of development studies, development education/transformative learning, participatory research, development organization and civil society, and the sociology of development. His research interests include international education, participatory research, and ethnic minorities, culture, indigenous knowledge, community management, engaged Buddhism/ecology, and development organizations. He has published in academic journals such as *International Education* (United States), *Canadian Journal of Development Studies, Alternative Journal in Social Sciences* (United States), and *Development Review* (Bangladesh). He has also contributed to several edited collections. He is a member of the international advisory board of Exploring Leadership and Learning Theories in Asia (ELLTA). He is a senior fellow of the *Journal of Alternative Perspectives in the Social Sciences* (United States). He is a recipient of the Ontario Graduate Scholarship and the 2002 Graduate Student Paper Award from the Canadian Association for the Study of Adult Education.

Dia Da Costa teaches in the Department of Global Development Studies, Queen's University, Canada. She develops her research and teaching at the intersection of global political economy and cultural studies. She is the author of *Development Dramas: Reimagining Rural Political Action in Eastern India* (2010) and editor of the book *Scripting Power: Jana Sanskriti On and Offstage* (2010). She has articles in *Third World Quarterly, Globalizations, Signs: Journal of Women and Culture,* and *Contributions to Indian Sociology*. She is currently working on a second book, tentatively entitled, *The Work of Theatre in an Age of Precarious Labour*.

Al-Karim Datoo is a sociologist of education and Assistant Professor at the Aga Khan University Institute for Educational Development (AKU-IED) in Pakistan. He heads initiatives related to social science education programs and teaches and does research in development and education and social studies. He is a founding member of a multi-disciplinary research group working in the area of globalization and cultural studies at AKU-IED. His primary research interest is studying the nexus between globalization, culture, and education. Dr. Datoo has a PhD in the cultural sociology of globalization and education from McGill University, Canada. His dissertation is a pioneering effort in conducting a critical ethnography of schooling in the Pakistani context. He has an MSc in educational research methodology from the University of Oxford, United Kingdom, and the graduate program in Islamic studies and humanities from the Institute of Ismaili Studies (IIS), London, United Kingdom.

Radhika Gorur is a Research Fellow at the Victoria Institute for Education, Diversity and Lifelong Learning. Her research interests include education policy and evidence-based policy. Approaching her research with a material-semiotic sensibility, she focuses on epistemic cultures, and more particularly, on the sociology of comparison and measurement. Her interest is in the exploration of new forms of knowledge production and the coordinating mechanisms that make these forms possible. Her current projects include an examination of the production, stabilization, mobilization and circulation of equity, inclusion, exclusion and difference in education policies and the institutional practices that promote them. She has also published in the area of the internationalization of education. More recently, working closely with Fazal Rizvi, she has contributed to the debates and discussions on the policy challenges in higher education in India.

Amita Gupta is a Fulbright Research Scholar, an Associate Professor at the City College of New York, and Doctoral Faculty for urban education at the CUNY Graduate Center. She has extensive cross-cultural experience with school administration, teacher education, and classroom teaching in urban schools in the United States and India.

Her research and scholarship is focused on the interdisciplinary, comparative, and international examination of early education and teacher preparation, and is characterized by the themes of cross-cultural perspectives on teaching, learning, and child development; sociocultural-historical constructivism in teaching and learning; and the impact of globalization on teacher preparation and practice. The integration of these themes also appears in the graduate courses she teaches on curriculum design, child development, and social studies. She earned her doctoral degree from Columbia University, serves on editorial boards, school boards, and has published extensively in books and journals.

Ehsanul Haque is Associate Professor in the Department of International Relations, University of Dhaka, Bangladesh. He also teaches in the Department of Social Sciences, East West University, as an adjunct faculty. He obtained an MA in international affairs from Ohio University, United States, with a specialization in Southeast Asian affairs. He has published on issues such as South Asian peace process, Chinese military power, democracy movement in Burma, ASEAN and regional security, North Korean nuclear program, ethnicity in South Asia, conflict and poverty, and rights of the indigenous peoples. From 1994 to 2003 he was the Associate Editor of the *Journal of International Relations* (a biannual journal of the Department of International Relations, University of Dhaka) and from 1995 to 1998 he served as the Assistant Editor of *Social Science Review* (a biannual journal of the Faculty of Social Sciences, University of Dhaka). He is a recipient of the US Department of State Fulbright Scholarship.

Dip Kapoor is Associate Professor in international education in the Department of Educational Policy Studies, University of Alberta, Canada, and Research Associate, Center for Research and Development Solidarity (CRDS), an Adivasi/Dalit rural people's organization in Orissa, India. His research interests include critical globalization and education studies, subaltern social movements/learning in the global South, NGO – social movement relations, and the political sociology of education and development. His most recent edited collections include *Critical Perspectives on Neoliberal Globalization: Development and Education in Africa and Asia* (Sense 2011), *Indigenous Knowledge and Learning in Asia/Pacific and Africa: Perspectives on Development, Education and Culture* (Palgrave 2010), *Learning from the Ground Up: Global Perspectives on Knowledge Production in Social Movements* (Palgrave 2010) and *Education, Participatory Action Research and Social Change: International Perspectives* (Palgrave 2009). *Complicity, Contradiction and Prospects: NGOization and its Discontents* (with Aziz Choudry, McGill University) is an edited collection currently in progress for Zed, London (2013).

Bikku Kuruvila, JD, MR P, has served as Senior Consultant to the National Institute of Public Finance and Policy in New Delhi and Legal Advisor to various state and nongovernmental agencies in India and the United States. He is the author of several reports and articles related to law, economic development, and public policy. He holds a Juris Doctorate degree from Cornell Law School, a master's in regional planning from Cornell University, and a bachelor's in political economy from Stanford University.

Tejendra J. Pherali is a Senior Lecturer in education studies at Liverpool John Moores University, United Kingdom. He is the coordinator of the international collaborative research project "Education for Peace building," involving Kathmandu University, Paññāsāstra University of Cambodia, and Search for Common Ground, Nepal. He also chairs the multi-institutional association Network for Research in Education and Conflict (NREC). His research primarily involves education, conflict, and international development but he is also interested in broader areas including political economy of education, globalization, ethnicity, identity, and post-conflict reconstruction. His recent work involves a political economy analysis of education in Nepal (with Prof. Alan Smith and Tony Vaux). He is also involved in UNICEF's global research project on education and peace building. His doctoral research examines the impact of armed conflict on school education in Nepal.

Fazal Rizvi is a Professor in education at the University of Melbourne and an Emeritus Professor at the University of Illinois at Urbana Champaign. Much of Fazal's recent research has focused on issues of identity, culture; global mobility of students; and theories of globalization and the internationalization of higher education. His current projects include an examination of the ways in which Indian universities are negotiating pressures of globalization and the knowledge economy, as well as a more theoretical exploration of the cosmopolitan possibilities of education. His recent books include *Youth Moves: Identities and Education in a Global Era* (Routledge 2007), *Globalization and the Study of Education* (Wiley 2009), and *Globalizing Educational Policy* (Routledge 2010). From 1993 to 2000, Fazal edited *Discourse: Studies in the Cultural Politics of Education,* and in 1996 was President of the Australian Association for Research in Education. He is a Fellow of the Australian Social Science Academy.

Azra Talat Sayeed, PhD, works with Roots for Equity, a nongovernmental organization in Karachi, Pakistan. Azra is an activist working for social, economic, and political rights of small and landless farmers in Pakistan. As part of the organization, she has worked for women's rights, including rights of landless rural women and home-based women workers. She is also a visiting faculty at the University of Karachi and has taught courses on the political economy of Pakistan, feminism and globalization, and food sovereignty. She is currently cochair of the People's Coalition on Food Sovereignty (PCFS) and has served as part of the governance team of Asia Pacific Forum on Women Law and Development (APWLD) and the Asia Pacific Research Network (APRN). Her major contribution as a member of the Women and Environment Task Force in APWLD was her editorship for the manual on food sovereignty and women.

Touhida Tasnima is Assistant Professor in the Department of Social Sciences at East West University, Dhaka, Bangladesh. She has earned an MA in development studies with specialization in public policy and management from the International Institute of Social Studies (The Hague, Netherlands). She also holds a master's in public administration from the University of Dhaka, Bangladesh. Her research interest broadly lies in the field of higher education in Bangladesh in the postcolonial period. She also has an interest in development policy and public sector reform.

Index

activism, 11, 147, 149, 150, 190, 201, 207
　political activism, 161, 164, 165
　SSM activism, 187, 198
Adivasi, 6, 9, 11, 129, 132–5, 141, 148–9, 187–207
　see also caste(s)
adult education, 4, 6, 125, 162, 203
agricultural laborers, 10, 155, 163
agriculture, 10–11, 76, 159, 171–84, 190–5
agrochemical TNCs, 11, 171, 173, 179, 181, 182, 184
Ali, Sajid, 6, 37–52, 211
anticolonial approach, 9, 142
anticolonial pedagogy/ies, 187, 190, 193, 198

Bajaj, Monisha, 3, 8, 123–38, 211
Bangladesh, 2, 4, 7, 9, 10, 53–69, 141–54
Barua, Bijoy, 1–13, 141–54, 211
Barua community, 4, 9, 141–54
benchmarking, 43, 61
Bengali community, 141, 149
Bt Cotton, 172, 174–8, 182

capitalism, 1, 2, 4, 55, 74, 104, 132, 145, 163, 171, 173, 187–210
caste(s), 6, 9, 11, 72, 75, 77–9, 84–5, 126, 129, 130–1, 135, 144–6, 177, 187, 189, 195, 200, 202, 206
　caste system, 19, 149, 150
　see also Adivasi; Dalits

centralized education, 42, 71
child development, 103, 105, 110, 116, 167
class-based education, 39
collaborative arrangements, 18, 21, 26
colonial difference, 90–1, 95, 98–9
colonial education, 9, 104, 141–54
colonialism, 1, 4, 18, 95, 117, 172–3, 190–1, 206
colonial legacy, 8, 18, 19, 198
colonization, 1, 2, 10, 11, 90, 113, 171–85, 189, 193, 206
commercialization, 8, 56, 103, 110–11, 174
　of higher education, 56
　of seeds, 178
community learning, 11, 178
community schooling, 7, 71–86
critical pedagogy, 128, 161, 163–4
cultural hegemony, 89–90
cultural heritage, 9, 62, 141–3, 150–1
cultural identities, 87, 91, 92, 99, 141–3, 146–51
curriculum, 7, 8, 9, 19, 24, 32, 38, 39, 48, 71, 76, 87–90, 98–9, 107, 108, 110, 112, 127–9, 147, 151, 168, 180

Da Costa, Dia, 2, 10, 155–70, 212
Dalits, 6, 11, 72, 75, 77–8, 129, 187, 189–90, 194–7, 200–2, 206
　see also caste(s)
Datoo, Al-Karim, 1–13, 87–101, 212
decolonization, 142–3, 171
democratization, 8, 114

Index

deregulation, 3, 7, 53, 64, 65, 72, 171
development, 6, 21, 40, 44, 78, 107–8, 114, 125, 164, 167, 174, 179
dispossession, 10, 11, 159, 187–90, 193, 198–210

early childhood education (ECE), 46, 105, 107–10, 112–14, 118
educational decentralization, 3, 44, 71–86
education for all (EFA), 6, 10, 44–5, 48, 125, 156–61, 167–8
educational reforms, 72, 74, 107, 111, 113, 117
education policy, 37–52, 103, 110, 115
  see also global education policy field; national education policy field
education policymaking, 6, 37, 45
education. *see* adult education; centralized education; class-based education; colonial education; early childhood education (ECE); education for all (EFA); education policy; higher education; human rights education (HRE); political education; preprimary teacher education
English (language), 14–16, 19, 26, 37, 39, 49, 62, 76, 113–14, 148–9, 179–80
ethnic identity, 9, 141–3, 147–51
exclusion, 87, 90–1, 95, 98, 148

farmers. *see* landless farmers; small farmers
food security, 171, 176, 183, 201
food sovereignty, 179–80, 183, 196–7

genetically engineered (GE) cotton/ crops/ seeds, 11, 171, 174–5, 177–9, 182
global collaboration(s), 6, 17, 18, 25, 27–8, 31–4
global education policy field, 37–48
globalization, 1–4, 7, 9, 18, 19, 24, 34, 37, 39, 40, 45, 53, 55, 74, 87, 89–92, 95–6, 98–9, 104, 114, 118, 141–2, 151, 173, 180, 184, 188, 190, 205
  see also neoliberal globalization
globalizing capitalism, 187–210
global knowledge economy, 17, 43
global policy, 47–50, 72, 84
global South, 104, 123, 190
grassroots activists, 9, 135
Green Revolution (GR), 11, 171–85
Gupta, Amita, 8, 103–21, 212–13

Haque, Ehsanul, 7, 53–69, 213
higher education, 4–7, 17–36, 48, 53–69, 107, 146
high yielding variety seeds (HYVs), 172, 178
human capital, 7, 8, 25, 43, 54, 59, 63–4, 103, 105, 110, 115, 124
human rights, 8, 9, 124, 126–32, 134–5, 157, 158, 161, 168, 202, 205
human rights education (HRE), 3, 8–9, 123–38

imperialism, 1, 2, 113
India, 4–6, 8–11, 17–36, 103–21, 123–38, 144–6, 155–86, 187–210
indigenous knowledge, 9, 19, 76, 142
information and communication technology/ies (ICT), 42, 74, 91, 111
internationalization, 8, 25, 32–3, 113
Islam, 38, 48

Jana Sanskriti (JS), 10, 155–70
JS pedagogy, 10, 157

Kapoor, Dip, 1–13, 187–210, 213
Knowledge. *see* local knowledge; western knowledge
Kuruvila, Bikku, 3, 8, 123–38, 213–14

labor market(s), 22, 24, 25, 28
land grabbing, 179, 181, 183, 184
land grabs, 191, 192

landless farmers, 10, 171, 177, 179, 182–3
landless peasants, 6, 11, 181, 188–9
learner-centered pedagogy, 112
liberalization, 10, 17, 22, 54, 57, 128, 134, 171, 188, 191
local capacities, 79
local-global dynamics, 91
local knowledge, 9, 21, 90, 98, 142
Lok Adhikar Manch (LAM), 188–90, 193–7, 202

Maldives, the, 2, 4, 8, 103–21
market forces, 18, 54, 57, 58, 60, 61
massification, 25
Millennium Development Goals (MDGs), 6, 10, 44–5, 48, 125, 156
modernization, 3, 9, 22, 142, 176, 187, 195, 200, 204

National Curriculum Frameworks for Teacher Education, 9, 128
national education policy field, 37, 48, 49
national policy, 32, 40–50, 112
neocolonialism, 103, 113, 162
neoliberal globalization, 7, 9, 10, 53–69, 103–21, 141, 142, 171, 172, 184, 190
neoliberal ideology, 40, 63, 106, 134
neoliberalism, 4, 5, 8, 40, 46, 54–6, 61, 72, 74, 103, 106, 115
neoliberal reforms, 24, 65
neoliberal turn, 11, 189, 191, 198
Nepal, 4, 7, 59, 71–86
NGOs (nongovernmental organizations), 5, 6, 26, 30, 38, 43, 45, 47, 105, 124, 127, 129, 132–5, 157, 201, 202
nostalgia, 95–6, 98–9

Orientalism, 90, 97, 99
Orissa (India), 5, 11, 133–4, 187–210

Pakistan, 4, 6, 10–11, 37–52, 59, 87–101, 171–85
Pakistan Kissan Mazdoor Tehreek (PKMT), 11, 177–84
People's Coalition on Food Sovereignty, 179–80
permanent critique, 10, 162, 164
permanent liberation, 10, 162, 164
Pherali, Tejendra, 3, 7, 71–86, 214
policy reform, 60, 72, 73, 75–6, 84
Policy. *see* education policy; global policy; national policy
political economy, 3, 6, 7, 71–86, 96, 165, 168, 198
political education, 6, 164, 179–80, 203
political engagement, 123–4, 131, 134–5
politicizing education, 155–70
postcolonial perspective, 8, 90–1, 119
postcolonial theory, 103–4
preprimary teacher education, 8, 103–21
preschool, 105, 108–10, 112, 114
private education, 22, 41, 44, 58, 78, 84
private sector, 41–2, 47, 58–9, 62, 74, 105, 107, 108
private universities, 21, 57–63
privatization, 5–8, 19, 24–6, 28, 41, 44, 53–4, 56, 62, 74, 106, 107, 110–11, 171, 190
public education, 41, 43, 71–4, 76, 84

resistance, 47, 123–38, 159, 165, 171, 184, 193, 201, 202
Right to Education (RTE), 111, 113, 125–7, 130
Roots for Equity, 10, 11, 172, 174, 176–84
rural communities, 41, 133, 142, 174–7, 180–1

Sayeed, Azra Talat, 2, 10, 171–85, 214
school-based management, 7, 71–3
school knowledge production, 87–101
school management, 72–3, 75–6, 79–82
school management committee (SMC), 72, 75–84

seed sector, 10, 171
sharecroppers, 172, 176–7
signature campaigns, 11, 178
small farmer campaigns, 11, 177
small farmers, 172–3, 176–8, 181, 183
social identity, 142, 145
social justice, 8, 38, 64, 118, 128, 135, 142
South Asia, 1–13, 103–5, 110, 112–14, 116–20
spect-actors of history, 10, 157, 165, 168
Sri Lanka, 4, 8, 59, 103–21, 147
standardization, 7, 27, 41, 43–4, 61, 74
structural adjustment policies, 61
subaltern rights, 191
subaltern social movement (SSM), 11, 187–210

Tasnima, Touhida, 3, 7, 53–69, 214–15
teachers, 44, 76–83, 105–19, 126–9, 131–5, 162, 167

teacher training, 4, 5, 105–16, 125, 127
textual constructions, 8, 87
theater of the oppressed, 157, 162, 164, 169
Theravada Buddhism, 9, 142, 147, 152
trade liberalization, 128, 171
transgenic seeds, 178, 182
transnational corporations (TNCs). *see* agrochemical TNCs

villagers, 10, 159–60, 165–6

West Bengal, 10, 20, 132, 155–70, 189, 205
westernization, 5, 8, 9, 103, 111, 141
western knowledge, 8, 19, 91, 98, 142
World Bank, 3, 40, 41, 44, 57, 60, 71–86, 105, 110, 117, 174

GPSR Compliance

The European Union's (EU) General Product Safety Regulation (GPSR) is a set of rules that requires consumer products to be safe and our obligations to ensure this.

If you have any concerns about our products, you can contact us on

ProductSafety@springernature.com

In case Publisher is established outside the EU, the EU authorized representative is:

Springer Nature Customer Service Center GmbH
Europaplatz 3
69115 Heidelberg, Germany

www.ingramcontent.com/pod-product-compliance
Lightning Source LLC
LaVergne TN
LVHW051913060526
838200LV00004B/116